Collective Violence

Steven E. Barkan

University of Maine

Lynne L. Snowden

University of North Carolina at Wilmington

Allyn and Bacon

Boston ■ *London* ■ *Toronto* ■ *Sydney* ■ *Tokyo* ■ *Singapore*

For Barb, Dave, and Joey
S.E.B.

For Jim, Mike, and Julie
L.L.S.

Editor in Chief, Social Sciences: Karen Hanson
Editorial Assistant: Karen Corday
Editorial-Production Administrator: Annette Joseph
Editorial-Production Service: Karen Mason
Electronic Composition: Karen Mason
Composition Buyer: Linda Cox
Manufacturing Buyer: Julie McNeill
Cover Administrator: Jenny Hart

Copyright © 2001 by Allyn & Bacon
A Pearson Education Company
160 Gould Street
Needham Heights, MA 02494

Internet: www.abacon.com

Library of Congress Cataloging-in-Publication Data
Barkan, Steven E.
  Collective violence / Steven E. Barkan, Lynne L. Snowden.
     p.   cm.
  Includes bibliographical references and index.
  ISBN 0-205-26782-3
   1. Violence. 2. Political violence. 3. Collective behavior. 4. Radicalism. 5. Cults.
  I. Snowden, Lynne L.   II. Title.

HM281 .B273 2000
303.6--dc21   98-020203

Printed in the United States of America
10 9 8 7 6 5 4 3 2 1   05 04 03 02 01 00

Contents

Preface   vii

1   *The Problem of Collective Violence*   1

Collective Violence Defined   4

Rationality versus Irrationality   6

Micro versus Macro Roots of Collective Violence   8

Interplay with State Authorities   10

Conclusion   11

2   *Explaining Collective Violence*   13

Individual-Level Explanations of Collective Violence   13

   Rationality, Irrationality, and Involvement in
     Collective Action   14

   Frustration and Relative Deprivation   17

   The Effect of Social Attachments   19

Social and Structural Explanations of Collective Behavior   20

   Smelser's Structural-Strain Theory   20

   Political Theories and Resource Mobilization   23

Recent Developments in the Study of Collective Behavior   25

Conclusion   27

3 *Riots*   **29**

Types of Riots   **29**
    What Do You Think?   •   31

A Brief History of U.S. Riots   **31**
    The Colonial Period   31
    Rioting in the Nineteenth Century   32
    Race Riots in the Early Twentieth Century   33
    The 1960s Urban Riots   34

Explaining Riots and Rioting   **34**
    Who Riots?   35
    The Underlying Conditions for Riots   38

The Consequences of Riots   **41**

Prison Riots   **42**
    Explaining Prison Riots   42
    The Consequences of Prison Riots   44
    What Would You Do?   •   45

Conclusion   **46**

4 *Revolution*   **48**

Explaining Revolution   **49**
    Marx and Engels's Theory of Revolution   49
    The Natural History of Revolution   51
    Relative Deprivation and Rising Expectations   52
    Structural Theories   53

Some Twentieth-Century Revolutions   **56**
    The Russian Revolution of 1917   56
    The Chinese Revolution of 1949   57
    Nicaragua and Revolution   59
    The Iranian Revolution   60

Conclusion   **61**

5 *Terrorism*   *63*

Defining Terrorism   64

Examples of Historical and Contemporary Terrorism   66
Vigilante Terrorism   66
    What Do You Think? • 69
Insurgent Terrorism   70
Transnational Terrorism   74
State Terrorism   76

Explaining Terrorism   79
Psychological and Social-Psychological Views   79
Structural Views   81
Media Coverage of Terrorism   83
    What Would You Do? • 83

Women and Terrorism   85

Countering Terrorism   86

Conclusion   89

6 *Cults, Militia, and Hate Groups   90*

Cults   90
What Is a Cult?   90
Charismatic Leadership in Cults   91
How and Why People Join Cults   92
Cults and Violence   96
    What Would You Do? • 97
Cult Beliefs and Cult Violence   98
The History of Cults in the United States   99
The Anticult Movement   101
Satanic Cults in the United States   102

Militia and Survivalist Groups   104

Hate Groups   105

Why Hate Groups Develop   106
The Social Structure of Hate Groups   106
A Historical Perspective on Hate Groups   107
Ethnic Conflict   112

Conclusion   **113**

7 *Conclusion: The Nature and Future of Collective Violence*   **114**

The Structural Roots of Collective Violence   **114**

The Rationality of Collective Violence   **116**

The Consequences of Collective Violence   **118**

Interplay with State Authorities   **120**

The Future of Collective Violence   **123**

References   **126**

Author Index   **143**

Subject Index   **147**

Preface

As we enter the twenty-first century, violence remains an important problem around the world. When we think of violence, we usually think of *individual* violence: One individual attacks another individual with the intent of inflicting physical injury. The result might be a homicide, an assault, a rape, or a robbery. Such individual violence is the type of violence that Americans fear and the type that prompts us to lock our doors at night, to buy weapons in self-defense, to carry pepper spray or other protective devices, and to pay princely sums for home security systems.

But there is another type of violence that affects our lives, and that is violence done by groups of people to advance or impede the goal of social change. This type of violence goes by many titles. *Collective violence* and *political violence* are the names given to just two broad categories into which many types of violent acts fall. Perhaps the most familiar type of collective and political violence to most of us is war, but that is not the subject of this book, as it has been treated extensively elsewhere. Instead, this book addresses the types of collective and political violence committed by cults, survivalist and militia groups, hate groups, terrorists, police and other governmental agents, rioters, and revolutionaries. One might have strong opinions about all of these groups and about the violence that they often commit, but they have at least two things in common: They act collectively, and they act to achieve or impede social, political, and economic change.

As we hope to make clear in the pages that follow, this sort of violence has marked the historical landscape for many centuries and has certainly highlighted U.S. history since colonial days. Yet it remains little understood by the general public. Our goal is to acquaint you with the sources, dynamics, and consequences of some of the most important types of collective and political violence in the world today. Our overriding view is that these types of violence are largely rational attempts to use violence to advance or resist social change. It is difficult to discuss objectively the collective and political violence depicted in this book because it easily arouses strong opinions from almost everyone. But we do our best in the book to provide a balanced perspective grounded in sociology and the other social sciences. We hope we have succeeded.

This book would not have been possible without the help of several people to whom we owe a considerable debt. Karen Hanson, Editor in Chief, Social Sciences, at Allyn and Bacon, showed quick interest in our project, and we appreciate her invitation to publish it. Karen Corday, Editorial Assistant, guided the book through production. Several reviewers provided valuable comments that greatly improved the book: Barbara Chasin, Montclair State University; Richard DeLung, Wayne Baptist University; Jerry Lewis, Kent State University; and Ron Weitzer, George Washington University. Any faults that remain are our responsibility.

We also wish to thank the academic departments at the University of North Carolina at Wilmington and the University of Maine for providing a collegial working environment that helped us write this book while meeting our other professional responsibilities. In more personal acknowledgments, Lynne Snowden thanks her children, Jim, Mike, and Julie, for their love and support that give her the strength to endure, and Steve Barkan thanks his family—Barb, Dave, and Joey—for their patience and support during his work on this book.

1

The Problem of Collective Violence

On August 7, 1998, simultaneous car bombs blew apart the U.S. embassies in Kenya and Tanzania, killing more than 250 people, including 12 U.S. citizens, and injuring some 5,000. A week later, another car bomb in a crowded shopping area in Omagh, a small town in Northern Ireland, killed 28 people, among them 11 children and infants, and wounded more than 200. Much of the world reacted with horror and disbelief to these terrible acts and found them difficult to understand.

A few years earlier, a group of Mexican rebels called the Zapatista National Liberation Army (EZLN) attacked forces of Mexico's ruling government, the Institutional Revolutionary Party (PRN), in the Mexican state of Chiapas. The PRN had ruled Mexico in corrupt fashion for 65 years. It also supported the efforts of large landowners in Chiapas to maintain their oppressive rule over the peasantry, who lived in abject poverty and, thanks to years of governmental neglect, suffered from starvation and disease. In its 1993 "Declaration of the Lacandon Jungle," the EZLN proclaimed:

> We have nothing to lose, absolutely nothing, no decent roof over our heads, no land, no work, poor health, no food, no education, no right to freely and democratically choose our leaders, no independence from foreign interests, and no justice for ourselves or our children. But we say enough is enough! We are the descendants of those who truly built this nation, we are the millions of dispossessed, and we call upon all of our brethren to join our crusade, the only option to avoid dying of starvation!

In January 1994, the EZLN's attacks on army troops and police stations began. Fierce fighting ended with an estimated 145 dead on both sides and the retreat of the rebels into the Chiapas jungle. Skirmishes between the EZLN and the army continued over the next several years, with the army attacking Chiapan villagers and harassing them in many other ways. In December 1997,

70 gunmen thought to be affiliated with the PRN walked into a Chiapan village as people prayed in church and began shooting. As hundreds of villagers fled, the gunmen continued firing. When they stopped, 45 villagers, most of them women and children, had been murdered. In another part of Mexico six months later, army troops opened fire on more than 50 villagers sleeping in a small schoolhouse, killing 12 and wounding 5 (Evans 1998; Kleist 1997; Ross [John] 1998).

In the United States, in October 1996, the Federal Bureau of Investigation (FBI) arrested seven members of a group called the West Virginia Mountaineer Militia for allegedly making illegal explosives and plotting to attack a new FBI fingerprint and database center in West Virginia. At about the same time, three alleged members of the Georgia Republic Militia went on trial in Georgia for making illegal pipe bombs. In July 1996, the government had arrested 12 members of another militia group in Arizona for allegedly plotting to blow up federal buildings (Wilmington News Journal 1996; U.S. News & World Report 1996).

A century earlier, a major riot broke out in New York City in July 1863 against the military draft in support of the Civil War. For three long days and nights, mobs roamed the city, setting fire to buildings and shooting blacks, police, and federal troops. When the dust had settled, more than 1,000 people had been killed or wounded (Bernstein 1990). More than a century later, at the other end of the country, another large riot occurred when in April 1992, thousands of people in Los Angeles protested the acquittal of four police officers of charges of beating an African American resident, Rodney King, whom they had stopped for an alleged traffic violation. The rioting lasted five days and ended with more than 50 dead, 4,000 injured, and $1 billion in property damage (Cannon 1998). These two riots are among the largest in U.S. history, but the country's landscape has been marked by hundreds of riots in the last two centuries. Nor is this form of behavior confined to that country, as Europe and other continents have seen their share of riots in the last several centuries.

Another form of collective violence binds the world community: revolution. The United States began, of course, as the result of a revolution whose guiding principles are so eloquently set forth in the Declaration of Independence. Although the American revolution remains the one with which U.S. citizens are most familiar, other revolutions since the 1700s have dramatically changed the international landscape. The French Revolution and the Russian Revolution perhaps come most readily to mind, but many other revolutions have occurred as well. Their numbers are exceeded by smaller-scale rebellions, which were not extensive or successful enough to win the label of revolution.

When we think of violence, we usually think of *individual* or *interpersonal* violence: for example, a homicide, an assault, a rape, or a robbery. In all of these acts, one individual attacks another with the intent of inflicting physical injury. This is the type of violence that we fear and that prompts us to lock our doors at night, to buy weapons for self-defense, to carry pepper spray or other protective devices, and to pay princely sums for home security systems.

However, as the examples earlier in the chapter indicate, another type of violence affects our lives, and that is violence done by groups of people to advance or impede the goal of social change. Called *collective violence*, perhaps its most familiar form is war (Bramson and Goethals 1968; Groebel and Hinde 1989; Lang 1972; Shaw 1984). This book, however, focuses on types of collective violence that you're probably less familiar with: riots, revolution, terrorism, and the violence committed by cults, survivalists, and hate groups. These forms of violence differ very much from each other, yet they share at least two traits: They are done collectively, and they are meant to achieve or impede social, political, or economic change.

Collective violence has marked the historical landscape for many centuries and has certainly highlighted U.S. history since colonial days. Yet it remains little understood by the general public. Why do people participate in collective violence? Why does collective violence occur? What are its dynamics and impact? These questions are central in the study of collective violence. This book's goal is to help you understand some of the most important types of collective violence today by answering these questions. Its overriding view is that these types of violence are largely rational attempts to advance or resist social change, broadly defined. Discussing collective violence objectively is difficult because it easily arouses strong opinions from almost everyone. But the book attempts to provide a balanced perspective grounded in sociology and the other social sciences.

Why study collective violence? One reason is that it has been so important in the history of the United States and other nations. To put it plainly, collective violence has changed the course of human affairs and "often has led to the achievement of a more equitable and just society," as two scholars put it (Short and Wolfgang 1972:8). On the negative side, it often has also been used for the opposite goal: to bring about inequality and to cause injustice. For better or worse, we cannot understand how and why nations have changed without understanding collective violence. Sociologist Charles Tilly (1989:62) once observed:

> Western civilization and various forms of collective violence have always clung to each other. . . . Historically, collective violence has flowed regularly out of the central political processes of Western countries. People seeking to seize, hold, or realign the levers of power have continually engaged in collective violence as part of their struggles. The oppressed have struck in the name of justice, the privileged in the name of order, those between in the name of fear. Great shifts in the arrangements of power have ordinarily produced—and have often depended on—exceptional moments of collective violence.

Studying collective violence tells us something about ourselves and the society in which we live. To the extent that collective violence reflects underlying social, political, and economic conditions, its study implicitly tells us something about these conditions. And to the extent that people feel impelled to join in collective violence, it also tells us something about the external forces that motivate human action.

When riots and other collective violence erupted in the United States in the 1960s, the media, the public, and many scholars were startled. Forgetting the importance of such violence in the American past, they viewed those events as a historical aberration and, in the words of one sociologist, as an "unexpected and, in some ways, inexplicable phenomenon which somehow suddenly appeared in a full-blown and extremely threatening form" (Grimshaw 1972:37). In response, several scholars said that the 1960s violence was not that surprising, especially in view of the violent U.S. past, and criticized the "myth of peaceful progress" that dominated the country's understanding of its history (Rubenstein 1970). In these scholars' work lay, in the words of one, an "emphasis on the continuity of violence as a characteristic of American society (and, more broadly, possibly of most societies)" (Grimshaw 1972:37).

Back then, many observers were cautiously optimistic that the collective violence in the United States and elsewhere would prompt state authorities and other established interests to produce the necessary changes in the status quo that would reduce the motivation for continued collective violence (Grimshaw 1972). More than three decades later, their cautious optimism has not been borne out. If the 1960s riots in U.S. cities ultimately stemmed from substandard social and economic conditions, then these conditions are still with us and in many ways have worsened (Hacker 1992). If rebellion, revolution, and at least some forms of terrorism are a response to governmental oppression, then oppressive governments still exist across the globe. Meanwhile, homegrown militia and hate groups pose a threat to civil order in the United States and to racial minorities and other groups despised for their race, religion, national origin, or sexual orientation. Because collective violence will not soon go away, this book gives you some insight into its essential features.

This chapter introduces several issues and themes in the study of collective violence that later chapters address further. Chapter 2 reviews the literature on the reasons for collective violence, while later chapters focus on riots, revolution, and terrorism and the violence committed by cults, survivalists, and hate groups. In these chapters on specific types of collective violence, the goal is to help you to understand their causes, dynamics, and consequences. The last chapter reviews the themes of the book and comments on the prospects for collective violence in the years to come.

Collective Violence Defined

An important issue in the study of collective violence is its definition. Until we can define collective violence adequately, we can't know what it is and isn't, and unless we know this, we can't begin to understand it. This is true not only for the term *collective violence,* but also for the terms *riot, revolution,* and *terrorism* and those for the other behaviors examined in later chapters. Unfortunately, defining collective violence is more difficult than you might think. A key problem is distinguishing it from individual or interpersonal violence, in which one individual attacks another, with the result being a homicide, an assault, a rape, or a robbery. Most such crimes do involve one individual attacking another, but in many two or more people attack one or more victims (Ringel 1997).

According to the dictionary definitions for the terms *collective* (of or pertaining to a group) and *violence* (the infliction of physical injury or the destruction of property), such crimes technically should be considered examples of collective violence. This should be especially true of gang violence, whether the gang is a collection of juveniles, as so vividly portrayed in the famous, if dated, musical *West Side Story,* or a collection of adults participating in organized crime, as epitomized by the activities of gangster Al Capone in the 1920s. When two or more persons attack another person, when a juvenile gang attacks another juvenile gang, or when an organized crime gang strikes out at another crime gang, their interaction is surely both collective and violent. But does that make their attacks collective violence?

Social scientists mostly say no. Although "ordinary" violence of this sort is collective in nature, according to a strict dictionary definition of the term "collective," it usually lacks a key component that makes a violent act an example of collective violence: social change. When, in ordinary crimes, one individual attacks another, the offender's desired result is not a change in social policy or in some aspect of the political and economic systems (which is what social change means). When juvenile gangs or organized crime gangs attack each other, social change is not their desired result. These acts of ordinary violence occur so as to harm their targets and, in some way, to help the attacker(s) or satisfy their emotions. The "change" the offenders want, if any, in these conventional crimes is thus individual or interpersonal. Their acts have no intended implications or repercussions beyond those for the immediate participants and perhaps their friends and relatives.

As conceptualized by social scientists, collective violence by contrast has the express goal of aiding or impeding change in the social, political, and economic arenas of society. The targets of collective violence typically are only a means to an end, and that end is social change, broadly defined. Acts of violence are not examples of collective violence unless they have this goal.

So far, so good. But what if a lone assassin kills, or tries to kill, a political official, as has occurred many times in U.S. history (Clarke 1982)? The assassin might be trying to bring about or impede social change, but if he or she is truly acting alone and not as part of some larger movement, the violence is not collective in nature. Such an assassination would be an example of political violence but not of collective violence as usually conceived.

The distinction drawn here between interpersonal (or ordinary) violence and collective violence roughly corresponds to a widely used distinction between *expressive violence* and *instrumental violence* (Champion 1997). Expressive violence is violence committed to express anger, frustration, or some other emotion. Instrumental violence is violence committed to improve one's own status or to achieve some other material, social, or political gain. Most ordinary violence is expressive (Gilligan 1997), whereas most collective violence is instrumental.

Collective violence is sometimes also called *civil violence* (Rule 1988). Chapter 2 shows that the first scholars of civil violence studied riots and other crowd behavior, as well as rebellion and revolution. Terrorism has begun to capture scholarly interest as international terrorism has increased during the last few decades. Scholars of collective violence have largely neglected three more types of violence, that by cults, survivalists, and hate groups. Chapter 6 addresses these. Survivalist and hate group violence fits the previous definition of collective violence, as it is committed by groups to slow down or even to reverse modern social change. Cult violence, however, fits this definition less clearly. Some cult violence is directed at external targets to advance or impede social change and is in many ways the equivalent of terrorism. However, other cult violence is directed inwardly, as when a cult abuses its own members or even prompts them to commit suicide to achieve the cult's spiritual or other goals. Such cult violence doesn't include the important social change component, even if it is collective in nature. But because cult violence receives so much attention when it does occur, and understanding of it remains so limited, it is included in this book.

Rationality versus Irrationality

In sociology, the study of collective violence traditionally falls under the larger rubric of collective behavior, which refers to relatively spontaneous behavior by large numbers of people (Marx and McAdam 1994; Turner and Killian 1987). Examples of collective behavior include crowds, mobs, fads, rumors, panics, mass hysteria, reactions to disaster, and the forms of collective violence outlined previously. Over the years, scholars have developed several general explanations of collective behavior, many focusing on riots and other forms of crowd behavior. Chapter 2 reviews these general explanations.

One of the many issues that these explanations raise is whether collective behavior is rational or irrational. This issue applies especially to collective violence, which by its very nature seems extreme. Because collective violence is harmful by definition and often deadly, understanding why people engage in it can be difficult. This is true even if we agree with their social change goals; it's even more true if we disagree with them. Terrorism and other forms of collective violence are often described as "senseless," and their participants are often depicted as irrational. When they are described this way, their actions lose whatever little credibility they might have had with the general public. Two related questions thus arise: First, how rational is collective violence, and, second, how rational are its participants?

If "rational" means goal directed (Weber 1968 [1921]), then most collective violence is indeed rational. The goals of its participants depend on the specific type of collective violence and the circumstances under which it occurs. However, their violence is indeed directed at achieving certain, social change-oriented goals, regardless of whether we agree with those goals or with the violent means used to attain them. If "rational" further means sound, wise, and logical, then available evidence indicates that collective violence is rational, at least from the perspectives of its participants, because it sometimes can help achieve their social change goals.

To reiterate this point, for better or worse, collective violence can and does "work." This is said neither to justify nor celebrate it, but rather to underscore its largely rational character. As later chapters indicate, riots and other forms of collective violence sometimes lead to social policy and other kinds of changes. Moreover, revolution by definition involves the overthrow of an existing government and thus achieves its participants' goals, regardless of whether the revolution's aftermath lives up to their collective vision for a new society and government.

Support for the effectiveness of collective violence comes from several studies (e.g., Button 1989; Piven and Cloward 1979). In a study that won wide attention, William Gamson (1990) examined the strategies and outcomes of a number of "challenging groups" in U.S. history. Those that used violence were more successful in achieving their goals than those that did not. Although Gamson's study is not the last word on the subject and was later criticized on methodological and other grounds (Frey, Dietz, and Kalof 1992; Goldstone 1980; Mirowsky and Ross 1981; Steedly and Foley 1979), it does indicate that collective violence can succeed, even if it can also be counterproductive (Burstein, Einwohner, and Hollander 1995).

Gamson's study also suggested, however, that protest using nonviolent direct action (e.g., picketing, sit-ins, and marches) can also succeed more than "orderly" social change strategies that stay within the electoral system. Although Gamson thus concluded that "disruptive" strategies—violent or nonviolent—were more successful than conventional, electoral strategies, his findings on nonviolent strategies suggest that protest can succeed even if it isn't violent. Unfortunately, few studies have explored the relative efficacy of violent versus nonviolent protest (Burstein, Einwohner, and Hollander 1995). Nevertheless, if collective violence does work, then it is rational, no matter what else we might think of it.

The second question is how rational are the participants in collective violence? Are they sane? Do they really know what they're doing? Are they suffering from symptoms of mental illness such as extreme paranoia? If they're so willing to cause what's often considered senseless suffering and death, can they really be rational?

Here again the available evidence favors rationality. Certainly some rioters, terrorists, revolutionaries, survivalists, and the like are irrational and mentally ill, but so are some members of the general public, some politicians, and some people in just about every walk of life. As later chapters demonstrate, although some explanations of collective violence stress psychological abnormality among its participants, studies on this issue suggest that in general they're as psychologically normal and rational as the average person.

One point should be emphasized. We should not automatically assume that people have psychological problems and are irrational just because they engage in collective violence that kills and maims many people. The generals who run wars and the soldiers who fight them kill more people than participants in collective violence, but few people would question their sanity and psychological adjustment. U.S. President Harry S. Truman ordered the dropping of atomic bombs on Japan in 1945 that killed tens of thousands almost instantly, but few people, even those who condemn his use of atomic weapons, question Truman's psychological fitness. The key point is this: Whether we like it or not, a person can maim and kill for various goals without being mentally ill or psychologically abnormal. If we're willing to accept this fact for war, then we should do the same for riots, terrorism, and other types of collective violence.

The groups engaging in collective violence all have belief systems, or ideologies, with which they justify their actions (Lofland 1996; Marx and McAdam 1994). As Short and Wolfgang (1972:31) said, "The eruption of violence comes with self-legitimation of the use of physical force. Injurious consequences are neutralized by explicit or implied virtuous ends." In adopting such an ideology, collective violence groups don't differ from other kinds of groups, including those planning and fighting the wars with which we're all too familiar. Sometimes the beliefs of collective violence groups prompt them to commit actions that are difficult for us to fathom, but that doesn't necessarily mean that these actions stem from irrational individuals.

Micro versus Macro Roots of Collective Violence

When sociologists and other social scientists try to understand the various social behaviors and problems that they study, such as divorce, crime, and teenage pregnancy, they typically try to answer one or both of two related questions. First, why does the behavior occur? This is the so-called macro question, and answers to it typically focus on macro aspects of the social environment, broadly defined, that make the behavior more or less likely to happen. Second, given that the behavior is occurring, why are some individuals more likely than others to engage in it? This is called the micro question, and answers to it usually focus on such individual or personal factors as someone's personality or psychological state. Some social scientists take a macro approach to understand social behavior, whereas others take a more micro approach. Both approaches together offer a fuller understanding than either one can alone.

In Chapter 2, explanations of collective violence try to answer a pair of similar questions. First, why does collective violence occur? Answers to this question typically focus on macro, structural factors such as the underlying social, economic, and political conditions that make collective violence more or less likely to happen. Second, given that collective violence does occur, why are some individuals more likely than others to participate in it? Answers to this question usually focus on personality and other micro factors. As with other social behaviors, to fully understand the origins of collective violence we need to be familiar with both its micro and macro roots.

An example from the study of ordinary violence should illustrate not only the difference between micro and macro explanations, but also how they complement each other. Suppose that we want to understand homicide in the United States. A full explanation would begin at a high level by discussing why homicide is more common in the United States than in other industrial nations. This explanation would focus on the possible historical, cultural, and structural reasons, such as high rates of inequality, that help produce a higher homicide rate there than elsewhere (Zimring and Hawkins 1997).

This explanation is fine as far as it goes, but it fills in only part of the homicide puzzle. Even if homicide is especially common in the United States, it remains true that most of its citizens don't commit murder. Homicide rates are higher among some groups than others. To find out why, we could focus on some social and cultural factors, such as poverty and masculinity, that produce higher homicide rates among some categories (e.g., the poor and males) than among others (Barkan 1997).

Yet even then our understanding remains incomplete because most poor people and most men, and even most poor men, don't commit murder. At this level, we now want to know why some individuals who are poor, male, and so on are more likely to commit murder than others having the same or similar characteristics. To answer this question, we'd probably focus on such individual-level factors as personality and other psychological components or on an individual's family and peer influences.

To understand homicide as fully as possible, we must pursue the two levels of explanation just outlined. First, we must understand the social, cultural, historical, and economic roots of the behavior. Given that murders happen, however, we must also understand why individuals commit it (and why other individuals don't). Although most criminologists favor one type of explanation over the other in their own research, the field of criminology as a whole undertakes both approaches.

The analogy to the study of collective violence is clear. We must get a sense of the (macro) historical, social, and economic conditions that make collective violence more or less likely. We must also understand in the more micro arena why some individuals are more likely than others to participate in the various types of collective violence once they occur. While this dual approach seems eminently sensible, the study of collective behavior (and thus of collective violence) historically takes an either/or approach. In explaining such behavior, some scholars have favored macro factors, whereas others have favored micro factors; over the years, the two approaches have competed for popularity (Klandermans 1997). This rivalry has limited a full understanding of collective behavior and collective violence. Thus this book stresses both macro and micro approaches as much as possible and thereby aligns itself with other scholars (e.g., Snow and Oliver 1995) who feel that a complete understanding of collective action is impossible without appreciating the influence of both the macro and micro dimensions of social life.

Interplay with State Authorities

To understand the dynamics and outcomes of collective action—violent or nonviolent—we need to appreciate the interplay between protest groups and state officials. Groups that challenge the status quo through disruptive tactics represent a challenge to civic order and to the rule of state authorities. Interaction between disruptive groups and state authorities—governmental officials, the police, and the military—is crucial to the development and outcomes of the groups' disruptive strategies and tactics (Barkan 1984; McAdam 1983; McAdam, McCarthy, and Zald 1996; Tarrow 1998).

This central dynamic of protest certainly applies to collective violence. Several years ago, sociologist Allen D. Grimshaw (1972), author of several works on racial violence in the United States, called attention to the "central importance" of state authorities as a factor in civil violence. If aggrieved groups believe that state authorities are biased, Grimshaw said, they're more likely to become violent than if they believe that state authorities are impartial.

Other aspects of this collective violence dynamic are apparent. Protest groups are more likely to be violent when they feel that conventional political means such as voting and lobbying offer little hope for the redress of their grievances and that social reforms promised by state authorities are moving too slowly or were made in bad faith (Oberschall 1973). Thus, collective violence is more likely to occur under authoritarian governments that violently repress dissent than in more democratic governments that allow dissent. This is because violence by the state encourages violence by dissenters, who feel that they have no other choice (Della Porta 1996; Tarrow 1998). When dissenting groups do engage in violence, they inevitably end up confronting police and/or the military, both of whom aim to maintain the civil order that collective violence tries to disrupt. In short, the state attempts to meet force with force, responding violently to collective violence. This response helps to determine whether collective violence succeeds or fails (Rasler 1996). Later chapters explore the state's role in specific types of collective violence.

Conclusion

Collective violence is not only a feature of modern life but also an important element of the history of nations worldwide. It has been responsible for beneficial social change for masses of people. It also has been responsible for the worst forms of injustice, inequality, and oppression. By studying collective violence, we learn something about the reasons for and dynamics of social change in many social, political, and economic contexts. We also learn about society itself. To the extent that collective violence results from grievances and negative conditions in the larger society, we learn something about these problems. Given the significance of collective violence in the world today and in the past, understanding collective violence is an important part of understanding social and political life.

This chapter introduced several themes and issues in the study of collective violence that later chapters address more fully, including the following:

- The definition of collective violence
- The degree to which collective violence is rational or irrational
- Whether collective violence is better explained by micro or by macro factors
- The nature and implications of the interplay between collective violence participants and state authorities and other antagonists

As we explore collective violence in the chapters ahead, keep in mind that scholars often find it more difficult to study collective violence than many other behaviors and social phenomena (Berk 1972). This is largely because they often don't know about any specific episode of collective violence until after it has occurred. In the case of a riot, for example, social scientists can interview riot participants and nonparticipants only after the riot is over. Because the riot might result in changed attitudes of people living in or near the scene of the riot, it's difficult to determine community attitudes preceding the riot.

Also, many participants in collective violence might be difficult to find, and be unwilling to be interviewed even if they are found. As Richard A. Berk (1972:114) wryly notes, collective violence participants "are unlikely to take time out from what they are doing to cooperate with an investigator. And even if they would, the suspicion that a researcher might be a police officer or informant would mitigate against a sincere interaction." This comment suggests that social scientists who do try to interview some collective violence participants, such as terrorists, might place themselves at risk.

Contrast these problems with the relative ease of studying a more conventional behavior such as voting. Because social scientists know when an election will occur, they can interview potential voters before the election and reinterview them afterward. They can chart changes in voting preferences for several months and tie them to current events, social conditions, and campaign strategies.

For these reasons, social scientists studying collective violence rely less on interviewing than do social scientists studying many other topics and rely more on understanding the underlying historical, social, economic, and political conditions that lead to collective violence (Berk 1972). Thus, while the picture that we have of the individuals involved in collective violence might be less clear than we would like, it still can help us understand collective violence. As noted previously and in Chapter 2, sociologists tend to focus on the macro, underlying conditions for collective violence. This is certainly a major emphasis of this book.

2

Explaining Collective Violence

Chapter 1 noted that the study of collective violence falls under the more general study of collective behavior. Not surprisingly, the various explanations over the years of collective behavior are very relevant for understanding the genesis and dynamics of collective violence. This chapter reviews these explanations and expands on some of the issues introduced in Chapter 1. Given the sheer volume of the collective behavior literature, this chapter can't hope to cover every single aspect of it. But it does highlight its most important points so that you will come away from it with an understanding of the major insights of social scientists regarding the genesis and dynamics of collective behavior. Each subsequent chapter on specific types of collective violence use this understanding as a starting point to help explain the type of collective violence addressed in the chapter.

As Chapter 1 noted, to understand collective behavior and collective violence we need to understand why such behaviors begin in the first place and why some individuals are more likely to take part in them once they have begun. We thus need to understand not only the macro conditions that underlie collective behavior and collective violence, but also the micro factors that affect individual involvement in them. This chapter begins our review of the collective behavior literature with the micro, or individual-level factors, that social scientists have identified over the years and then turns to the macro, or structural factors, that they've also discussed.

Individual-Level Explanations of Collective Behavior

Although several types of micro explanations of collective behavior exist, they all seek to answer the question, "Why are some individuals more likely than others to participate in collective action?" In answering this question, most explanations focus on individual psychological states and attitudes as causes of collective behavior. Another type of individual-level explanation is more sociological, focusing on individuals' involvement in social and organizational networks as important influences on their decisions to participate in collective action. This chapter begins with the more psychological explanations and focuses on the degree to which irrationality and/or frustration underlie individual decisions to engage in collective behavior.

Rationality, Irrationality, and Involvement in Collective Action

A lengthy literature addresses the degree to which individual involvement in collective behavior is the result of irrational impulses and thinking and thus irrational itself. As we consider the question of irrationality, one thing becomes clear. Whether scholars attribute collective behavior to irrationality depends on many things, including the political atmosphere, for want of a better term, of the period in which a particular theorist is writing, the type of behavior that the theorist is trying to explain, and the theorist's own political biases. Theorists who dislike a behavior are apt to depict the individuals who engage in it as irrational, whereas those sympathetic to a behavior might hold the opposite view. Not surprisingly, opinions about irrationality have changed over the years.

The question of irrationality arose during the nineteenth century in Europe and was stimulated by the political and social turmoil of that century and by developments in psychoanalytic theory focusing on the unconscious (Rule 1988). All of this came on the heels of the French Revolution of 1789, as the intense violence and bloody success of this revolution frightened not only the aristocracy throughout Europe, but also many intellectuals. The latter began to fear that a breakdown of social order would occur in the absence of a strong society, that is, strong social bonds and social institutions and effective socialization (Collins 1994; Coser 1977).

The events of the nineteenth century only heightened their anxiety. Mob after mob of the poor roamed the streets of major European cities and, somewhat later, their U.S. counterparts. Property destruction, death, and injury were common. In Europe, several governments regularly battled violent left-wing movements. Living themselves in privileged positions, many intellectuals were horrified by what was happening. Not surprisingly, they began to write about mob violence in negative terms, with much of their work depicting the individuals taking part in such violence as irrational actors swayed by irrational impulses and crowd influences.

About the same time, Sigmund Freud was writing that human behavior is influenced by unconscious forces. The intellectuals' view of collective violence and Freud's view of the unconscious complemented and reinforced each other and together helped popularize the supposed irrationality of collective violence and the view that it "could never be a reasonable reaction to real needs or conditions" (Rule 1988:93). In one of his later works, *Group Psychology and the Analysis of the Ego,* Freud (1967 [1921]) said that crowds act irrationally on unconscious impulses and think more like children or primitive people than like intelligent adults.

Perhaps the most noted proponent of the irrationality thesis was Gustave LeBon (1841–1931). In 1895, LeBon wrote a famous book, *The Crowd: A Study of the Popular Mind,* that has been excerpted many times since. When individuals are isolated, LeBon wrote, they think rationally and without undue emotion. But they begin to feel, think, and act differently when in a crowd and succumb to the crowd's emotions. "In the collective mind" of the crowd, LeBon wrote, "the intellectual aptitudes of the individuals, and in consequence their individuality, are weakened" (LeBon 1978:8).

Noting that unconscious psychological phenomena and hidden motives can affect our thinking and behavior, LeBon added that individuals in crowds lose their ability to control their unconscious instincts. They are little different, he said, from hypnotized individuals under the control of the hypnotist. Just as the hypnotist controls all thoughts and movements of the person hypnotized, so does the crowd control the thinking and behavior of the individuals it contains. This individual "is no longer conscious of his acts" and instead "has become an automaton who has ceased to be guided by his will" (LeBon 1978:8–9). He becomes as savage and ferocious as primitive people and is easily "induced to commit acts contrary to his most obvious interests" (p. 9). To LeBon, then, people who take part in mobs, riots, and other forms of collective violence were little better than irrational savages who don't really know what they're doing.

Shortly after LeBon published his book on the crowd, Vilfredo Pareto (1848–1923), an Italian social scientist, came out with a series of books in the early 1900s (e.g., Pareto, 1935 [1916]) that tied the unconscious to collective violence (Coser 1977; Rule 1988). People, he said, often behave for reasons of which they're not aware. Thus, their behavior can be manipulated by political and economic elites. By the same token, without leadership by these elites, mass political behavior, including violence, is apt to be both senseless and aimless. Elite direction is necessary to channel the mass violence into politically effective directions.

Although the view of the "irrationalists," as they are now called (Rule 1988) began in Europe, it was popularized even further in the United States in the 1920s by Robert E. Park and other sociologists at the University of Chicago who began what came to be called the *collective behavior tradition* (Blumer 1939; Park and Burgess 1921). Park and his colleagues viewed riots, revolts, rumors, fads, and other processes as "noninstitutional" forms of behavior that represent a breakdown of social norms and a departure from the standards of normal behavior. Compared to conventional behavior, collective behavior was, in their view, "more irrational, more emotional (even frenzied), completely spontaneous, disorganized, disruptive, and totally without rules or boundaries," as Erich Goode (1992:4) observes. In depicting collective behavior as more *expressive* than *instrumental*—as more emotional than directed at achieving specific goals—the early collective behavior theorists in effect depicted all collective behavior, including the collective violence that falls into this category, as largely *apolitical,* since it was intended not to achieve political aims but rather to express various emotions and to fulfill various personal needs.

Since the time of these early theorists, the view of collective behavior has changed gradually to a more rational and political one, as collective behavior has come to be seen as less different from conventional behavior than the early theorists assumed. Among the first to adopt this new view were Ralph H. Turner and Lewis M. Killian, who in various works presented their "emergent norm" theory (Turner 1964; Turner and Killian 1957; Turner and Killian 1972; Turner and Killian 1987). This view emphasized that when people begin to interact in collective behavior, how they're supposed to behave or what they're supposed to do might initially be unclear. As they interact with each other, they discuss potential behavior and other related matters, and norms governing their behavior emerge. Social order and rationality, then, exist amid collective behavior, even that which is violent.

Despite the influence of Turner and Killian's emergent *norm theory,* the irrationality view continued into the 1960s. This is perhaps best illustrated in Neil J. Smelser's 1963 book, *Theory of Collective Behavior* (1963). One part of this theory, which is discussed further later in the chapter, emphasized that before collective behavior can occur in response to some social problem, people must first develop "generalized beliefs" about why the problem exists and what should be done about it. Often, Smelser wrote, these generalized beliefs are akin to magical, and even mythical, beliefs. Despite other valuable components of Smelser's theory, his discussion of generalized beliefs did harken back to the irrationality of the early collective behavior view (Currie and Skolnick 1970).

Irrationality received even greater emphasis in Lewis S. Feuer's 1969 book, *The Conflict of Generations,* in which he traced youths' involvement in protests to hostile relationships with their parents, including unresolved Oedipus complexes, whereby they hate their parents of the opposite sex. Feuer's view immediately proved very controversial and was severely criticized (Flacks 1970–1971).

At the turn of the 1970s, however, a new generation of sociologists began to critique this view. Many of these were involved in the Southern Civil Rights movement, Vietnam antiwar movement, and other social change efforts of the period. To these scholar-activists, any suggestion of irrationality in these movements was anathema because it implicitly challenged their legitimacy and high moral purpose. In an effort to establish a new understanding of individual involvement in collective behavior, these sociologists thus wrote many books and articles attacking the collective behavior view and emphasizing the rationality, purposefulness, and effectiveness of political protest (Currie and Skolnick 1970; Gamson 1975; McAdam 1982; Oberschall 1973). New models of rationality in crowd behavior were developed and presented (Berk 1974; McPhail and Miller 1973) in what became known as the *resource mobilization theory* (see later in this chapter).

The dominant view today is that most individuals involved in most types of collective behavior, especially social movement behavior, are indeed acting rationally and instrumentally, not just expressively, to use terms introduced previously. People involved in social movements do have emotions, just like people not so involved, but that does not mean that their behavior is any less rational or political (Jasper 1998; Snow and Oliver 1995; Taylor and Whittier 1995). This view applies to collective violence at least as much as to other forms of collective action. No matter what we might think of the means and ends of collective violence such as riots and revolution, its participants differ very little from those involved in conventional political activities in trying to achieve dearly felt political objectives. No matter how extreme their behavior might seem, it remains political behavior and they are political actors.

Frustration and Relative Deprivation

A popular social-psychological approach in the study of social movements and collective violence concerns the degree to which feelings of deprivation and frustration underlie individual decisions to engage in collective action. The origins of this *deprivation-frustration-aggression approach* (McPhail 1994) go back at least to Aristotle, who felt that inequality would lead to frustration among the masses and thus to social unrest (Rule 1988). A more modern underpinning of the approach is the *frustration-aggression theory*. Developed in the late 1930s by psychologist John Dollard and his associates (Dollard, Doob, Miller, Mowrer, and Sears 1939), this theory argues that frustration leads to aggression and that aggression results from frustration.

In the early 1960s, James C. Davies (1962) built on this view to develop a theory of collective violence based on the related concepts of rising expectations and relative deprivation. When social conditions are improving, Davies reasoned, deprived people begin to hope for improvement in their lives. If these conditions then stop improving, their hopes are sorely dashed. Their resulting disappointment leads to much frustration and then to violence. Thus it's not their *absolute* deprivation but rather the *relative* deprivation that they feel is the crucial source of their individual decisions to join in collective violence.

Davies's theory echoed the argument of the great French social observer, Alexis de Tocqueville (1955 [1856]), who sought a century earlier to explain why revolution occurred in France in the late 1700s but did not occur in

Germany, even though German peasants led worse lives than their French counterparts. The answer, said Tocqueville, lay in the fact that the lives of French peasants had been improving, whereas those of German peasants had not. Once the French peasants had gotten a taste of a better life, they were especially frustrated when they found that things weren't improving even more.

A few years after Davies presented his theory, Ted Robert Gurr published his book *Why Men Rebel* (1970) to much acclaim. After asserting the importance of the frustration-aggression theory described previously, Gurr observed that frustration arises from feelings of relative deprivation, which can be defined as a perceived discrepancy between one's hopes and one's reality. Increasing relative deprivation leads to more frustration, more frustration leads to more anger, and more anger leads to more violence. In the discussion of relative deprivation, the concept of perception is crucial, Gurr noted, as not everyone in the same objective situation feels relatively deprived. One person might feel quite happy with, or at least resigned to, her or his situation, whereas another might feel deprived and even resentful. By the same token, people who, objectively speaking, are better off than other people may nonetheless *feel* more deprived, especially if the latter have given up hope.

Thanks to Davies and especially to Gurr, *relative deprivation theory* became quite popular, as it seemed an intuitively appealing explanation for the rise of collective violence. All of us can think of times when our hopes and expectations were thwarted and can recall the hurt and anger that we felt as a result. Some of us might have lashed out angrily and even violently at the individual that we held responsible for our frustration. If these same processes apply to masses of individuals angered by social conditions, then relative deprivation could well be a very sound explanation for collective violence.

Despite its inherent appeal, however, relative deprivation theory might be weaker than first thought, as critics have noted several shortcomings (Gurney and Tierney 1982; Rule 1988; Salert 1976; Sederberg 1994). First, contemporary work in psychology notes that frustration leads to aggression much less often than the authors of the original frustration-aggression theory thought; many responses other than aggression are possible. For example, people can blame themselves for the deprivation that they feel; if they do blame themselves, they're not likely to be violent toward others. Second, the frustration-aggression theory applies to individual behavior, whereas the relative deprivation theory really applies to groups of individuals. It's not clear that a process that might affect one person's behavior can be assumed to explain the behavior of groups of individuals, since individuals likely differ markedly in their psychological makeup.

Third, and perhaps most important, several empirical studies, many of them of U.S. riots in the 1960s, have not found a relationship between various measures of relative deprivation and collective violence. Thus, they provide little support for relative deprivation theory (Gurney and Tierney 1982;

McPhail 1994; Rule 1988). In some studies, relative deprivation is measured by asking individuals about their feelings about their socioeconomic status and other aspects of their lives. Contrary to what relative deprivation theory would predict, those who are most frustrated about their lives are not more likely to support or engage in collective violence (Muller 1979). Other studies measure relative deprivation with aggregate (e.g., nationwide or city-wide) data such as unemployment rates or the income differences between the richest and poorest segments of a community. Again contrary to what relative deprivation theory would predict, localities with the greatest deprivation are not more likely than those with less deprivation to experience rioting and other collective violence (e.g., Snyder and Kelly 1976).

Despite the criticism that it has received, relative deprivation theory still has its advocates. In particular, David E. Snow and Pamela E. Oliver (1995:579) recently termed the dismissal of the theory "premature." They note that most studies testing the theory infer felt deprivation from objective conditions (objective deprivation) such as unemployment rates instead of measuring the amount of deprivation that people actually *feel* (subjective deprivation), which is what adequate tests of the theory need to do. They also observe that relative deprivation might be a necessary condition for collective action even if it's not a sufficient condition. Although people might not engage in collective action even if they feel relatively deprived, they will not engage in such action *unless* they feel so deprived. Finally, Snow and Oliver (1995) point out that some studies have indeed found subjective deprivation related to involvement in collective action (e.g., Useem 1980). The authors conclude that it's "likely that . . . something like relative deprivation, appropriately measured and contextualized, can affect differential recruitment and participation" in collective action (p. 579).

Taking a more skeptical view, Goode (1992:127) notes, "Actually, a few, but only a very few, instances of collective violence or revolution are illuminated by this model. History notes countless uprisings in which relative deprivation has been entirely absent." He also observes that relative deprivation theory says little about how and why people who feel deprived end up becoming involved in collective violence, whereas others feeling the same way do not. As the recent comments by Snow and Oliver (1995) suggest, however, the debate over relative deprivation theory promises to continue for some time.

The Effect of Social Attachments

A final, individual-level perspective on collective behavior is more sociological, addressing the issue of whether individuals who become involved in such behavior are isolated from society or very much involved in it. Empirically, the question becomes whether actors in collective action are loners (or "social isolates," to use some sociological jargon) or people with extensive friendships and organizational memberships.

The "loner" image of individuals in collective violence was popular for much of this century, as various writers advanced the view that "violent social movements sprang disproportionately from the ranks of the socially dislocated," who were manipulated into being violent by cynical leaders (Rule 1988:108). This view reached its fullest expression in William Kornhauser's (1959) book, *The Politics of Mass Society.* Kornhauser wrote that in industrialized and urbanized societies, society as a whole becomes more impersonal and social ties and social institutions become weaker. Individuals with the weakest social attachments—for example, those who are unmarried and unemployed, who don't belong to religious or other organizations, and who have few friends—become alienated and are the most vulnerable to inducements to take part in social movements, including violent movements, because these efforts provide them the sense of belonging that they lack in their normal lives.

Although this view remains popular, the empirical evidence clearly indicates that the loner image is "fatally flawed" (Goode 1992:421). Many studies, some of them of riot participants (see Chapter 3), find that the people most likely to participate in collective action are those with extensive friendships and organizational involvements, not those who are socially isolated. In fact, one of the most consistent findings mentioned in recent social movement literature is that these friendships and organizational memberships serve as a catalyst for recruiting people into collective action (McAdam, McCarthy, and Zald 1988; Snow, Zurcher, and Ekland-Olson 1980). As Rule (1988:109–110) says of the mass society loner view, "It is hard to think of another influential idea [in the study of collective violence] that has received such wide refutation."

Social and Structural Explanations of Collective Behavior

Although several types of social and structural explanations of collective behavior exist, all seek to answer the question, "Why are some locations in some periods of history more likely than other locations in other periods of history to experience collective behavior?" The emphasis here is not on why individuals become involved but on why the behavior arises in the first place. Despite their many differences, social and structural explanations focus on certain society-wide problems and processes that generate the motivation and willingness for collective action. The two most important explanations are discussed next.

Smelser's Structural-Strain Theory

Earlier in the chapter Neil Smelser's discussion of generalized beliefs was critiqued as a necessary condition for collective action. Though his notion of generalized beliefs smacked of the irrationality found in earlier explanations, his larger *structural-strain theory* remains an influential macro explanation of collective behavior (Marx and Wood 1975). At its heart are six factors that must be present for collective action to occur.

The first factor, says Smelser, is **structural conduciveness;** that is, how a society's organization makes some types of collective action more or less likely than others. Violent social movements are less likely to occur, for example, in democratic societies than in totalitarian ones, as the former permit various kinds of legal protest and other political activities aimed at redressing grievances. Lacking these opportunities, aggrieved groups in totalitarian societies are more apt to turn to violence as their mode of protest.

Smelser's second factor, **structural strain,** is perhaps his most important. It refers to various kinds of social problems, including a general breakdown in conventional social institutions, such as the family and religion, that result from rapid social change and that lead to people being upset about the existing social, economic, and political systems. Their frustration, anger, and other such manifestations of discontent in response to structural strain underlie their efforts to become politically active as they try to change conditions to reduce the strain. As should be clear, Smelser's treatment of strain is the macro equivalent of the deprivation-frustration-aggression theory discussed earlier in the chapter and that operates at the individual level. This is because strain can be said to lead to feelings of deprivation and frustration and thus to violence and other collective action. The two approaches are thus often treated as one general approach that emphasizes the importance of grievances for the origins of such activity (e.g., McPhail 1994).

Before efforts to reduce structural strain can begin, people need to develop **generalized beliefs,** Smelser's third factor. These are explanations for structural strain that serve to justify what measures are necessary to deal with it. As noted previously, Smelser's discussion of this concept in the context of exaggeration and mythical thinking led to criticism that his theory harkened back to the irrationality of LeBon and others with similar views. However, if we think of generalized beliefs as more level-headed ideological beliefs, as Smelser also did, then contemporary theory would agree that such beliefs are a necessary if hardly sufficient condition for much collective behavior (Goode 1992; McAdam, McCarthy, and Zald 1988).

Smelser's first three factors set the stage for collective action. For such action to occur, **precipitating factors** must also take place. These are events that trigger particular episodes of collective action, such as an arrest in an urban area that angers people and leads them to throw things at the police and even to riot.

Mobilization for action must next take place in order for collective action to continue. At this stage, leaders specifically, and social movement organizations more generally, must effectively do the "nuts and bolts" of recruiting people into collective action and organizing their protest and other activities. Without such organizing, any collective action ignited by a precipitating factor is apt to be aimless and fleeting.

How long collective action lasts and whether it succeeds also depend on how authorities respond with **social control,** whose operation is Smelser's sixth and final factor. Authorities can either try to do something about the social conditions leading to the structural strain that is underlying collective action or try to stop the collective action itself without addressing the reasons for the underlying discontent of its participants. A violent response by the government can effectively end a movement. However, it can also lead a movement to engage in violence in response and thus prompt a reform social movement to become a revolutionary one (Rasler 1996; Wood and Jackson 1982).

For Smelser's theory to be valid, two things must be true at a minimum (Rule 1988; Wood and Jackson 1982). First, all six factors or stages must be present before a sustained collective action develops. Second, collective action must develop if all six factors occur. On both counts, empirical support for Smelser's structural-strain theory is mixed (Rule 1988). While it might be true that collective behavior does not generally occur without these six factors occurring, it is also true that it does not always occur when the six factors do occur. His theory is also hard to falsify, as it's difficult to imagine sustained collective action occurring without the six stages (Rule 1988). Finally, the theory also suffers from a lack of clarity. As Goode (1992:424) points out, "For collective behavior generally, some of Smelser's factors are so broad and vague as to explain both everything and nothing." As an example of this problem, the theory doesn't say how much strain is needed to generate collective behavior (Rule 1988).

Despite these criticisms, however, the stages that the theory discusses do play an important role in the onset of collective behavior. Research since its introduction continues to explore the complex ways in which these stages operate and their implications for the onset, dynamics, and success or failure of collective action. In particular, the theory's emphasis on structural strain continues to stimulate scholarship on whether and to what degree such strain underlies collective violence and other social movement activity (Myers 1997; Useem 1985). Indeed, a recent review concluded that the societal breakdown emphasized in the theory has a much stronger impact on collective action than the theory's critics assume (Useem 1998).

The Ethnic Competition Model.   One specific type of strain emphasized in recent research is that resulting from *ethnic competition,* which is often said to promote collective violence. An ethnic competition model is increasingly being regarded as an important explanation for collective violence (Belanger and Pinard 1991; Bonacich 1972; Olzak 1989; Olzak 1992; Olzak, Shanahan, and McEneaney 1996; Tilly, Tilly, and Tilly 1975; Tolnay and Beck 1995). According to this model, conflict results when groups compete for scarce resources. Such competition can increase when, for example, the economy takes a turn for the worse or immigration increases. Thus, when two or more ethnic groups living in the same nation or a smaller setting find themselves competing for jobs, housing, and other resources, ethnic hostility and eventually conflict in the form of ethnic violence are likely to develop, provided that one or more of the ethnic groups perceives that the competition is unfair (Belanger and Pinard 1991). The ethnic competition model has received much empirical support and promises to continue to explain many examples of collective violence and other collective action.

Political Theories and Resource Mobilization

Beginning in the 1970s, a new view began to dominate the study of social movements and collective action (Gamson 1975; McCarthy and Zald 1977; Oberschall 1973; Tarrow 1998; Tilly 1978). In this view, collective action is the response of rational political actors to harsh social conditions. These conditions, and thus the strain and discontent resulting from them, are said to be relatively constant and thus cannot account for the beginning of collective action. As Charles Tilly, this approach's major proponent, observes, "Grievances are fundamental to rebellion as oxygen is fundamental to combustion. But just as fluctuations in the oxygen content of the air account for little of the distribution of fire in the workaday world, fluctuations of grievances are not a major cause of the presence or absence of rebellion" (quoted in Sederberg 1994).

Instead, collective action begins when resources of the populace—such as money, time, and communication skills—are mobilized by social movement leaders and when political and social conditions change in ways that facilitate such mobilization. Movements succeed when they can mobilize sufficient resources to counter social control efforts by the state. They are especially likely to succeed when political events have weakened the state's ability to respond effectively to movement challenges (McAdam, McCarthy, and Zald 1996).

This new view of collective action goes under several names: political theory, political process theory, resource mobilization theory, and political opportunity theory to name just a view. These theories differ in several ways from each other and even dispute each other, but they all share the basic elements summarized previously. In emphasizing the importance of mobilization, organization, and resources, they explicitly deemphasize the importance of psychological and social-psychological factors such as grievances and discontent. While it is true, they say, that certain attitudes (for example, sympathy with the goals of a movement) are necessary for involvement in a social movement, it also remains true that most people with these attitudes do not become involved (Klandermans and Oegema 1987). If this is true, then, as Gary T. Marx and Doug McAdam (1994:89–90) observe, "The role of individual attitudes in shaping activism must be regarded as fairly limited." The key question then becomes why some people with the necessary attitudes do get involved and why most do not. The friendship and organizational networks discussed previously provide one important answer to this question, as mobilization efforts often work through these channels.

As noted earlier in the chapter, the theorist in this new approach most associated with the study of collective violence is Charles Tilly, whose work has greatly enriched our historical and sociological understanding of collective violence in Europe (Tilly 1978; Tilly 1986; Tilly 1989; Tilly 1995; Tilly, Tilly, and Tilly 1975). Tilly sees collective violence as a common aspect of the more general "contention" that marks almost every society. By "contention" he means "one set of people making claims that bear on the interests of another set of people" (Tilly 1989:64). Most contention is nonviolent, but some involves violence. Tilly (1989:65) observes, "Since contention is the very stuff of normal politics, collective violence belongs to the everyday world of political struggle." To this extent, then, collective violence is "normal," whatever one thinks of it, and does not represent an incomprehensible departure from everyday life and politics.

Despite their important contributions, Tilly and other political theory proponents have been criticized on at least two grounds. First, their approach might well underestimate the significance of structural strains, grievances, and other social-psychological states for collective action (Klandermans and Oegema 1987; Snow and Oliver 1995; Useem 1998; Walsh and Warland 1983). In particular, several critics point out that strain and discontent are not as constant as the political approach assumes and that sometimes collective action is indeed prompted by changes in social, economic, and political conditions that lead to new grievances and a heightened sense of dissatisfaction and discord.

Three examples from different parts of the world in early 1998 illustrate this dynamic. In the first, 40,000 people demonstrated on February 5 in Germany to protest rising unemployment, which had reached a post–World War II high of 12.6 percent nationwide and over 21 percent in the east. One demonstration leader said, "People are more willing to protest now. The situation is more severe" (Neuffer 1998:A2). In the second example, riots broke out in Zimbabwe in January after the government said that it would raise food prices 21 percent in order to reduce food consumption in view of an impending drought and low crop output. A month earlier, the announcement of huge new taxes had sparked a national strike in that nation (Shillinger 1998). At about the same time, people were also rioting daily in Indonesia because of a rapidly declining economy and rising food prices. The situation led one scholar to warn, "If you are unemployed and don't have food for your family, people get desperate. [There's] a sense of having nothing to lose, and that's dangerous" (Lakshmanan 1998:A25). The political theory's assumptions notwithstanding, these examples indicate that deteriorating economic and other conditions can increase discontent and spark collective violence and other protests.

The political theory has also been criticized for painting a view of activism that is overly rational, too unemotional, and too political (Jasper 1998;

Johnston and Klandermans 1995a; Rule 1988; Taylor and Whittier 1995). Not all collective violence and other forms of collective behavior are planned in the cold, calculated way often depicted by political and resource mobilization theorists, and not all episodes of collective violence are as explicitly political as they assume. Moreover, collective violence and other social movement activity are much more emotional than the new view assumes. In trying to avoid the irrationality and emotionality that biased older views of collective behavior, the new theorists have perhaps gone too far in the other direction.

These criticisms notwithstanding, the writings of Tilly and other recent theorists have significantly advanced our understanding of collective violence and other forms of collective behavior. They have reinforced the rationality of political protest and called attention to important processes involved in the mobilization of political action. The continuing discussion between the political approach and its critics promises to enrich the field of collective behavior for many years.

Recent Developments in the Study of Collective Behavior

During the 1970s and early 1980s, the political approach described in the previous section dominated the study of social movements. Beginning in the middle 1980s, however, a new wave of work criticized this approach for ignoring the social-psychological dimensions of collective behavior. More important, new studies began to explore these dimensions (Klandermans 1984; Snow and Oliver 1995; Zurcher and Snow 1981). This new body of work has been called the *social constructionist perspective*, or *social constructionism* (Snow and Oliver 1995).

Among other things, the social constructionist perspective emphasizes how individuals decide to participate in collective behavior and how they interpret the meanings that they attribute to specific collective behavior events. It also calls attention to the cultural aspects of collective behavior, including the ways in which social movements draw on religious and other beliefs to mobilize their supporters and construct collective identities that involve a shared understanding of how they define themselves and the goals that they're pursuing (Abrahams 1992; Johnston and Klandermans 1995b; Melucci 1989). This body of work also emphasizes that identity and culture are as important as organizations and structural change to social movements, and perhaps even more so (Polletta 1997; Whittier 1995). For example, movements can succeed not only when they affect social policy and bring about other structural changes, but also when they change the larger culture and achieve a collective identity (Darnovsky, Epstein, and Flacks 1995; Johnston and Klandermans 1995b).

To illustrate the social constructionist perspective, this section discusses briefly two of its most important themes (Snow and Oliver 1995). The first involves what is called *framing*, the attempt to affect the meanings and understandings that social movement actors, their antagonists, and the public attach to movement grievances, goals, and justifications for protest (Benford 1997; Snow and Benford 1992; Snow, Rochford, Worden, and Benford 1986). In this regard, the struggle between social movements and their antagonists is in large part an effort to control the view that the public has of the struggle. Social movements seek to convince the public to accept their analysis of the reasons that social change is needed, whereas the state and other foes try to do just the opposite, often painting movements as dangerous threats to the public order. Framing, then, is the attempt to affect the "public perception of protest" (Turner 1969).

When it comes to collective violence, framing takes on special importance, as the public would normally be reluctant to accept the claims of protesters whose actions lead to death or injury (Ball-Rokeach 1972). Partly for this reason, the Southern Civil Rights movement was committed to nonviolent direct action. It realized that violent acts by Civil Rights protesters would delegitimate their cause and reduce their potential support from the news media, Northern whites, and the president and the Congress in Washington, D.C. The movement also hoped that brutal repression by Southern police and white citizens against nonviolent protesters would win it sympathy from these same parties. Violence by the movement would have thus undermined the perception that it wanted its potential supporters to have. Fortunately for the movement, Southern whites played into their hands by indeed acting violently. This white violence greatly helped the movement to win significant legislative victories in Washington (Barkan 1984; Garrow 1986; McAdam 1983).

Given the normal concern of social movements for their public image, why, then, does collective violence take place? One reason is that not all movements and collective violence actors share the concern of the Civil Rights movement over their public image. Terrorists, for example, commit violence not to win public sympathy, since it is the public that their violence often victimizes, but to force concessions from state officials or other antagonists. Revolutionaries aim to force similar concessions, but because their violence is directed at the state and not the masses in whose name they are revolting, they also hope to win public support to their cause, often through the type of framing efforts described previously.

Another reason that collective violence occurs despite the normal concern of movements for their public image is that some collective violence, particularly riots, are fairly spontaneous (see Chapter 3). Because of this, rioters do not normally sit down and weigh in advance whether their rioting will win support from the public or, instead, alienate it. Instead they riot, and the outcome of their rioting for public support and other matters starts to become clear only after the rioting ends. From the rioters' perspectives, their riot might do no good at all or it might force concessions from governmental officials and prompt at least some members of the public to consider whether the grievances underlying the riots ought to be addressed.

A second theme in the new social constructionist perspective concerns collective identity. As William A. Gamson (1992:56) notes, "Participation in social movements frequently involves enlargement of personal identity for participants and offers fulfillment and realization of self." It also involves identification with a larger cause and with the people working for that cause. Protest might aim at tangible victories such as changes in social policy. However, it also aims to develop a sense of collective identity among the actors engaging in it. Such collective identity develops in part from the emotional bonds that collective action actors develop with each other and from their shared commitment to the goals for which they are working together (Gamson 1996; Melucci 1989; Taylor and Whittier 1992).

Recent work on collective identity has drawn to a large degree on the women's and gay rights movements in the United States, ones in which collective violence has been rare, as well as on various social movements in Europe that have used violence somewhat more often. Because this work is still so new, its implications for our understanding of collective violence remain unclear. That said, the development of collective identity and the ways in which this development occurs should be at least as important for collective violence as they are for other forms of collective behavior. If anything, the "shared commitments and bonds of solidarity" (Snow and Oliver 1995:588) that are essential for the development of collective identity should be even stronger in groups that use collective violence, if only because their means are so drastic and the consequences of detection and apprehension by state authorities so severe. Future research on collective identity that involves collective violence will thus contribute greatly to our understanding of an important aspect of the development and dynamics of collective behavior.

Conclusion

Theories of social phenomena often reflect the political and social currents of the times in which the scholars writing the theories live (Coser 1977). However objective that they try to be, social scientists' explanations of the world around them are to some degree influenced by what is going on in that world. Explanations of collective behavior illustrate this pattern. To a large degree, the development of theories of such behavior reflects changing political and intellectual climates. When intellectuals have opposed the collective behavior of their times and of their recent pasts, they have tended to depict the behavior negatively and the people engaging it as apolitical actors cut off from society who are expressing personal needs instead of aiming for political goals. When scholars have instead supported the collective behavior of their eras and their recent pasts, they have painted a more positive portrait of both the behavior and the individuals participating in it.

When the study of collective behavior began more than a century ago, the French Revolution was still a recent memory and the political turmoil in Europe an even fresher one. Accordingly, scholars such as LeBon and, later, Freud and others, wrote of participants in crowds and other forms of collective behavior as irrational actors, with some scholars terming them a serious threat to public order. These views carried over, if often in more muted fashion, into the study of collective behavior for much of the 1900s in the United States. Scholars such as Turner and Killian began to develop a richer understanding of collective behavior that served as a bridge between the views of the earlier irrationalists and the new emphasis beginning in the 1960s on the rationality and high moral and political purpose of collective action. Although this new political approach—or resource mobilization perspective, as it's also called—dominated the study of collective action for some time, it has arguably given way in the last decade to a social constructionist perspective. This perspective considers collective action as both rational and political, but it also reminds us of its various social-psychological dimensions. Because of these trends, the study of collective action is today richer than ever before. It promises to increase our understanding of collective violence. In turn, the study of collective violence promises to increase our understanding of the larger phenomenon of collective action.

3

Riots

Although U.S. residents were shocked by the urban riots of the 1960s, rioting goes back to the colonial period and has occurred throughout U.S. history. Nor have riots been limited to American shores. In Europe throughout the 1700s and into the early 1800s, food riots were common. As Europe urbanized, fewer people were producing food on their own, as they no longer worked on farms, and thus had to buy food from others. Many were too poor to do so. As a result, poor Europeans would seize grain that was being transported through their towns and would force other grain to be sold at a price lower than the listed one. To accomplish these goals, they would sometimes attack the people who owned, transported, or sold the grain. Other Europeans during this time rioted because of opposition to the military draft, taxation, the use of new farm machines that threatened their jobs, and other issues (Hobsbawn 1962).

This chapter examines the riot as a significant form of collective violence. It first outlines the types of riots and then reviews the history of riots in the United States. Next it discusses the various explanations that scholars have of riots and also considers their consequences. The last section discusses prison riots, many of which have occurred in the United States and other countries during the last few decades.

Types of Riots

A **riot** is a fairly spontaneous, noisy, and violent outburst of disorder by a large group of people. Like *terrorism*, the term *riot* sounds very negative to many. Thus to characterize the urban violence that broke out in cities across the United States in the 1960s, many social scientists preferred terms such as *urban revolt* or *ghetto uprising* (Balbus 1977; Feagin and Hahn 1973). Some riots are explicitly political in nature, while others are very apolitical, or, as Gary Marx (1972) calls them, "issueless riots." Given this book's theme of group violence aimed at political and social change, the discussion in this chapter highlights the political nature of many riots, while recognizing the apolitical nature of others.

Several scholars have presented typologies of riots according to the motivation and goals of their participants. Usually we don't actually *know* their motivation and goals. Rather we *infer* them from the physical and social characteristics of the location in which the riot occurs, the precipitating event that sparks the riot, and the social backgrounds of the people who participate in it.

A basic distinction in these typologies is between riots that have political underpinnings and consequences and riots that are largely apolitical in their origins and dynamics. Clark McPhail (1994) refers to these as *protest* and *celebration* riots, respectively. A **protest riot** occurs in response to discontent with existing social, political, and/or economic conditions. A **celebration riot,** as the name implies, occurs as part of the general rejoicing that accompanies a major event, such as the victory of a favorite athletic team.

Some riots contain elements of both types. A recent example is the riot that occurred in Chicago on the night of June 14, 1992, after the Chicago Bulls basketball team won the National Basketball Association title. Boisterous celebrations began across the city, but in the black ghetto areas they took an ugly turn as hundreds of stores were looted, more than 1,000 people arrested, and almost 100 police officers injured (Rosenfeld 1997). Although the Bulls had won the NBA title both before and after 1992, the rioting that year was probably by far the most extensive. Rosenfeld (1997) argues that it resulted from discontent over a massive welfare cut in April 1992 and from continuing dismay over the acquittal that same month of the four Los Angeles police officers for beating Rodney King. Thus the motivation for the rioting was both celebratory and political.

Erich Goode (1992) categorizes riots according to their participants' motives and goals. The first type is the **purposive riot** (also called **instrumental riot**), which results from discontent over specific issues and aims to achieve specific goals. Examples include riots by workers as part of labor-management strife, the New York City antidraft riot discussed previously, and many prison riots. The second type is the **symbolic riot** (also called **expressive riot**), which is meant to express discontent but not to achieve a specific goal. Many of the urban riots of the 1960s fit into this category. A third type is the **revelous riot,** which occurs after a celebration by a crowd that gets out of hand and is equivalent to the celebration riots discussed previously. Such celebrations often involve a lot of drinking, which can easily promote violence in this sort of setting. A final type is the **issueless riot,** which has no observable motivation or goal. An example is the rioting and looting that sometimes occur when police go on strike (Goode 1992; Marx 1972).

What Do You Think?

As the text notes, many social scientists sympathetic to the conditions facing African Americans prefer terms such as *urban revolt* or *ghetto uprising* to characterize the urban riots of the 1960s (Balbus 1977; Feagin and Hahn 1973). To these scholars, those riots were ultimately an expression of discontent over negative social conditions and not simply the acts of irrational, criminalistic individuals. Robert M. Fogelson (1971:21) summarizes this view: "The 1960s riots were articulate protests against genuine grievances in the black ghettos. . . . [T]hey were attempts to call the attention of white society to the blacks' widespread dissatisfaction with racial subordination and segregation."

Other observers at the time were much more critical of the 1960s riots. There was no place for these riots in a law-abiding society, they said, and even if the riots were an expression of grievances, in a democracy people have other avenues for expressing their discontent and attempting to change political and economic policy.

A later section examines the evidence on the degree, if any, to which social conditions motivated the 1960s rioting. In the meantime, try to answer the following questions. Is *riot* the appropriate term for the 1960s urban violence, or would a term such as *urban revolt* be more appropriate? Are riots ever justified in a democratic society? Are they justified if the people engaging in them have few other ways of making their grievances known?

What do you think?

The next section discusses the history of riots and rioting in the United States, focusing on *protest riots,* to use McPhail's (1994) category.

A Brief History of U.S. Riots

The Colonial Period

As noted at the beginning of this chapter, rioting in the United States goes back to the colonial period. We cannot fully understand the history of this country without appreciating the role that rioting has played in it (Rubenstein 1970).

In the 1700s, taxation, as you surely remember from your colonial history lessons, was a sore point with the colonists, and they often rioted against tax collectors and other officials appointed by England. Rioting also occurred for other reasons, such as land disputes. An estimated 75 to 100 riots of all types occurred between 1641 and 1759. Once hostilities with England escalated, rioting became a favorite colonial tactic, with at least 44 riots occurring from 1760 to 1775 as "an instrument of resistance to and rebellion against British policy" (Brown 1975:51). After the victory over England, many people, and particularly farmers, faced prison because of their debts, and they often rioted and otherwise fought with state militia. The famous Shays' Rebellion, which involved a group of farmers, began with a riot of six hundred people in front of the courthouse in Springfield, Massachusetts, in protest against the legal punishment they were facing.

Rioting in the Nineteenth Century

In the first half of the nineteenth century, rioting was "as much a part of civilian life as voting or working" (Rosenfeld 1997:484). Common in Northern cities, it usually took the form of mob violence by native-born whites against blacks, Catholics, and immigrants. From 1830 to 1865, at least 70 percent of U.S. cities with populations over 20,000 experienced at least one major riot. One historian has dubbed this period the "Riot Era" (Brown, 1975:19), and another observer calls it the "Turbulent Era" (Feldberg 1980). Abraham Lincoln himself despaired in 1837 of "the worse than savage mobs" and "the increasing disregard for law which pervades the country." He continued, "Accounts of outrages committed by mobs form the every-day news of the times. . . . Whatever their causes be, it is common to the whole country" (quoted in Feldberg 1980:4).

From 1824 to 1849, at least 39 riots were directed against blacks in cities such as Philadelphia, Cincinnati, New York, Buffalo, and Pittsburgh. As historian Richard Maxwell Brown (1975:206) observes, "The underlying causes of these riots were white fears of social amalgamation with blacks, distrust of black education, dislike of black efforts at self-improvement, and hatred of abolitionism." Underlying these fears, he continues, was a "deep-seated racial prejudice . . . in which whites saw blacks as 'something less than human.'" As one example of the rioting to which this prejudice led, in August 1834 a mob of whites, worried about black job competition, ransacked a black neighborhood in Philadelphia and beat up many of its residents.

Blacks were not the only targets in the Riot Era. During the 1850s, the so-called Know-Nothing Party, discussed in more detail in Chapter 5, was virulently anti-Catholic. Its members roamed the streets in cities such as Baltimore and New Orleans, beating and sometimes killing Catholics (Anbinder 1992). Mob violence in Northern cities also broke out during that decade against abolitionists and, again, against blacks. As discussed earlier, New York City was the scene of perhaps this country's worst riot in 1863, when Irish Americans rioted against the military draft and killed several hundred blacks, whom they blamed for the draft (Bernstein 1990). Rioting against blacks also marred the Southern landscape after the Civil War, as whites worried about gains being made by the newly freed slaves (Brown 1975).

Rioting after the Civil War was more economic in motivation, with some of it fitting the ethnic competition model outlined earlier. During the

1870s, Chinese immigrants, who had come to this country to help build the railroads, presented a threat to white labor when railroad construction began to decline. Native-born whites feared that the Chinese were competing for the relatively few jobs that remained, not only taking jobs away from native-born whites but also forcing down wages. Riots against Chinese immigrants in cities in California and other states led to several deaths and the passage by Congress of the Chinese Exclusion Act in 1882 that prohibited Chinese immigration (Hing 1993; Kim 1994; Salyer 1995).

On the heels of the anti-Chinese riots came labor riots, especially during the railroad strikes of 1877 during which rioting broke out in several cities that resulted in dozens dead (Bruce 1959; Lens 1973; Taft and Ross 1990). Perhaps the most famous labor riot of this period was the Haymarket Riot that began during a labor protest in Chicago in May 1886 after someone threw a bomb that killed several police and spectators (Henry 1963). Labor riots continued into the next century, especially in 1919 at steel industry plants in several states and in 1934 at sites of the cotton and textile industry.

Race Riots in the Early Twentieth Century

The early 1900s also saw several large race riots, as whites, many of them fearing that blacks would compete for their jobs and move nearby, attacked blacks in several cities. One of the worst riots occurred in East St. Louis, Illinois, in 1917 and ended with 39 blacks and 9 whites dead (Rudwick 1964). Then, in the summer of 1919, riots, instigated by whites but meeting black resistance, broke out in at least seven cities, including Washington, D.C., and Chicago, that resulted in dozens more dead (Waskow 1967).

The Washington riot began when several hundred white sailors, Marines, and civilians began beating blacks after a report that two black men had jostled a white woman. The Chicago riot started when a black man died after he was stoned by whites for entering a "white" area of a Chicago beach. When a white police officer refused to arrest any of the whites and then arrested a black man for a minor offense, he was attacked by black bystanders. Fights broke out between blacks and the police and then between whites and blacks; the rioting continued for seven days. Later that summer, riots broke out in Knoxville, Tennessee, and Omaha, Nebraska, after white mobs tried to break into a jail in each city to capture and lynch a black prisoner.

Racial rioting continued periodically over the next few decades. Two notable riots occurred in the Harlem area of New York City in 1935 and again in 1943. Harlem residents had long resented white police and been dismayed by their economic circumstances. Many had also been active in the socialist movement that was so popular during the 1930s. Against this backdrop, the 1935 and 1943 riots were perhaps not that surprising (Fogelson 1971). The 1935 riot began when a black youth was caught shoplifting in a Harlem department store and detained in a back room for the police. When, coincidentally, a hearse parked near the store, a crowd that had gathered assumed that the youth had been killed. The rumor of his death quickly spread, and rioting began. The 1943 riot started when a white police officer tried to arrest a black woman for disorderly conduct and then shot a black soldier who tried to help the woman. Although the solder suffered only a minor wound, the rumor grew that he had been killed, and rioting again broke out. The two riots combined killed six people and injured several hundred (Capeci 1977; Fogelson 1971).

The 1960s Urban Riots

During the 1960s, major riots involving black participants occurred in cities throughout the northern United States. Many of these riots were precipitated by reports of police brutality or unfair treatment against blacks. At least 239 riots occurred from 1964 to 1968. These civil disorders involved more than 150,000 participants, of whom approximately 50,000 were arrested. About 75 percent of the outbursts were limited to window breaking and car burning; 20 percent included looting and greater destruction of property; and 5 percent involved more widespread looting and property destruction, including arson (Downes 1968). Another estimate puts the number of urban riots from 1963 to 1970 at 500. These involved an estimated 350,000 participants and resulted in almost 250 people dead—most of them shot by police and the National Guard—9,000 injuries, and more than 50,000 arrests (Gurr 1989c).

As mentioned in Chapter 1, when the 1960s urban riots occurred, many scholars and other observers were shocked and assumed that the riots represented a historical aberration unique to that decade. As this historical overview suggests, this view falls prey to the "myth of peaceful progress" (Rubenstein 1970). Instead, the 1960s riots and more recent ones in Miami in 1980, as well as Los Angeles in 1992 after the acquittal of the police officers for beating Rodney King, are best seen as falling squarely into the American historical tradition (Brown 1990; Button 1989; Rubenstein 1970). To acknowledge this is not meant to glorify the riots but rather to underscore their underlying political and social character.

Explaining Riots and Rioting

Explanations of riots are subsets of the explanations of collective behavior reviewed in Chapter 2. When we try to understand why riots occur, we are really asking about the social conditions that help lead to riots and also about the factors that make some individuals more likely than others to take part in them. A riot will not occur unless people choose to take part, but they will not be motivated to riot unless certain social conditions exist beforehand. Explanations of riots thus ask what kinds of people take part in riots and what kinds of social conditions underlie those riots.

Who Riots?

The "Scum of the Earth" View.   Let's start with the "kinds of people" explanations. For many years, the dominant view of the types of people who riot was what Rule (1988) calls a "scum of the earth" perspective. From LeBon and the other "irrationalists" of the late nineteenth and early twentieth centuries through Kornhauser's (1959) more sophisticated "mass society" view, rioters were depicted as criminals, insane, and/or socially isolated. Italian theorist Scipio Sighele (1868–1913), one of LeBon's contemporaries, characterized rioters and collective violence participants as "criminals, madmen, the offspring of madmen, alcoholics, the slime of society, deprived of all moral sense, given over to crime" (in Rule, 1988:95), while Kornhauser viewed them as "socially atomized" individuals who, because they lack friendships and ties to conventional institutions, feel alienated and anxious.

How correct is this "scum of the earth" perspective? Today, most scholars would say that it's hardly correct at all. While some rioters in some riots might fit the "scum of the earth" model, most do not. The most extensive evidence on this point comes from studies of rioters in nineteenth-century Europe and in the urban disturbances in the United States in the 1960s. Rioters in both periods were remarkably similar to nonrioters in their friendships and organizational involvement, criminal pasts or lack of them, and other aspects of their lives (Caplan and Paige 1968; Fogelson 1971; Kerner Commission 1968; Murphy and Watson 1971; Skolnick 1969; Tilly 1978). Far from representing the "scum of the earth," rioters instead seem fairly typical of the areas in which they live.

Data from the 1965 riot in the Watts district of Los Angeles illustrate this point with regard to criminal background and other dimensions. Of the 3,371 adults who were arrested, more than half had no previous criminal convictions, and the remainder had convictions for relatively minor offenses. Overall their criminal backgrounds were less serious than those of Los Angeles adults who were arrested throughout the year for nonriot reasons. Most rioters had lived in Los Angeles for at least five years and thus were not recent migrants to the area. Their median educational level, slightly more than ten years of schooling, was similar to that of residents of South Los Angeles in general (Oberschall 1967)

In short, rioters seem representative of the people in the communities from which they come. However, rioters do tend to differ from nonrioters in certain respects (Goode 1992). First, they tend to be more "socially available" for rioting, meaning that they have fewer social obligations that prevent them from being at the site of a riot. Thus, they are less likely than nonrioters to be married, or, if married, to have children. They are also somewhat less likely to be employed (McPhail and Miller 1973). Second, rioters tend to be fairly young—in their teens and twenties. This might be because people in this age range are more socially available. However, it might also be because people in this age range are more apt than older people to engage in daring, unconventional behavior, including rioting and other law-breaking behavior (Steffensmeier and Allan 1995:97). Third, rioters are far more likely to be men than women. The reasons for this gender difference have not been studied. However, it's likely that men are much more apt than women to engage in the type of behavior that rioting involves—violence, vandalism, and the like—because of their socialization into "masculine" ways of behaving. A similar explanation helps account for the greater involvement of males in criminal behavior (Barkan 1997; Messerschmidt 1997).

Beliefs and Attitudes.   Another focus of the "kinds of people" approach centers on beliefs and attitudes. Are certain people more likely to take part in riots because of their beliefs and attitudes? To put it another way, do rioters have beliefs and attitudes that differ from those of nonrioters and that also lead them to riot? To assess this possibility, researchers have investigated whether the attitudes of participants in protest riots, to use McPhail's (1994) term noted previously, differ from those of nonrioters. Ideally, researchers would be able to examine these attitudes *before* a riot occurs and then see whether people with certain attitudes are more likely to take part in the riot. However, this sort of research design is almost impossible because we can never know in advance when a riot is about to occur. As a result, the typical study assesses rioters' attitudes after a riot and compares them with those of nonrioters. However, even if rioters have some different attitudes, it's possible that these attitudes stem from taking part in the riot and did not precede it. Another problem is that it is not easy to interview rioters, so relatively few comparisons of rioters' and nonrioters' attitudes exist.

The studies that we do have indicate that rioters' beliefs differ somewhat from those of nonrioters but are less different than we might expect (Goode, 1992). Once again, the most extensive evidence on this point comes from studies of participants in the U.S. urban uprisings of the 1960s. In one such study, David O. Sears and T. M. Tomlinson (1971) interviewed 124 blacks arrested in the 1965 riot in the Watts area of Los Angeles and a random sample of 586 blacks who lived in the area of the rioting. Although the riot participants generally had more favorable views about the riot than the random sample, about two-thirds of both groups nonetheless called the riot a "protest" and also felt that the targets of the riot "deserved" to be attacked. Two-thirds or more of both groups attributed the riot to long-standing grievances and frustration in the black community, and over half of both groups also felt that the riot would have "favorable" effects. The authors concluded that the similarity of views between riot participants and nonparticipants suggested that the former "were not particularly unusual or deviant in their thinking" (Sears and Tomlinson 1971:380). Further, the general support for the riot found in the random sample meant that the Watts community as a whole did not view the riot "as an alien disruption of their peaceful lives, but as an expression of protest by the Negro community as a whole, against an oppressive majority" (Sears and Tomlinson 1971:386).

An additional study supports the view that rioters' attitudes were generally similar to those of nonrioters. Clark McPhail (1971) analyzed data on participants and nonparticipants in several of the 1960s urban riots and found that the two groups differed significantly in only a few of the several dozen attitudes that he examined. In particular, the rioters didn't generally feel more deprived or frustrated than their nonriot counterparts. This suggested that relative deprivation didn't explain their decisions to riot. The overall similarity of views between the two groups led McPhail to conclude that attitudes by themselves were insufficient to explain riot participation.

However, other studies of attitudes in the 1960s riots reached a different conclusion. James A. Geschwender and Benjamin D. Singer (1971) compared the views of 499 people arrested during the 1967 Detroit riot with the views of a like number of their neighbors who had not taken part in the riot. The rioters were twice as likely (26 percent compared to 13 percent) to report feeling angry about whites or pleased that whites had been the targets of rioting. Similarly, in a study of the Detroit and Newark riots of 1967, Nathan S. Caplan and Jeffery M. Paige (1968) found that people who took part in both cities' riots held more militant, "black power" beliefs than people who lived in the areas of the riots but chose not to take part. Paige (1971) also found that participants in the Newark riot were more likely than nonparticipants to be both knowledgeable about the political process and distrustful of it. This finding led him to conclude that rioting should be considered a "form of disorganized political protest engaged in by those who have become highly distrustful of existing political institutions" (Paige 1971:820).

Although these studies do point to ideological differences between rioters and nonrioters, it remains unclear whether the rioters' beliefs motivated their rioting or instead resulted *from* their rioting and, especially, from their treatment if they were arrested (McPhail 1971; McPhail 1994). This "causal order" methodological problem makes it difficult to conclude that attitudes played a large role in decisions to join the rioting. Another problem is that it's possible that the attitudes identified in these studies merely reflected the rioters' gender (male) and age (young).

One way to avoid these methodological problems would be to study the willingness of people to engage in a hypothetical riot or similar situation and to study whether people who would be willing to take part hold different attitudes from those unwilling to participate. Using such an approach, H. Edward Ransford (1967), in a sample of Los Angeles black residents taken shortly after the Watts riot, examined responses to the question, "Would you be willing to use violence to get Negro rights?" Willingness to use violence was higher among people who felt more politically powerless and more dissatisfied with their living conditions. Because this study involved willingness to take part in a riot but not actual participation in a riot, its results must be regarded as provocative but not quite conclusive on the attitudes-rioting issue.

Organizational and Interpersonal Contacts.   In view of the mixed results on this issue, a fair conclusion is that attitudes sometimes matter but don't seem sufficient by themselves to explain involvement in rioting. Whatever attitudes people taking part in a particular riot do have, many more people with similar attitudes don't take part. As noted in Chapter 2, recognition of this basic fact of collective action has recently led scholars to emphasize the organizational and interpersonal contacts that pull people into such activity, including riots (McAdam, McCarthy, and Zald 1988). When the 1960s riots were studied, however, these contacts were not yet enjoying such scholarly emphasis. Thus we lack detailed information on their importance for individuals' decisions to take part in the riots.

In one of the few studies of this issue, Benjamin D. Singer (1968) analyzed data from interviews of several hundred people arrested for participating in a major riot in Detroit in the summer of 1967. One question put to the arrestees was how they found out about the riot. About one-fourth, 26.9 percent, knew about it from firsthand experience; 8.8 percent received a phone call about it; 39.0 percent were informed by someone in person; 16.5 percent heard about it on the radio; and 9.0 percent heard about it on TV. Thus almost half heard about it from someone, either in person or by phone. If those who learned about the riot from firsthand experience are disregarded, the percentage who heard about it from someone rises to almost two-thirds. This figure underscores the importance of interpersonal contacts for participating in the Detroit riot, but it does not tell us what percentage of those who heard about the riot from a friend did *not* participate.

The Underlying Conditions for Riots

So far we've been looking at micro explanations of riot behavior, examining possible characteristics about people and their interpersonal networks that might motivate them to take part in riots. Let's now turn to the more macro explanations of riots that focus on the social conditions that precipitate them. Here the key question is not why some individuals take part in riots and others do not, but why riots occur in the first place. This line of research focuses not on the characteristics of people who take part in riots but on the characteristics of the communities that experience them.

A key question here is the degree to which poor socioeconomic conditions and other sources of strain in a community help account for rioting, as the structural-strain theory would predict (see Chapter 2). The dozens of riots in U.S. cities in the 1960s once again gave social scientists valuable data with which to answer this question. In doing so, they sought to explain why some cities experienced riots and others did not, and, in the cities that had riots, why some cities were more likely than others to have severe riots. Their research led to a large number of studies but not to definitive answers to the question just raised (Bloombaum 1968; Downes 1968; Downes 1970; Eisinger 1973; Kerner Commission 1968; Lieberson and Silverman 1965; Lieske 1978; Morgan and Clark 1973; Spilerman 1970; Spilerman 1971; Spilerman 1976; Wanderer 1969).

Let's examine this body of research carefully. Implicit in much of the research was the view that the 1960s riots were ultimately an expression of discontent over negative social conditions and not simply the acts of irrational, criminalistic individuals (Fogelson 1971). Thus, several studies found that rioting tended to be most common and most severe in cities with the greatest poverty, highest unemployment, and most dilapidated living conditions. For example, Bryan T. Downes (1968) collected information on 239 riots, or *outbursts*, as he called them, that occurred from 1964 to 1968. These civil disorders involved more than 150,000 participants, of whom some 50,000 were arrested. As noted earlier, about 75 percent of the outbursts were limited to window breaking and car burning; 20 percent included looting and greater destruction of property; and 5 percent involved more widespread looting and property destruction, including arson.

Downes compared the cities in which the outbursts occurred to those in which none occurred. Not surprisingly, the former cities tended to be larger and more densely populated and to have higher proportions of African Americans than the latter. Compared to the outburst-free cities, the outburst cities were poorer and had significantly higher unemployment and more dilapidated housing. All of these factors also helped explain the intensity of the violence of the outbursts in the cities that experienced them: the worse the living conditions, the more intense the violence. Downes concluded that the cities experiencing the outbursts, including the most violent outbursts, had distinctly worse social and economic characteristics than those not experiencing them and that these structural differences helped explain why some cities had outbursts and others did not.

However, other scholars discounted the importance of structural differences among cities for their odds of experiencing a riot. To these scholars, such differences were much less important than the development of a "riot ideology" that made rioting acceptable in the major cities of the time. As T. M. Tomlinson (1968:30) observed, "What produces riots is the shared agreement by most Negro Americans that their lot in life is unacceptable coupled with the view by a significant minority that riots are a legitimate and productive mode of protest. What is unacceptable about Negro life does not vary much from city to city, and the differences in Negro life from city to city are irrelevant."

Supporting this view, Seymour Spilerman (1970, 1971, 1976) found that the key variable affecting both the likelihood and severity of rioting from 1961 to 1968 was the proportion of a city's population that was African American: The higher this proportion, the more likely the city was to have a riot. The social and economic conditions besetting riot-prone cities were, he argued, simply "incidental characteristics of cities with large Negro populations" (Spilerman 1970:645). Thus cities with more African Americans were more likely to have riots simply because they had such a high African American population. The frustrations that led to the riots were, Spilerman (1971:771) argued, "nation-wide in impact and not rooted in circumstances peculiar to the stricken communities." Spilerman's conclusion that structural conditions did not influence the odds of rioting is widely interpreted as evidence against a structural-strain explanation for the rioting (McPhail 1994; Myers 1997).

Other scholars disputed the view by Spilerman, Tomlinson, and others that structural differences among cities mattered little for their riot potential. In a study of 1967 riots, William R. Morgan and Terry N. Clark (1973) found that housing inequality, total population, police force size, and the size of the African American population predicted both the likelihood and severity of rioting, but that the size of the African American population was less important than the other factors. The authors concluded that differences in the structural conditions facing African Americans from city to city did indeed affect the potential for cities to have riots. In response, Spilerman (1976) found fault with much of Morgan and Clark's (1973) methodology and stood by his earlier conclusion that rioting potential had little to do with structural differences among cities. Instead, he argued, the rioting was best understood as the result of the nationwide riot ideology outlined previously. This ideology was fostered by TV coverage of Civil Rights protest and urban disorders that helped create a "black solidarity that would transcend the boundaries of community" (Spilerman 1976:793).

In one of the most recent studies on the issue, Daniel J. Myers (1997: 108) reanalyzed Spilerman's data with advanced statistical techniques and found that "local conditions did indeed contribute to the occurrence of racial rioting in the 1960s," but in a very complex manner. For some conditions, rioting was more likely in cities that were "worse off," as might be expected, but for other conditions rioting was *less* likely in such cities. Supporting the ethnic competition theory (see Chapter 2), rioting was more likely in cities with higher African American unemployment (see also Olzak and Shanahan 1996; Olzak, Shanahan, and McEneaney 1996). Finally, a "diffusion" process was also at work, as cities were more likely to have riots if they were near other cities that had already experienced rioting.

Although the link between cities' structural conditions and their rioting potential remains in dispute, a cautious conclusion based on the work of Myers (1997) is that some of these conditions, and especially African American unemployment, did indeed matter. Moreover, even if a nationwide sense of frustration and thus riot ideology fueled riots in cities despite any differences among them, as Spilerman and others argued, this frustration and ideology still stemmed from the poor living conditions of African Americans in *all* of these cities, regardless of whether the conditions in some cities were not quite as bad as those in others (Downes 1968). Put another way, the 1960s riots would not have occurred if conditions in the urban ghettos had been more like those in their much wealthier suburbs. If this is true, then the structural-strain theory better explains the 1960s riots than the theory's critics assume.

The Consequences of Riots

The literature on riots devotes more time to trying to explain why they occur than to documenting their consequences. However, several studies do explore the consequences of riots and generally find that they're quite effective in dramatizing grievances and bringing them to the attention of the public, state officials, and other parties. Less clear are the practical consequences of riots and in particular whether they lead to changes in public policy. The general view is that such changes do occur, although they are fairly limited in scope.

The best evidence on this point comes, not surprisingly, from studies of the 1960s urban riots in the United States (Button 1989; Button 1978; Isaac and Kelly 1981; Schram and Turbett 1983). After the urban riots, the U.S. government generally increased its spending for programs that benefit African Americans. This consequence was especially true for welfare benefits. However, funding in other areas, for example low-income housing, increased only slightly. Efforts by local governments to increase spending to improve urban conditions were even more limited and sporadic, and many cities did little at all. Moreover, any positive consequences that the riots did have for improving living conditions tended to be more short term than long term. As James Button (1989:296) observes, "While the black riots clearly had an impact on certain social and economic programs in the short run, it is less certain that these outbursts had any direct effect on longer term changes in the living conditions of ghetto residents." But he does think that the riots helped lead to equal employment opportunity legislation that eventually helped improve the socioeconomic status of African Americans by the early 1970s.

In 1968, however, the response of local, state, and federal governmental officials to the riots became more punitive, involving an increasing number of arrests and the growing use of deadly force (Button 1989; McAdam 1983). This shift in tactics was partly due to the intensity of several riots during that year, which prompted the federal government to mobilize the National Guard and U.S. Army to deal with the riots. As Button (1989:298) observes, "It was clear by the late 1970s that forceful repression from the national level would be used if necessary to quell the massive riots." Thus over time the reaction of government at all levels changed from a positive response focused on improving living conditions in urban areas to a negative response involving legal control, in the forms of arrests and deadly force.

One other consequence of the 1960s riots remains to be noted, and that is the strengthening of "black pride" and the mobilization of political change groups in African American communities and the election of African Americans to local political office (Button 1989). By the 1970s, African American mayors were more likely to be found in cities that had experienced riots in the 1960s than in cities that had not. As Button (1989:300) concludes from the evidence, "Although the linkage here may not always be easy to trace, it does seem that the ghetto violence helped provide some of the local organizational and other prerequisites for successful electoral representation of blacks."

All in all, the consequences of the 1960s riots were mixed at best for African Americans. Although they did lead to increased expenditures in African American communities and other political and economic benefits, they also eventually led to a punitive, law-and-order response that stigmatized African American residents and delegitimated their violent protest. The riots also prompted a white backlash, alienating potential white supporters for addressing the grievances of black communities (Button 1989). This was a marked change from the situation earlier in the 1960s, when the nonviolent Civil Rights protests in the South and the violent white brutality that greeted them won many white supporters to the Civil Rights cause. As Button (1989:301–302) observes of the 1960s riots, "By late in the decade, however, the massive violence eroded some of this support and the resulting backlash contributed to changes in the systemic response to black grievances."

Prison Riots

Most of the discussion so far has concerned the 1960s urban riots, as they were the subject of so much research. However, prison riots have also captured scholarly and public attention. Since the first such reported riot in 1774, more than 300 prison riots have occurred in the United States, with an estimated 90 percent of those occurring since the early 1950s (Martin and Zimmerman 1990). A substantial literature now examines the causes, dynamics, and consequences of prison riots (Braswell, Dillingham, and Montgomery 1985; Colvin 1992; Irwin 1980; Mahan and Lawrence 1996; Martin and Zimmerman 1990; Useem 1985; Useem and Kimball 1989). What do we know about them?

Explaining Prison Riots

Although many studies have tried to make sense of the causes of prison riots, it remains true that "there is relatively little reliable and valid information" about why they occur (Martin and Zimmerman 1990:712). One problem is that the conditions popularly thought to account for prison riots—such as poor food, overcrowding, harsh treatment by prison guards, and inadequate vocational and educational programs—exist in most prisons, yet most prisons don't have riots. While prison riots might well not occur without these poor conditions (just as the 1960s urban riots would not have occurred without poor structural conditions in the cities that experienced them), these conditions only rarely lead to riots. Indeed, a recent study found little relationship between variation in prison conditions and the likelihood of prison riots (McCorkle, Miethe, and Drass 1995). Thus, when riots do break out other processes must be at work.

One of these processes might be a weakening in the formal and informal social control mechanisms that characterize any prison. By "formal social control" is meant the rule of prison officials and guards over the inmates, and by "informal social control" is meant the understandings that inmates have among themselves and with prison staff about how the daily routine of prison life should operate (Irwin 1980). When these mechanisms are disrupted, social control in the prison breaks down and the potential for a riot increases (Martin and Zimmerman 1990).

Another process underlying at least some prison riots harkens back to relative deprivation theory (see Chapter 2), which assumes that dashed expectations can lead to frustration and discontent and thus to collective violence. If inmates expect improvements in their lives and then find that these improvements are not forthcoming, their increased discontent might lead to rioting. Although, as noted in Chapter 2, relative deprivation theory has received little support in the collective violence literature, it does seem to explain some of the prison riots that have occurred during the last few decades.

An example of both of these processes is the West Virginia State Penitentiary (WVSP) riot that broke out on January 1, 1986 (Martin and Zimmerman 1990; Useem and Kimball 1989). In the years before the riot, the conditions at WVSP were widely viewed as substandard, and in 1983 the West Virginia Supreme Court ordered massive changes; these, however, were not implemented because of lack of funds. Then, in September 1985, a new warden, the third in three years, assumed command and restricted visitation, limited private possessions, and imposed other controls, thereby making it even clearer than before to the inmates that the promised reforms would not occur. On January 1, 1986, several guards on the evening shift called in sick, and some critical guard posts were left empty. This situation required a lockdown, but none occurred, thus reducing the formal control that the inmates would face if they rebelled. Taking advantage of this opportunity, the inmates took control of the dining hall during dinner and then captured the prison's north wing, along with 16 hostages. After three days of negotiations with the governor that led to a promise to improve prison conditions, the inmates surrendered. The uprising had most likely been planned by members of a motorcycle gang.

Although conditions at the WVSP had been substandard, many other prisons at the time had similar conditions and did not experience riots. Thus the conditions by themselves cannot explain why the WVSP uprising broke out on New Year's Day of 1986. Instead, the harsh new measures of the new warden were responsible, as they antagonized the inmates, who saw their rising expectations of improved prison conditions dashed. This weakened their interest in helping to maintain order in the prison. Thus by January 1, the prison's "informal control system was in disarray" (Martin and Zimmerman 1990:729) and the reduced staff numbers gave the inmates the opportunity for which they evidently had been waiting.

Another example is a riot that occurred six years earlier in the Santa Fe, New Mexico, state prison on February 2, 1980. This riot was arguably the worst in U.S. history, costing $200 million and resulting in the deaths of 33 inmates and the injuring of approximately 400 others (Colvin 1982; Colvin 1992; Mahan 1985; Morris 1983; Useem 1985; Useem and Kimball 1989). It started when some inmates attacked and beat four prison guards in the south wing, after which the other guards in this wing were captured. Inmates then began to attack, beat, torture, and kill other inmates. Most of these targets were inmates thought to be informants, or prison snitches, and inmates who wanted revenge against other inmates for previous perceived wrongs. Several guards were also beaten and raped.

Interviewed later, most inmates blamed the riot on the substandard living conditions of the prison. One inmate said, "It's been too crowded, the food is bad, the goddamned guards talk to you like you're a dog. We're not dogs" (in Useem 1985:672). Another recalled, "There was one dormitory designed for 45 men, and they had 120 in there. It is a jungle after lights out. You couldn't go to the restroom at night without stepping on someone, and that was all it took for a fight to break out" (in Useem 1985:672).

Although prison conditions are typically substandard and thus by themselves cannot explain why a riot begins, the New Mexico inmates, similar to their West Virginia counterparts, felt that the conditions had worsened since a change in prison warden occurred five years earlier. In addition, the reduction of educational and vocational programs during this period angered inmates, weakened their informal social control networks, and reduced their incentive to behave. The establishment of a system of prison snitches during this time led inmates to distrust each other further. Thus, as with the West Virginia prison riot, an increased sense of deprivation combined with weakened social controls set the stage for the New Mexico uprising.

The Consequences of Prison Riots

While most attention in the scholarly literature on prison riots is on their causes, several studies also explore their consequences. The immediate consequences are obvious: property destruction, injury, and death. Inmates sometimes kill each other and sometimes kill prison guards and other prison personnel, and guards, police, and other law enforcement agents often kill the inmates who riot. Perhaps the most notable example of this latter dynamic occurred after inmates in the Attica, New York, state prison rioted in 1971. The inmates, most of them black, had been angered by their alleged mistreatment at the hands of the white prison guards. They rioted, held prison guards as hostages, and took control of the prison, holding it for four days while they negotiated with state officials for the release of the hostages in exchange for improvements in prison conditions. Then, acting on the orders of the New York governor, state troopers stormed the prison and in the process killed 32 inmates, as well as 11 guards whom the inmates had been holding hostage. Critics denounced the governor's decision to storm the prison and said he should have allowed more time for the negotiations to work (Mahan 1985; Wicker 1975).

The longer-term consequences of prison riots are less obvious but perhaps just as important. Often, they lead to improved living conditions in the prison that experienced the riot (Useem, Camp, and Camp 1996; Useem and Kimball 1989). From the perspective of prison officials, the goal is to reduce inmates' anger and frustration over their living environment and in this way to prevent future outbursts. Yet any such improvements in living conditions are fairly limited at best, and, for better or worse, most prisons remain horrible places in which to live even after these improvements are implemented (Kappeler, Blumberg, and Potter 1996).

Another long-term consequence of prison riots concerns the way that prisons are administered. A growing literature identifies prison management problems that might make riots more likely and proposes changes in prison management and administration to prevent future riots (Boin and Duin 1995; DiIulio 1987; Montgomery 1997; Useem and Kimball 1989). The debate here is whether a strict, disciplinarian style of management is more effective than a more relaxed style in which inmates are allowed freedom of movement and other privileges designed to keep their frustration to a minimum (Boin and Duin 1995). This debate carries over into the prisons in which riots have occurred. In response to the riots, some prison administrators have strengthened their control over their inmates with stricter rules on their behavior, whereas others have loosened their control while still maintaining proper security measures. The dilemma for prison administrators is how to strike the right balance between these two styles of management. Prison discipline must be maintained, but not at the expense of inhumane treatment that increases the chances of future prison violence.

What Would You Do?

As the previous examples indicate, prison riots often involve the taking of hostages. Inmates hold hostages for at least two reasons. First, they hope to gain concessions from the prison warden and state officials on improving the prison conditions that helped to prompt the riot in the first place. Second, they hope that the holding of hostages will prevent or at least reduce a violent response by police, state troopers, and other law enforcement officials.

Suppose that you are the assistant to a governor in a state in which the major prison has just had a riot. The violence has ended for now, but the inmates hold about two dozen hostages, most of them prison guards but some of them cooks and other nonguard workers. The inmates are demanding better living conditions, including reduced crowding in their cells, more exercise time, better food, and better plumbing facilities.

Having taken a criminal justice course in college, in which the terrible living conditions in prisons were discussed extensively, you're at least somewhat sympathetic to the inmates' grievances and partial to their demands. At the same time, you're concerned that while granting them concessions in return for the release of the hostages and an end to the crisis might help in the short run, it will only make future rioting and hostage-taking more likely. The governor asks for your advice. You must decide whether to urge the governor to grant the inmates the concessions that they want.

What do you tell the governor?

Conclusion

Riots are probably the most spontaneous of the forms of collective violence treated in this book and hence the least predictable and perhaps the most difficult to explain. History suggests that we should not be surprised when they occur, but that doesn't mean that we shouldn't try to understand their causes and consequences.

In explaining riots, we need to consider both why they occur and, once they do occur, why some individuals are more likely than others to choose to take part in them. The historical evidence from Europe and the United States suggests that rioters aren't very different from nonrioters in their beliefs, attitudes, and social backgrounds. They might be younger than average and more likely to be male than female, but their beliefs and backgrounds don't seem to fit the "scum of the earth" model popular in earlier conceptions of riots and rioters.

In considering why riots occur in the first place, most scholarly attention focuses on the underlying negative social, economic, and political conditions said to prompt frustration, strain, and other social-psychological states that make rioting seem to be an appropriate response. But a puzzle remains. While it's true that almost all protest riots occur amid these conditions and almost certainly wouldn't occur if these conditions didn't exist, it's also true that these conditions usually exist without any rioting occurring at all. As an example, U.S. cities are in many ways worse off now than two decades ago (Hacker 1992; Wilson 1996), and yet they're not experiencing riots, at least at the time of this writing. By the same token, most prisons are greatly overcrowded and beset by many kinds of the structural problems thought to underlie riots and other forms of collective violence, yet most prisons don't experience riots. The lack of rioting in such circumstances suggests the need to merge macro perspectives with micro ones to develop a fuller understanding of why riots occur and why people take part in them.

4

Revolution

Riots often reflect discontent with existing social, economic, and political conditions and might lead to some limited reforms, but they don't by themselves constitute a *revolution,* or a popular overthrow, usually violent, of a nation's government and often a fundamental change in its political, economic, and social structure. In the grand scheme of protest and rebellion, revolution represents the most extreme outcome, whereas riots are, relatively speaking, minor skirmishes. Sometimes, however, riots can spiral into open rebellion and even outright revolution (Goldstone 1986; Gurr 1989c). This dynamic led to the revolutions of 1848 in Europe, when rioting by workers, students, peasants, and others helped lead to the overthrow of King Louis Philippe in France and played a key role in violent uprisings in other European states (Hobsbawn 1962; Jelavich 1987).

A central task of this chapter is to explain why revolutions occur. On the surface, this might seem to be an easy task, for we all know that revolutions ultimately arise from popular dissatisfaction with existing social, economic, and/or political conditions. But the equation is not that simple because over the centuries there have been many societies with such terrible conditions but only a relatively few revolutions. If human misery led automatically to revolution, then, as Leon Trotsky, one of the leaders of the Russian Revolution, put it, "the masses would be always in revolt" (quoted in McAdam and Snow 1997:3). Revolution scholar Jack A. Goldstone (1986:1–2) similarly observes, "Oppression and misery have been widespread throughout history, yet revolutions have been rare."

One reason for this is that the masses might react to their conditions with despair or passive resignation rather than with outrage and thus not revolt. Or they might accept their fate as God's will and, again, not see fit to engage in political struggle. Even if they do react with outrage, they might fear the consequences of protesting or lack the skills, leadership, and organization that rebellion and revolution require.

As these considerations suggest, an adequate explanation of revolution must go beyond popular dissatisfaction with existing conditions. Although probably no revolution occurs without a good deal of such dissatisfaction, the extent of human suffering far exceeds the number of revolutions. Thus, given such suffering, some other processes must come into play for a revolution to occur. Perhaps something changes the masses' reaction to their conditions. Perhaps leaders come along to incite them to revolt. Perhaps something else weakens the power of the state and gives the masses hope that their protests will succeed without too much personal cost.

Theories of revolution build on these and other possibilities. They incorporate components of the theories of collective violence already reviewed but apply them in a distinctive way to an understanding of the most extreme example of such violence. Some focus on the structural conditions underlying revolutions, whereas others focus on the factors that motivate individuals to take part in them. Scholars continue to debate the merits of these theories, and the discussion here will incorporate their critiques (Greene 1990; Kimmel 1990; Malecki 1973; Moshiri 1991b; Rule 1988; Salert 1976; Sederberg 1994). Following this theoretical review, this chapter sketches some of the major revolutions of the twentieth century to illustrate the social, political, and economic forces that helped to produce them.

Explaining Revolution

Outlined here are the major theories of revolution, which are presented in the chronological order in which they first appeared. While all seek to explain why revolutions occur, they differ in the emphasis that they place on structural versus social-psychological factors and in the attention that they give to the role of the state and the importance of mobilizing efforts by revolutionary actors. Let's see what they have to say.

Marx and Engels's Theory of Revolution

Karl Marx's (1818–1883) theory of revolution, written with Friedrich Engels (1820–1895), remains the most famous theory of revolution and certainly the most influential on scholarship and actual worldly events. It traced the causes of revolution to economic conditions that, over time, would become intolerable for those at the bottom of society and prompt them to revolt.

Marx and Engels (Marx 1906 [1867]; Marx and Engels 1962 [1848]) wrote that every society is divided into two classes, one that owns the means of production and one that doesn't. This basic fact permeates all social and political life and is the inherent source of conflict between the two groups. As Marx and Engels (1962 [1848]:1) wrote at the beginning of *The Communist Manifesto*, "The history of all hitherto existing society is the history of class struggle." In capitalist society, the bourgeoisie, or ruling class, owns the means of production—factories, tools, and so on—and thus holds economic and political power, whereas the proletariat, or working class, lies at the bottom of society in a condition of oppression and exploitation.

Capitalism, Marx and Engels wrote, contains the seeds of its own demise because it involves structural contradictions that make revolution inevitable. For example, the major goal of economic production becomes the maximization of profits and not the fulfillment of human needs. To maximize profits, capitalists often reduce wages, maintain shoddy workplaces, and otherwise act in a way that oppresses the proletariat. Further, because some capitalists will lose out to others, the number of capitalists eventually decreases, while the defeated capitalists swell the ranks of the proletariat. Their increased numbers in turn reduce wages even further. These forces prompt workers to develop class consciousness, or an awareness of the true nature of, and reasons for, their oppression. Increasing class consciousness leads in turn to increasing discontent and in time to a revolution of and by the proletariat that abolishes private property.

This too-brief summary of Marx and Engels's theory doesn't do it justice, but it does indicate its essential points. Over the years, the theory has generated much debate, as scholars have dissected virtually every word that Marx and Engels wrote. Many scholars support the theory's view of revolution and other collective violence rooted in economic conflict, whereas others say that it overemphasized the importance of economic divisions for revolution and underemphasized the role of other factors (Foster 1974; Paige 1975; Sederberg 1994).

One thing does seem clear: History does not generally support Marx and Engels's prediction of revolution in capitalist societies. As many observers have noted, the United States, the quintessential capitalist society, has never had a working-class revolution, partly because various aspects of American society and ideology have minimized the development of working-class consciousness (Kimmel 1990). One reason for this is the political freedom that even poor Americans theoretically enjoy. This helps convince them of the inherent justness of their political, economic, and social systems, thereby minimizing the discontent they might otherwise feel. Another reason is the American belief in equal opportunity for all, symbolized by the Horatio Alger myth and the story of Abraham Lincoln's being born in a log cabin and later becoming president. This helps keep even poor Americans at least somewhat hopeful for improvement in their lives or else minimizes the blame they place on the "system" for the conditions in which they live.

Another shortcoming of the theory lies in its treatment of peasants. As Kimmel (1990:24) points out, Marx considered the peasantry "solidly reactionary" and thus a source of support for capitalism. The reason for this, Marx wrote, lies in the nature of the agricultural work that peasants do, as their "mode of production isolates them from one another instead of bringing them into mutual intercourse" (quoted in Kimmel 1990:24). Because they work in isolation from one another, Marx felt, they can't develop either community bonds or political organization. Thus, they can't develop class consciousness and become united against capitalism. For these reasons, Marx thought revolution would be far more likely in the most industrialized societies than in agricultural ones.

Once again, however, history has proven Marx wrong. Most of the key revolutions of the twentieth century occurred in largely agricultural nations such as Algeria, China, Mexico, Nicaragua, and Vietnam, where the peasantry became "the chief revolutionary actors in the development of socialist society" (Kimmel 1990:25; Wolf 1969). Even in Russia, which was more industrial, the peasantry played a key role in the revolution that toppled that nation in 1917. While all of these revolutions fit the basic Marxian model of revolt stemming from economic conflict, the role played in them by the peasantry was not something that Marx predicted.

Another problem with the theory is that much civil violence stems from conflict rooted in racial, ethnic, and other such hostility rather than in class divisions. As Sederberg (1994:185) notes, "Even a cursory review of various civil conflicts around the world reveals that cleavages other than class—for example, race, linguistic, and religious identities—seem far more significant sources of violent discord and even revolution than presumed economic class divisions." Marx and Engels's neglect of these sources of revolution remains a serious weakness of the theory.

These criticisms notwithstanding, Marx and Engels's theory remains one of the most valuable explanations that we have today for revolution. It stimulated many of the theories developed later, as scholars tried to point to key variables and processes that Marx and Engels overlooked.

The Natural History of Revolution

In the first half of the twentieth century, several writers outlined the stages that they felt revolutions typically go through (Brinton 1938; Edwards 1927; Hopper 1950; Pettee 1938). Their work has since come to be known as a *natural history approach,* as it likened the stages of a revolution to those that a body experiences as it deals with disease. Just as a disease might build slowly and then wrack the body with sudden, violent symptoms, so does a revolution begin slowly until it overtakes a whole society. Afterward, both body and society face a period of relatively quiet convalescence with perhaps a few relapses. As Lyford Edwards, one of the original natural history proponents, put it, "A country in revolution is like a person suffering from a deadly cancer" (quoted in Kimmel 1990:48). Another natural history proponent, Crane Brinton (1938), observed that just as a person might acquire some immunity after a disease has run its course, so might a society be stronger after a revolution has succeeded.

Goldstone (1986) summarizes several stages put forth by the natural history proponents. First, economic and other problems lead the intellectuals of a society to criticize the existing regime and to call for major reforms in political, economic, and social conditions. The intellectuals' disillusionment implies "an unusually widespread and pervasive dissatisfaction with regime performance" (Goldstone 1986:3). Second, the state tries to implement these reforms, but its very attempt to do so signals its weakness and encourages further demands for reforms. Third, an economic, political, or other crisis begins and triggers a revolt, which leads to the regime's demise. The actual nature of the crisis is less important than the fact that its occurrence indicates that the regime is too weak to deal with it.

Fourth, after the revolution occurs the revolutionary forces become internally divided, usually into a conservative faction that wants to take a slow course, a radical faction that wants rapid and extreme changes, and a moderate faction that advocates a course between the positions of the other two. In the next stages, the moderates take temporary control and undertake substantial but not far-reaching reforms. However, these reforms typically leave the radical faction wanting more, so the radicals eventually take over and establish a coercive "reign of terror." In the ensuing struggle between radicals and moderates, new leaders, often military figures, then fill the power vacuum and institute moderate reforms, as a more quiet period begins.

This early natural history approach added several insights to the process of revolution that were ignored by Marxian views, but it also neglected other issues (Kimmel 1990; Goldstone 1986). On the plus side, its attention to the disunity within revolutionary forces was a useful corrective to the Marxian view of a united proletarian class striking out against the ruling class. On the minus side, the natural history approach exaggerated the role that intellectuals play in revolutions. As Kimmel (1990) observes, intellectuals might have been important to the French Revolution, but they have been less important to some other revolutions. As this criticism suggests, the natural history approach might have relied too much on the French Revolution, as other revolutions differed in several ways from the French experience.

Relative Deprivation and Rising Expectations

As discussed in previous chapters, several scholars trace collective action, including collective violence, to feelings of relative deprivation and/or rising expectations in the general population or in significant segments of it (Davies 1962; Gurr 1970). In a brief reiteration, when people feel deprived relative to some other group or find that their hopes and expectations for improved conditions have been frustrated, their discontent and thus likelihood of engaging in protest increases. According to this view, a government that improves social and economic conditions finds itself dancing on a razor's edge because these improvements raise the public's expectations for continued improvements. If conditions suddenly worsen, people will become especially frustrated and could rebel. This social-psychological approach has been popular in the study of revolution.

James C. Davies (1962:5) summarizes this process: "Revolutions are most likely to occur when a prolonged period of objective economic and social development is followed by a short period of sharp reversal. . . . [This leads to] an expectation of continued ability to satisfy needs . . . and then . . . a mental state of anxiety and frustration when manifest reality breaks away from anticipated reality." A century earlier, the great social theorist Alexis de Tocqueville (1955 [1856]:176–177) had similarly observed, "It is not always when things are going from bad to worse that revolutions break out. On the contrary, it oftener happens that when a people which has put up with an oppressive rule over a long period without protest suddenly finds the government realizing its pressure, it takes up arms against it. . . . [T]he most perilous moment for a bad government is one when it seeks to mend its ways."

This keen insight challenges the Marxian notion of revolution springing from continued and worsening misery and oppression. Instead of arising from worsening conditions, revolution ironically arises from improving conditions. Unfortunately, as Chapter 2 noted, empirical research has not often supported the relative deprivation/rising expectations model (Kimmel 1990; Rule 1988; Salert 1976). Although in many nations, relative deprivation occurs and rising expectations are frustrated, revolution is not the usual outcome. This fact, says Kimmel (1990:80), makes us "suspicious of [relative deprivation] as the decisive element in the historical trajectory." In fact, revolution seems to occur more often under continuing or worsening misery than when conditions have been improving. Further, the model does not indicate why some groups respond to deprivation by revolting and others remain quiet.

Structural Theories

Structural theories of revolution emphasize that weaknesses in state structures encourage the potential for revolution (Goldstone 1986). According to this view, a government beset by problems such as economic and military crises is vulnerable to challenges by insurgent forces. Some of these crises result from competition with other states, others result from internal problems within a particular state, and still others reflect both external and internal problems. As one example of the latter, the crushing blows that Russia suffered during World War I led to severe internal problems that helped set the stage for the 1917 Russian Revolution (see later in this chapter).

Other governments run into trouble when their fiscal or other policies alienate and even anger elites within the society, who might then plot a revolt or, at a minimum, collaborate with other rebellious forces. When the loyalty of the state's army shifts to these forces, revolution becomes even more likely. Goldstone (1986:8) summarizes this dynamic: "Where a powerful elite outside the state bureaucracy has the resources to paralyze the state in times of conflict, and outside allegiances weaken the army, severe political crises are liable to occur."

For a revolution to occur when a state is so weakened, Goldstone (1986) continues, popular uprisings play a crucial role. These traditionally take the form of either peasant revolts or urban workers' uprisings. In agrarian societies, he notes, peasants have long been oppressed with heavy rents and taxes and other problems, and peasant revolts have been quite common (see also Paige 1975; Scott 1977). When these revolts occur in conjunction with the state weaknesses described previously, revolution becomes that much more likely, especially if urban elites help the peasantry achieve tactical and organizational strength.

If urban revolts are occurring at the same time as peasant revolts, the state is even more ready to crumble. Historically, such urban revolts stem primarily from two causes: the high cost of food and a high rate of unemployment. Riots protesting both of these have been quite common during the last few centuries. Yet even these urban revolts will not become full-scale revolutions, and especially successful ones, unless the state has previously been weakened in the ways outlined earlier.

As this analysis should imply, structural theories place the state, or, as some would call it, governmental apparatus, at the center of attention. In the Marxist view, the state is a rather passive agent that awaits the inevitable takeover by revolutionary forces. In the structural view, the state plays a more active role, including one that ironically could set up its own demise as it implements policies and engages in actions, including international conflict, that might weaken it (Kimmel 1990).

Much of this structural view comes from the work of Theda Skocpol (1979; 1994; 1978), who placed the state at the center of her analysis of revolution. She rejected Marx's idea that the internal contradictions of capitalism help set the stage for revolution against a state controlled by the capitalist class. Instead, she argued, revolution stems from an autonomous state's military, political, and economic competition with other states that leads to several internal problems that make the state vulnerable to insurgency. In response, the state often tries to enact reforms whose successes in staving off revolt depends heavily on whether the upper classes go along with them. If, however, an organized peasantry is in revolt at the same time, the state may well not withstand being overtaken. If a revolution does succeed, a stronger, more bureaucratic state will usually result. Skocpol's theory contradicts Marx's idea that the state will "wither away" after a revolution.

Skocpol's theory has been criticized for overemphasizing the role of the state and underemphasizing the role of insurgent forces (Kimmel 1990; Walton 1984). Some critics feel that she gives insufficient attention to ideologies that could impel people to revolt, to the importance of protest and organizing by insurgent forces, and to the ways in which such protest and organizing develop. Her defenders believe that her critics overlook her discussion of these issues (Goodwin 1996).

If Skocpol does underplay the importance of the organizational and other factors that make revolt possible and help it to succeed, other writers give these factors prime attention. Eric Wolf (1969), for example, argues that the peasants most likely to revolt are those who are small landowners rather than those who are poorer and landless. The former have greater resources that may aid in political struggle. They also tend to live further from landlords and other officials and thus are freer to act without fear of reprisal.

The organizational and political factors that facilitate insurgency lie at the heart of the resource mobilization theory developed by Charles Tilly and others. Although Chapter 2 criticized that theory for neglecting the role that changing discontent plays in collective action, it remains valuable for the attention that it gives to the processes involved in such action. While the theory recognizes the importance of state vulnerability to insurgency, it also emphasizes the importance of resources and organization, especially social networks, for the mobilization that is essential for insurgency to begin and then succeed. Thus, Roger V. Gould (1991) documents the importance of informal neighborhood networks for participation in the Paris Commune uprising in the spring of 1871 and for maintaining the commitment of protesters to the uprising.

In an effort to synthesize various structural theories, Jack A. Goldstone (1991a, 1991b) emphasizes three factors whose mutual occurrence helps lead to revolution. First, the state faces an economic crisis that it can't deal with adequately. Second, elites become alienated from the state and then try to take control of it. Third, the populace has the potential for mass mobilization, such as when it is concentrated in urban areas and thus able to communicate easily. In all of these factors, he notes, population growth can play an important role. For example, such growth leads to rising prices for grain and other commodities; the resulting inflation reduces the value of taxes. In response, the state might need to raise taxes, which in turn alienates elites. Further, rising population can also decrease the land available to peasants, thereby increasing their discontent. All of these processes increase the potential for revolution.

Drawing on these and other explanations of revolution, James A. DeFronzo (1996) outlines several factors whose joint occurrence comes close to making a revolution inevitable. First, the populace, whether urban or rural, experiences mass discontent. Second, elites are alienated from the state and also challenge its authority. Third, the state experiences a major crisis that makes it vulnerable to revolt. The crisis might result from wartime losses, a natural disaster, severe economic problems, or other causes. Finally, other nations must be unwilling or unable to intervene to help the state resist revolutionary challenges. When these factors occur simultaneously, a revolution is likely to follow.

Some Twentieth-Century Revolutions

This section discusses some of the most important revolutions of the twentieth century to illustrate the factors and processes discussed in the preceding section. The purpose is not to make you an expert on these revolutions but rather to help you understand how their histories tie in with the explanations just reviewed.

The Russian Revolution of 1917

The Russian Revolution of 1917 remains the most famous revolution of the twentieth century, partly because it was the first that sought to achieve socialism. It has been extensively recounted and analyzed (e.g., DeFronzo 1996; Fitzpatrick 1994; Read 1996; Skocpol 1979).

From the Middle Ages through the early 1900s, Russia was ruled by a series of czars, whose governments were repressive in every respect. When Alexander II became czar in the mid-1800s, he instituted several reforms, including freeing serfs, developing railroads, and implementing self-government in several villages, all in an attempt to improve the Russian economy and to strengthen the nation more generally. However, his efforts did little to solidify his rule, as some Russian dissidents thought his reforms were too limited and ironically the serfs' situation worsened in some ways after they were freed because they ended up with little land and heavy debt. Several small-scale revolts by various groups finally ended with Alexander's assassination in 1881. A decade later weather conditions produced several bad harvests and increased starvation among the peasantry, while workers in the cities grew increasingly discontented because of their living conditions. An economic depression in 1899 led to student protests, peasant revolts, and strikes by workers in Russia's major cities. A war with Japan in 1904 further weakened the Russian government and led to more internal dissent.

Finally, on January 22, 1905 thousands of workers marched to the home of czar Nicholas II in St. Petersburg. Although the workers were unarmed, troops shot and killed or wounded hundreds in what is now known as the "Bloody Sunday" massacre. The massacre led to more strikes and uprisings throughout Russia and rising dissent among both the peasantry and the military. The following October, a general strike brought the country to a halt; strikes and violent skirmishes continued for several more years.

After World War I began in 1914, Germany and Russia engaged in some major battles, with Russia suffering losses numbering in the millions. Domestic supplies were diverted to the war effort, and thus the Russian people, 85 percent of whom were peasants, didn't have nearly enough food or coal. People from all walks of life blamed the czar, Nicholas II, both for their domestic problems and for the battlefront losses. In early 1917, riots and strikes threw Petrograd (formerly St. Petersburg) into chaos; national troops joined the dissidents instead of trying to stop them. Nicholas abdicated his throne in March of that year. Skirmishes among the dissident forces over control of the country continued for several more months, until one faction, the Bolsheviks, seized control of both Petrograd and Moscow in the fall. The Russian Revolution had succeeded in toppling the old regime. Shortly afterward, Russia signed a peace treaty with Germany, but fighting among various factions within Russia continued for several more years.

This brief account of the Russian Revolution of 1917 illustrates several of the factors and processes previously discussed. Internal problems aggravated by a wartime economy weakened the existing regime and increased discontent. The dissident forces included both peasants and industrial workers. DeFronzo (1996) notes that social ties between these two groups increased their communication and helped unite them against the old regime, as at least one-half of urban workers had previously been peasants or had peasant parents. These ties were especially important because the conditions in which the peasantry lived had significantly worsened in the latter years of the nineteenth century and the beginning years of the twentieth. Thus, the importance of the peasantry for the Russian Revolution cannot be underestimated. As DeFronzo (1996:30) observes, "Intense peasant discontent with the czar's regime constituted one of the essential elements of the revolutionary situation in the early twentieth century."

Certain "marginal elite" groups, especially the young, educated classes, also played an important role in the Russian Revolution (Skocpol 1979). Many of them had been educated in Western Europe and became committed to the democracy that Russia lacked. As a result, they chafed under the czarist regime and were willing to join both peasants and workers in opposing it. The confluence of all of these events and processes created a powerful impetus for the rebellion that was to become the Russian Revolution of 1917.

The Chinese Revolution of 1949

About three decades after Russia's revolution came another momentous one, this time in China. In a country that was almost entirely agrarian, Chinese peasants had suffered terrible living conditions that led to many rebellions in China's long history and meant that the peasantry was a potentially revolutionary force (DeFronzo 1996; Wolf 1969). This force built slowly in the first half of the twentieth century until it finally exploded in 1949.

Because China's history had been filled with peasant uprisings, it was no surprise that the decades leading to 1949 were tumultuous (Skocpol 1979; Thaxton 1983; Wolf 1969). During the 1800s, China suffered severe economic losses as Great Britain, France, the United States, and other colonial powers carved it into spheres of influence and drove it into debt. To pay its debt, the Chinese government had to raise taxes and poor peasants had to pay higher rents for land on which they worked. A series of uprisings beginning in mid-century with the Nian Rebellion in central China and the Taiping Rebellion in south China lasted into the 1870s but failed to topple the existing regime. By the end of the century, China's prosperous economy began to worsen further because of its efforts to expand into foreign markets and a persisting poor balance of trade with Britain and other countries. Conditions worsened further when China lost the Sino-Japanese war in 1895 and had to give up Taiwan and other land and pay war reparations.

After more tumultuous years, in 1911 Chinese students, merchants, soldiers, and other groups engaged in a series of uprisings that led to the establishment of a new government called the Republic of China headed by a military general. Within a few years, increasing disillusionment with what they regarded as Western imperialism led young, educated Chinese intellectuals to look to the Soviet Union and its experiment in socialism as a possible solution to China's own problems, and the Chinese Communist Party was established in 1921. Seven years later, however, General Chiang Kai-shek took control of the government by bribing local warlords and attacking and killing hundreds of members of the workers' militia of the Communist movement in Shanghai and elsewhere (Jordan 1976).

Fearing for their lives, many Communists went into hiding. The most prominent of these was Mao Zedong (also known as Mao Tse-tung), who felt that the peasantry could be turned into a revolutionary force. Thus, he went into the rural areas to mobilize them (Wei 1985). Skirmishes between governmental and Communist forces continued for several years. Meanwhile, the government also had to contend with Japan during the 1930s. By the end of that decade, China's economy had worsened from severe inflation and its government had weakened from internal factionalism. At the same time, the Chinese Communists grew rapidly from 80,000 troops in 1937 to an estimated 900,000 by 1945 (Bianco 1971). Thus, while Chiang's government was weaker by the end of World War II, the Communists were stronger.

Civil war between the two sides broke out by 1947 even as the government continued to be wracked by internal dissent and soaring inflation. Still recovering from World War II, other nations did not come to the government's aid. In 1949, the Communists won, and Chiang's government fled to the island of Taiwan. Decades of conflict had ended in the Chinese Revolution.

Once again, a cluster of factors led almost inexorably to revolution (DeFronzo 1996). Discontent among peasants had always been high, but it increased in the decades leading up to the revolution because of a declining economy and a corrupt and repressive government. The government itself was weakened because of economic exploitation and military defeats by other nations and because of its own internal corruption and factionalism. Communist leaders were well educated and able to fuse Marxist ideas with traditional Chinese philosophies to forge a revolutionary ideology that helped convince peasants of the need to engage in revolutionary struggle. In this regard, the Communist emphasis on land reform had special appeal for peasants, who were worried about their increasing poverty and weakening family structures (Stacey 1983). Meanwhile, other governments were either unable or unwilling to come to China's aid. This combination of factors eventually resulted in the revolutionary overthrow of Chiang's government.

Nicaragua and Revolution

From a revolution in China on the Asian continent, we move closer to home to Central America, where a revolution in Nicaragua in 1979 overthrew a widely unpopular regime. Like other revolutions examined so far, this one resulted from several familiar factors (Chavarria 1986; Grynspan 1991; Walker 1985; Woodward 1985).

After Nicaragua won its independence from Spain in the early 1800s, a few wealthy families essentially ruled the country for many years. In 1909, U.S. Marines landed in Nicaragua to help force out President José Santos Zelaya, who had frustrated U.S. investments in Nicaragua and its efforts to build a canal across it. In 1912, additional Marines arrived to help oppose rebel forces trying to stop U.S. economic influence in the country; they skirmished with the rebels for the next two decades and finally left in 1933. Three years later, the head of the Nicaraguan army (called the National Guard), Anastasio Somoza Garcia, was elected president of the country after running as the only candidate. He was assassinated in 1956, and his son Luis took his place until 1963, when he and his family permitted one of their supporters to win the presidency in an uncontested election. Another son, also named Anastasio, became president in 1967. During this whole period, the rule of the Somoza family was marked by increasing corruption and repression. Even though the country prospered economically, much of this prosperity came at the expense of the peasantry, whose land had been taken. U.S. support of the Somoza family amid all of these problems thus "heightened nationalist and anti-U.S. sentiment among the popular sectors and further delegitimized the government" (Grynspan 1991:92).

The Nicaraguan economy declined during the 1970s as job growth lagged behind population growth and the demand for jobs. Certain elite groups continued to be excluded from a role in the government. As the economy continued to worsen, these groups became especially disenchanted with Somozan rule. A devastating 1972 earthquake further worsened the economy and allowed the latest Somoza president and his allies to misappropriate international aid funds. These combined problems then "exploded in increasing unrest at all levels of Nicaraguan society" (Grynspan 1991:95).

Rebel revolts against the Somozan government accelerated in the mid-1970s. Many of the rebels belonged to the Sandinista National Liberation Front (FSLN), which was named after a rebel leader that the original Somoza had assassinated in 1934. The FSLN had been founded in the early 1960s but was defeated by the National Guard. By the mid-1970s, however, it "was able to take advantage of the deepening economic and political crisis" (Grynspan 1991:95) to launch a series of attacks, which were supported by students, teachers, workers, and intellectuals. The Somozan government met these attacks with more repression that strengthened popular support for the FSLN. One crucial FSLN supporter was the Nicaraguan church, which, influenced by the doctrine of "liberation theology," had been advocating greater economic and social justice. The church's opposition to the Somozan government further weakened it.

Full civil war between the rebel forces and the government finally broke out in 1978. The United States, despite having supported the repressive Somozan government for many decades, declined to come to its aid after Jimmy Carter, a human rights advocate, became the U.S. president in January 1977. Without U.S. help, Somoza could not defeat the FSLN. In July 1979, he resigned and left the country.

The Nicaraguan revolution resulted from many of the same forces discussed previously: a corrupt and repressive regime, a deteriorating economy, disenchantment by elite groups, and the refusal of other governments to help the regime. These factors combined to set the stage for the 1979 revolution that ended decades of Somozan rule.

During the 1980s, the FSLN faced its own problems, first from dissent within its own ranks and then from rebellion by the so-called *contra* forces, many of them former members of the Somozan National Guard, which were supported by the United States after Ronald Reagan was elected president in 1980. The war with the contras cost many lives and worsened the Nicaraguan economy, eventually leading to elections in 1990 that the FSLN lost. Ironically, some of the same factors that led to the FSLN victory in 1979 led to its downfall 11 years later.

The Iranian Revolution

Iran, north of the Persian Gulf, has long been of interest to foreign powers because of its strategic location and rich oil depositories. During World War II, British and Soviet troops invaded Iran to force it to let them ship war supplies across Iranian territory. This in turn led Iranian nationalists to call for Britain to remove its oil operations. In 1953, the nationalists forced the Iranian ruler, or shah, to leave the country, but a few days later the U.S. Central Intelligence Agency (CIA) helped the shah return to power. Over the following years, the CIA and other U.S. agencies continued to bolster the shah's government.

During the early 1960s, the shah instituted several social and economic reforms, including the redistribution of land to peasants. He also used oil revenues to improve the country's economic base. Even as he was making these changes, however, the shah continued to use political repression, including a secret police force known as the Savak, as a primary means of controlling his people. His harsh rule alienated Iranian students and intellectuals. Meanwhile, his economic and other programs to improve Iran's international standing alienated influential economic elites, who feared a loss of economic status, and, more important, led conservative Muslims to denounce the shah for violating traditional Islamic beliefs (Abrahamian 1986; DeFronzo 1996; Green 1986; Moshiri 1991a). Sharply rising inflation in the late 1970s hurt the middle classes and aggravated the already dire economic circumstances of Iran's poor. By that time, Iran had become so dependent on the United States for economic and other support that its government had lost legitimacy: "The Iranian state could no longer claim nationalistic credentials, and was viewed as a surrogate of the United States by many Iranians" (Moshiri 1991a:124).

These various oppositional elements quickly came together in the late 1970s under the flag of a religious leader named Ayatollah Ruhollah Khomeini. A rapid series of uprisings began that included strikes and riots. The shah's attempts to repress the revolutionary movement only spurred further uprisings (Rasler 1996). Faced with defeat, the shah finally fled Iran in January 1979 and Khomeini became the head of the new government, which was now based on Islamic teachings. Khomeini had hundreds of officials from the previous government executed and otherwise engaged in his own brand of political repression. After the United States let the shah come to that country for medical treatment, Iran captured the U.S. embassy in Iran in November 1979 and held several dozen hostages for more than a year. When Khomeini died in 1989, he was replaced by another religious leader.

The Iranian revolution of 1979 resulted from some, by now, familiar factors: a bad and worsening economy, elite disunity and alienation, and lack of help from other nations. Although some scholars have questioned whether the Iranian government was as "structurally vulnerable" as is usually thought, it remains true that the revolutionary opposition perceived that their protest would succeed and acted on that perception (Kurzman 1996). Coupled with the religious fervor of Iranian nationalism, all of these factors finally led to the end of the shah's repressive regime in 1979.

Conclusion

Revolution is one of the most important types of collective violence that so often fills world history. This chapter called attention to several factors that when combined greatly increase the odds that a revolution will occur. These factors include increasing discontent with economic and other conditions, a weakened state and a divided elite, and the disinclination of other nations to lend assistance. Even with these factors operating simultaneously, however, many nations do not experience revolution. But most revolutions have not occurred unless these factors were present.

For better or worse, the world would look very different today if thousands of people had not been willing to risk their freedom and even their lives in revolutionary acts of violence intended to address deeply felt concerns and grievances. The American Revolution of the 1770s is the example of this dynamic with which you're undoubtedly most familiar. But it's also true that revolutions have occurred without ultimately improving the masses' lives or giving them political freedom. Sometimes one authoritarian regime ends up replacing another, while at other times a more democratic regime initially emerges only to lose out to more authoritarian forces. Of the four revolutions summarized in the previous section, three—Russian, Chinese, and Iranian—resulted in authoritarian rule.

Whether or not the lot of the masses improves after revolutions topple existing regimes, it remains true that revolutionary violence isn't the only recourse for social change. In a democracy, of course, the usual avenue is to work within the electoral system, but such activity isn't possible in an authoritarian regime. Although political dissidents under both types of rule might resort to political violence, nonviolent direct action can be a viable and even more effective alternative to violent protest (Sederberg 1989; Sharp 1973). As Peter C. Sederberg (1989:57–58) remarks, "We might overvalue violence as a necessary component of the revolutionary process. . . . We exaggerate the efficacy of violence, despite its bloody costs and many failures, while at the same time ignoring the power of nonviolent (though not necessarily noncoercive) action." We must not forget that in the late 1980s and early 1990s, the former Soviet Union collapsed under the weight of nonviolent resistance, with Poland, East Germany, and other nations turning to democracy after decades of Communist rule. This revolution was arguably as important as any in the twentieth century, yet it was not a violent one.

This issue aside, the treatment of riots in the last chapter and revolution in this one has stressed their structural sources and viewed them as rational attempts to change social, economic, and political conditions. Whether or not we admire the violent acts committed to achieve such change and applaud the outcomes of these acts, they remain as fully understandable, if often desperate, as other political acts. For better or worse, riots, revolution, and other collective violence will continue to mark the international landscape in our lifetimes. A fuller understanding of these efforts at social change is essential if we are to understand some of the major events of historical and social life.

5

Terrorism

In April 1995, a bomb hidden in a pickup truck parked outside of the Oklahoma City Federal Building exploded, ripping apart the building and leaving it in rubble. As a nation watched in horror and wondered who was responsible, rescue crews spent hour after hour looking for survivors and collecting and identifying corpses. The number of known dead reached 168, including 19 children in a day care center in the building. The deadly bomb had been manufactured from fertilizer and other common materials.

After the Oklahoma City bombing, commentators wondered why this senseless act, as it was called again and again, occurred. What could lead individuals to murder dozens of people they did not know, people against whom they held no personal grudge, and people—such as the day care children and the many persons just visiting the Federal Building—who weren't even part of the federal government that the bombing suspects had obviously targeted? Were the suspects mentally unstable? Were they merely carried away by their feelings about the government? What purpose could the bombing possibly serve?

Two years before the Oklahoma City bombing, similar questions were asked after a February 1993 bomb destroyed part of the World Trade Center in New York City, killing 6 people and injuring more than 1,000. If Americans had been unfamiliar with terrorism before the Oklahoma City and World Trade Center tragedies, they became all too familiar with it after those events.

These bombings followed on the heels of a December 1988 bomb that cost many American lives when it blew up Pan American (Pan Am) flight 103 over Lockerbie, Scotland, killing 270 passengers, crew, and people on the ground. The World Trade Center and Pan Am bombings were later attributed to Middle Eastern terrorists (Fried 1998). After the Oklahoma City bombing, much speculation again centered on Middle Eastern terrorists, prompting Arab Americans to complain about stereotyping and verbal harassment (Alter 1995). Finally, two U.S. citizens, both young white males with ties to right-wing militia groups, were arrested and later convicted (Russakoff and Kovaleski 1998). We learned that terrorism is not just something that other people do.

Even as we continue to think about these acts of terrorism, they remain difficult to understand. Perhaps this is primarily because terrorism so often involves innocent victims who die or are injured only because they happen to be in the wrong place at the wrong time (Kressel 1996). This basic fact of terrorism makes it easy to think that it's senseless and irrational. However popular this characterization of terrorism might be, it is too simple.

This chapter explores terrorism's complexity by examining its nature and dimensions. *Terrorism* defies any easy definition, so this chapter, after first discussing the conceptual difficulties surrounding the term "terrorism," then develops a straightforward typology that captures terrorism's most important features. Later sections of the chapter sketch the historical and contemporary use of terrorism. By the end of the chapter, you should have a better idea of what terrorism is, why it occurs, and what, if anything, can be done about it.

Defining Terrorism

The terrorism literature is filled with discussions of the difficulties in deciding just what *terrorism* means. Not surprisingly, many definitions of terrorism exist, with one estimate putting the number at more than a hundred (Schmid and Jongman 1988). This plethora underscores the problems in defining terrorism and led one analyst to despair that "a comprehensive definition of terrorism . . . does not exist nor will it be found in the foreseeable future" (Laqueur 1977:5).

This pessimistic appraisal notwithstanding, most definitions of terrorism highlight several key dimensions that characterize a given behavior or pattern of behavior as one of terrorism (Hoffman 1998). Before outlining these dimensions, let's explore why the concept is so difficult to define precisely.

One problem in defining terrorism is that the word "terrorism" can be confused with words such as "terror" and "terrorize," both of which connote violence or the threat of violence and stem from the Latin term *terr(ēre)*, meaning "to frighten." (The term "terrorism" originated from the Reign of Terror that characterized the French Revolution.) Thus a common criminal commits vicious acts of violence against a terrorized victim; a violent street gang terrorizes a whole neighborhood; a stalker forces a woman to live in terror of attack. These unfortunately common, tragic acts all involve the fear that "terror" and "terrorize" connote, but they do not involve the essentially *political* activity that lies at the heart of most standard definitions of terrorism.

Another, more important definitional problem is that the word "terrorism" raises all sorts of emotions. It immediately brings to mind hideous, irrational acts of violence committed by desperate and often slovenly individuals. With this image in people's minds, terrorism takes on a negative connotation that makes it difficult to discuss the concept objectively. To complicate matters, terrorism is sometimes viewed positively by bystanders who share its goals. As is often said, "One person's terrorist is another person's freedom fighter." Thus, for example, many people in Northern Ireland, and many Irish Americans in the United States, view the Irish Republican Army (IRA) as heroes struggling valiantly against a British government that is denying Ireland its independence, whereas many others condemn the IRA's bombings and other terrorist tactics as sickening and beyond contempt. Many people in the Middle East regard the actions of the Palestinian Liberation Organization (PLO) and other terrorist groups as necessary acts of liberation, while others regard them as the worst sort of terrorism.

In a related definitional issue, the usual equation of "terrorists" and "terrorism" with individuals obscures the fact that governments themselves sometimes use terrorism to achieve their ends. In both contemporary and earlier periods, nations worldwide, including the United States, have engaged in or otherwise supported acts of terrorism to achieve political ends. This chapter returns to this point shortly.

Australian terrorism expert Grant Wardlaw (1989) summarizes these definitional problems by saying that terrorism is, at heart, a "moral problem." By labeling certain behaviors as acts of terrorism and the people who commit them as terrorists, we implicitly condemn both the acts and the actors. By not labeling other, similar acts as terrorism and their perpetrators as terrorists, we implicitly approve those acts and actors. As a result, says sociologist Jack P. Gibbs (1989:329), any definition of terrorism "may reflect ideological or political bias." To be useful, then, a definition of terrorism must dispassionately highlight its essential dimensions in a way that covers the various acts that comprise terrorism and the various actors that do terrorism.

This discussion suggests three dimensions that should be considered when defining terrorism: violence, fear, and political change. To the extent that this is true, the term *political terrorism* favored by some commentators is, as argued here, redundant, because terrorism necessarily implies a political component.

Many definitions that include these three dimensions abound. A simple dictionary definition would thus be "the use of violence and threats to intimidate or coerce, especially for political purposes" (Webster's 1983). A definition proposed by political scientist Ted Robert Gurr (1989b:201) goes one step further in highlighting the random, sudden nature of terrorism that makes it so frightening: "the use of *unexpected* violence to intimidate or coerce people in the pursuit of political or social objectives" (emphasis added). This definition underscores the fact that anyone—including innocent people— can be victims of terrorism and the fact that innocent people are often *the* targets of choice for terrorists. As philosopher Loren E. Lomasky (1991:107) observes, terrorists, unlike Robin Hood, typically don't distinguish between the guilty and the innocent or between justifiable victims and unjustifiable victims: "The enemy is only incidentally particular individuals who cross the terrorist's path; more fundamentally it is civil order."

Thus although there might not be one perfect definition of terrorism, these definitions and others like them underscore its essentially political nature, its use to provoke fear in the general population, and its use both by and against the state. Viewed dispassionately, terrorism is a violent tactic aimed at winning political objectives.

One reason terrorism is so difficult to define is that there are so many types of terrorism. Recognizing this, scholars have developed typologies of terrorism that consolidate these many types into a much smaller number of categories. The intent is to clarify the key characteristics distinguishing one form of terrorism from another. Most typologies incorporate at least two of three important features of terrorism: its purpose, its actors and supporters, and its location (e.g., White 1991; Wilkinson 1986). The typology favored here comes from political scientist Gurr (1989b). It has the advantage of being comprehensive but not too complex. It consists of four categories based on the "political status and situation of the perpetrators" (p. 204).

Gurr's first type is **vigilante terrorism,** which is committed by private citizens, for example, the Ku Klux Klan (KKK or the Klan), against other private citizens to express hatred or to resist social change. This type is the most common form of terrorism in U.S. history and is neglected in most terrorism typologies. Gurr's second type is **insurgent terrorism,** in which private citizens commit terrorism against their government to win political goals. Next is **transnational terrorism,** in which terrorists living in one nation strike inside another nation. Gurr's final category is **state terrorism.** Sometimes called *repressive terrorism,* this type is used by a government to intimidate its own citizens.

Gurr's typology is followed here in the discussion of historical and contemporary examples of terrorism in the United States and elsewhere. These examples illustrate how common terrorism has been and continues to be, while underscoring its rational, political nature, and should help you to become familiar with some of the most important periods and uses of terrorism in the historical and contemporary world.

Examples of Historical and Contemporary Terrorism

Vigilante Terrorism

Vigilante terrorism is perhaps as old as the United States itself and represents some of the ugliest moments of the American past. This is certainly a harsh assessment, but the historical record supports it. Native Americans became victims of random, unexpected violence shortly after white Europeans arrived in the New World in the early 1600s. Their victimization began in Virginia in 1607 and continued for almost 300 years, ending with the infamous massacre of an estimated 300 Sioux Indians at Wounded Knee, South Dakota, in 1890. Their assailants were first white settlers and later both settlers and governmental troops. In that sense, the violence that Native Americans suffered might be considered a combination of both vigilante terrorism and state terrorism. The use of this violence was part of a larger pattern of "broken treaties, unkept promises, and the slaughter of defenseless women and children" (Brown 1989:40), all designed to force and intimidate Native Americans into giving up their land to Europeans. The effort worked. Before the European influx, an estimated one million Native Americans lived in the future United States. During the next three centuries, settlers and troops killed tens of thousands of them, while settler-introduced disease claimed the lives of thousands more. By 1900, the Indian population was fewer than 240,000 (Brown 1971; Guillemin 1989).

The anti-Indian violence was just the first of many U.S. examples of vigilante terrorism directed against racial, ethnic, and religious minorities. Here the Ku Klux Klan stands out as perhaps the most notorious practitioner (Chalmers 1965; MacLean 1994; Trelease 1971). As historian Eckard V. Toy, Jr. (1989:131), observes, "The remarkable resilience of the Ku Klux Klan is a sad reminder of the persistence of racial and religious bigotry in the United States. No terrorist organization can match the Klan's mystique or long history, and few can match its success. Like Coca Cola, McDonald's, and Levis, the Ku Klux Klan has a name and image recognized throughout the world. As a social movement and as a cultural symbol, the Klan is a virtual synonym for terror and violence."

The three major periods of Klan activity were the reconstructionist years following the Civil War, the 1920s, and the post–World War II period. Formed in 1865 by a small group of Confederate Army officers in Tennessee who named their new organization after the Greek word *kyklos,* or circle, the Klan soon became a powerful force in opposing Reconstruction, terrorizing Southern blacks and white officials with beatings, torture, and murder. Although the Klan's influence diminished greatly during the 1870s after hundreds of arrests of its members by federal troops, its activities set the stage for more than three thousand lynchings of Southern blacks from 1882 to 1930 as "lynch-mob violence became an integral part of the post-Reconstruction system of white supremacy" (Brown 1989:37; Tolnay and Beck 1995). The aim throughout this period was to intimidate ex-slaves into accepting a subordinate position to Southern whites.

The Klan was revived in 1915, and during the next decade its influence and activity extended nationwide in response to growing anti-immigration fervor and the movement of rural Southern blacks into Northern cities (Toy 1989). Its targets in this period included not only African Americans but also Jews and Roman Catholics and, more generally, immigrants not from Anglo-Saxon backgrounds.

The Klan faded in the 1930s but revived again after the landmark U.S. Supreme Court decision, *Brown* v. *Board of Education,* in 1954 that banned school segregation. During the next decade, the Klan was at the forefront of the white violence committed against Southern blacks in general and Civil Rights activists in particular. Klan members reportedly committed dozens of bombings of black churches and other establishments and are thought to have been involved in many murders, shootings, and other violent acts meant to intimidate the Civil Rights movement (Toy 1989). Chapter 6 discusses the Klan further.

The Klan's anti-immigrant violence during the 1920s reflects a larger trend of anti-immigrant violence that has characterized U.S. history. This violence in turn has been part of a larger anti-immigrant, or nativist, movement that pervades the American past (Bennett 1988; Jenkins 1995). As shown in Chapter 3, mob violence against Roman Catholic and other immigrants occurred between 1850 and 1880 in cities across the country. During the 1850s, Irish Catholics in cities such as Baltimore, Louisville, New York, and St. Louis, were attacked by mobs comprised of, and instigated by, members of the American Party. This group formed in the early 1850s in response to a great wave of immigration into the United States that began in the 1820s. During the next three decades, an estimated five million immigrants, most of them Catholic, came from Europe. The members of the American Party feared growing Catholic influence in U.S. affairs and held many secret meetings to discuss what action to take. When asked any questions about the group or its policies, its members, as instructed, responded with "I don't know." This common response led to the American Party's familiar nickname, the Know-Nothing Party. The Know-Nothings coupled their violent attacks on Catholic immigrants with more standard electoral activity, as they ran candidates in state elections in several Northern states and won the governorships in 1854 in Delaware and Massachusetts. They later suffered serious internal dissension over the slavery issue and by the late 1850s had faded away (Anbinder 1992).

Today, vigilante terrorism manifests itself primarily in the form of hate crime. When we think of terrorism we don't usually think of hate crime. However, it clearly falls into Gurr's (1989b) vigilante terrorism category because it consists of acts intended to preserve the status quo by intimidating members of the targeted groups.

We discuss hate crime further in Chapter 6. Suffice it to say here that today it's very common (Hamm 1993; Jenness and Broad 1997; Levin and McDevitt 1993; Mullins 1993). Aimed at damaging both people and property, hate crime's targets most often include African Americans and other people of color, Jews, and gays. Still other people are targeted on the basis of their ethnicity, national origin, or disability. Regardless of the reason, individuals are beaten or killed and their property is defaced or destroyed. According to the best estimates, more than one hundred people died in hate crimes in the first half of the 1990s (Southern Poverty Law Center 1994c). Despite many estimates, we can never know exactly how many other people are victims of nonlethal hate crime violence, since so much of it goes unreported. This seems especially true of hate crime committed against Native Americans, whom the Southern Law Center calls "hidden victims" (Southern Poverty Law Center 1994b).

Since the early 1990s immigrants to the United States have been increasingly targeted by hate crime. They've come under both symbolic and real attack, as both anti-immigration talk and anti-immigrant hate crime reflect growing anti-immigrant sentiment. Asians, Latinos, and other immigrants have been attacked, beaten, and sometimes murdered (Southern Poverty Law Center 1994a). This anti-immigrant violence is the modern echo of that committed by the Know-Nothings and the Klan decades earlier.

Another important example of contemporary vigilante terrorism in the United States is anti-abortion violence, which aims at intimidating women from having abortions and physicians and other health practitioners from helping them in this manner. Several dozen bombs have exploded at abortion and family planning clinics in the last two decades, and several physicians and other workers at such clinics have been murdered (Bragg 1998; Clemetson and Gegax 1998; Cullen and McGrory 1994; Jacobs 1999). The individuals committing these acts and their supporters would no doubt object to the label "terrorism" being applied to their behavior. Indeed, they consider the killings that have occurred "justifiable homicides" designed to prevent a greater harm (Rogers 1994). Not surprisingly, the courts have rejected this argument.

What Do You Think?

Rape and domestic violence, or battering, are common crimes of violence committed against women every year in the United States. The U.S. Department of Justice estimates that about 300,000 rapes and sexual assaults occur annually, and other studies estimate that 20 to 25 percent of women experience a rape or attempted rape at least once in their lifetimes (Bachman and Saltzman 1995; Koss, Godoman, Browne, Fitzgerald, Keita, and Russo 1994; Rand 1998; Skorneck 1992). About one-fourth of these rapes are committed by "intimates"—husbands, ex-husbands, boyfriends, and ex-boyfriends—and one-half by other men that the women know. The Justice Department also estimates that more than one million women are assaulted annually by male intimates, while national surveys of married couples conclude that about one-fourth of all wives are attacked by their husbands sometime during their marriages (Bachman and Saltzman 1995; Straus and Gelles 1986).

The United States is not the only country with high levels of violence against women. Amnesty International and other organizations have documented such violence worldwide. "Dowry deaths" claim the lives of many women in India and Pakistan; thousands of women have been routinely raped during wartime and ethnic strife; and tens of millions of girls and women have suffered genital mutilation (Brownmiller 1975; Curtius 1994; Heise 1994).

Some writers term this worldwide pattern of violence against women "sexist terrorism" (Caputi and Russell 1992:15), which, they say, is directed against women *because* they are women and is "part of the ongoing attempt by men . . . to ensure the continuance of male supremacy" (Hester 1992:36). Thus philosopher Claudia Card (1991:296) calls rape a "terrorist institution" designed to scare women into complying with men and into depending on them for protection. Other scholars take a similar view (Bart and Moran 1993; Griffin 1971; Ward 1995).

Taken this way, rape, battering, and other such violence could be considered the equivalent of vigilante terrorism against women. Another view would be that violence against women, however tragic, lacks the clearly political motivation and objectives of more conventional forms of terrorism and thus does not merit a "terrorism" label. Is violence against women a form of terrorism? What do you think?

Insurgent Terrorism

Insurgent terrorism "is directed by private groups against public authorities and aims at bringing about radical political change" (Gurr 1989b:204). The term *radical* should be regarded here as synonymous with "drastic" and not be taken as connoting "left-wing" change, as both right-wing and left-wing groups can commit insurgent terrorism. Regardless of who does it, insurgent terrorism is probably the type with which you're already familiar and one that is common in the world today. Such terrorism has ebbed and flowed throughout U.S. history as well.

Schmid and de Graaf (1982) identify three types of insurgent terrorism. The first is **single- issue terrorism,** terrorism committed by an individual or small group of terrorists to pressure the government to change a specific policy. The second is **separatist terrorism,** terrorism that aims to help an ethnic group secede from a state. The third is **social revolutionary terrorism,** terrorism to overthrow the government and bring about dramatic economic, political, and social change.

Insurgent terrorism in the United States goes back at least to the colonial period, which was filled with violence against Britain and its supporters (Hoerder 1977). Both before and during the American Revolution, "the meanest and most squalid sort of violence was put to the service of revolutionary ideals and objectives" (Brown 1989:25). One common example was tarring and feathering Tories, which involved smearing hot tar over their naked bodies and then covering them with feathers. In the years leading to the Revolution, this practice was a "terrifying part of the vendetta that violent patriots carried on against British sympathizers and customs officials" (Brown 1975:56). Many Tories in South Carolina and Virginia were also lynched (which at that time usually meant whipping and not hanging, with the term deriving from a leading Virginian citizen, Colonel Charles Lynch, who presided over illegal trials of the Tories).

Insurgent terrorism also highlighted the labor strife that followed the Civil War, as workers committed many acts of violence against company property and personnel. Though workers were quite willing to perform these acts, much of their violence was in fact provoked by the violence and other abuse of the companies, guards, and police with whom labor struggled: "The unyielding attitude of capitalists in regard to wages, hours, and working conditions inspired union activity and precipitated strikes. The violent attempts by capital to suppress unions and break up strikes frequently incited workers to violence" (Gurr 1989a:6-47). As two historians have noted, the United States "has had the bloodiest and most violent labor history of any industrial nation in the world" (Taft and Ross 1990:174).

Some of the establishment violence committed against labor is discussed shortly, but we note here some of the insurgent violence used by labor (Lens 1973). Perhaps the most well known such act was that of the Molly Maguires, a secret organization of Irish American miners in Pennsylvania in the 1870s that took its name from a similar group formed in Ireland during the 1840s potato famine to fight established interests. As part of their struggle against Pennsylvania mine owners, the Molly Maguires assassinated company officials and committed other acts of terrorism. After being infiltrated by a member of the Pinkerton Detective Agency, the Molly Maguires saw several of their members tried, convicted, and executed for murder (Broehl 1964).

Some of the most famous incidents of labor violence involved bombings. In one example, members of the American Federation of Labor blew up the Los Angeles Times building with dynamite in 1910. Ten years later another bomb ripped apart a Wall Street bank owned by financier J. P. Morgan, killing more than 30 people and injuring more than 200.

In the more recent past, during the 1960s and 1970s insurgent terrorism was a tactic of some black militants, white revolutionaries, and Puerto Rican nationalists (Gurr 1989b). Members of all three groups used other means to achieve their objectives, but violence played an important, controversial role.

The violence committed by African American militants occurred primarily from 1968 to 1974. It capped more than a decade of Civil Rights activism that began in the South in the mid-to-late 1950s and reached an emotional peak with marches and sit-ins during the first half of the 1960s, during which Southern whites engaged in their own brand of terror against Civil Rights activists. This activism then evolved into the black power movement that rejected the nonviolent, integrationist stance of Martin Luther King, Jr., and the mainstream Civil Rights movement. From early 1968 until the end of 1970, more than 60 incidents occurred in which black militants attacked whites or engaged in shootouts with police that claimed approximately 49 lives (Gurr 1989c). As one example, 16 members of the Black Nationalists of New Libya engaged in a July 1968 shootout with Cleveland police that left 7 people dead; it's not clear who fired first.

Having mentioned the clashes with police, it's also necessary to point out that the police, not black militants, initiated many of these. This was especially true of the Black Panther Party (the Panthers), the group that is most associated in the public consciousness with insurgent violence during this time, in large part because it adopted a militant image, was sharply critical of police, stockpiled weapons, and advocated violence for self-defense. This stance "led to heightened police surveillance, confrontations, police raids, and shootouts" (Gurr 1989b:211–212). Although the shootouts numbered more than a dozen, most were begun by police, not by the Panthers.

Other black militant groups better fit the label of insurgent terrorism. Perhaps the best known is the Black Liberation Army (BLA), which was formed in New York City in 1971 by some former Panthers and ex-convicts and which targeted police for ambush and banks for armed robberies. An estimated 26 police died from these ambushes from 1970 to 1974 (Gurr 1989b).

About the same time, some white radicals, unhappy with the failure of the Vietnam antiwar movement to end the fighting in Southeast Asia, split off from Students for a Democratic Society (SDS) to form a revolutionary group that eventually became known as the Weather Underground. This group carried out a series of bombings beginning in 1970; its targets included the New York police headquarters and the Capitol and Pentagon in Washington, D.C. Near the end of the decade, members of the Weather Underground joined with BLA members and others to form the May 19 Communist Organization, which carried out a series of armed robberies and bombings on the East Coast into the 1980s. Three other terrorist groups in this period were the New World Liberation Front, which bombed businesses belonging to International Telephone and Telegraph, Pacific Gas and Electric, and other concerns on the West Coast in the mid-1970s; the Symbionese Liberation Army, which murdered the Oakland, California, school superintendent in 1973 and, in probably its most publicized act, kidnapped heiress Patty Hearst in 1974; the Sam Melville-Jonathan Jackson Unit, which robbed several banks and bombed several buildings in the mid-to-late 1970s; and the United Freedom Front, which bombed corporations in New York City in the early 1980s to protest apartheid and U.S. imperialism (Gurr 1989b; Marin 1987; Terry 1994).

These many examples notwithstanding, terrorism by Puerto Rican nationalists has been even more common in the United States. Two nationalists tried to kill President Harry S. Truman in 1950, and others shot five members of Congress in 1954. From 1970 through the 1980s, Puerto Rican nationalists are thought to have committed an estimated three hundred bombings and other terrorist acts in Puerto Rico and on the U.S. mainland (Gurr 1989b).

In the last 10 to 15 years, insurgent terrorism in the United States has taken on a more right-wing bent, as members of militia and white supremacist groups have engaged in numerous terrorist acts against government and other targets and have been more violent than their left-wing counterparts of a generation ago (Dees 1996; Smith 1994; White 1991). Perhaps the most infamous such act was the 1995 Oklahoma City bombing. Chapter 6 discusses these groups further. Suffice it to say here that right-wing terrorism now poses "the most serious threat," according to one terrorism expert, who notes that these right-wing groups are quite adept with weapons and explosives. "Although one might be inclined to dismiss the members of these groups as intemperate hot-heads, country bumpkins, or mentally unstable alarmists," he continues, "they have demonstrated that they are serious in their beliefs and dedicated to their causes—and that they are willing to use violence in pursuit of their goals" (Hoffman 1993:224).

If insurgent terrorism has marked the American landscape, it has found even more fertile ground in other nations. During the last several decades, Western Europe, the Middle East, and Latin America have been sites of repeated bombings, kidnapping, assassinations, and other terrorist acts. Space limitations allow only some of the most notable terrorist groups to be sketched here.

In Western Europe, one of the best-known terrorist groups is the IRA, which originated about 80 years ago to help Ireland win independence from Britain. In the 1920s, Britain divided Ireland into separate political units, with the Southern region eventually becoming the independent Republic of Ireland in 1949. Meanwhile, tensions in Northern Ireland between Catholics and the ruling Protestants escalated over the years, leading to increased conflict in the late 1960s. In response, British troops were sent to Northern Ireland in August 1969, and they have stayed there since. About the same time, the Catholic IRA split into two groups, the Provisional IRA and the Official IRA, with the Provisional IRA since carrying out numerous bombings, assassinations, and other terrorist acts in Northern Ireland and in England (Clarity 1992; Weitzer 1995; White 1993). Protestant terrorist groups were established to fight the IRA. Since the late 1960s, more than 3,000 people have died in terrorist acts and violent clashes among the IRA, the Protestant groups, and British troops. In August 1994, the IRA declared a cease-fire, but various acts of violence since then have continued in the British Isles (Cullen 1996). In 1996, the IRA exploded a bomb in London in February that killed 2 people and injured approximately 100 and in June bombed a shopping center in Manchester, England.

Two terrorist groups elsewhere in Western Europe were more active several years ago than today. The first, the Red Army Faction, was formed by student activists in West Germany in 1968 and later committed numerous bombings, assassination attempts, and bank robberies. In the mid-1980s, it turned its attention to U.S. military personnel in Germany to protest the influence of the North Atlantic Treaty Organization (NATO) in Western Europe (Wright 1991). The second group, the Red Brigades, began in 1970 in Italy and, among other terrorist activities, set off bombs in Rome and Milan and kidnapped and murdered the Italian prime minister. The group waned by the mid-1980s in the face of intense efforts by Italian police (Drake 1995; Segaller 1987).

When you hear the word "terrorist" today, a Middle Eastern face probably comes to mind more than any other. That can often translate into prejudice against people from the Middle East, but it is also true that insurgent terrorism has been quite common in the Middle East for several decades. Probably the best-known group is the PLO, the confederation of other groups that was formed in 1964 to try to wrest control of Palestinian land from Israel (Cobban 1985; Wright 1986). By the late 1960s, the PLO had come under the leadership of Yasser Arafat, whose al-Fatah group advocated violent means to achieve its objectives. Among other terrorist acts, the various PLO groups over the years have engaged in repeated bombings of public buildings, buses, and other targets in Israel and elsewhere. In 1972, one of these groups, Black September, killed two Israeli athletes and took nine others hostage during the Munich Olympics. The hostages were later killed during a shootout with the police.

Another region rife with insurgent terrorism is South America. Over the years, most of the governments there have been repressive, right-wing dictatorships ruling over poverty-stricken nations. In many of these countries, left-wing rebel groups, some of which have used terrorism, arose in response (Duff and McCamant 1976; Halperin 1976; Herman 1983). One such group was the People's Revolutionary Army in El Salvador, which was part of a larger coalition of left-wing groups formed in the 1970s to fight El Salvadoran authoritarian rule. Despite the insurgent terrorism in the region, most of the terrorism there is in fact state terrorism (see later in this chapter), often in the form of right-wing death squads, because it is committed by and on behalf of the government against private citizens to quell dissent (White 1991).

Asia has also been the site of terrorist acts. Among the most recent incidents was a 1995 poison-gas attack in a subway in Tokyo that killed 12 people and made 5,500 ill. Members of a religious cult were later arrested for the gas attack (Kaplan and Marshall 1996). We discuss this group further in the next chapter.

Transnational Terrorism

Transnational terrorism begins in one country but takes place in another. This category also includes terrorism that occurs in one's own country against foreign targets or against domestic targets but "in the name of an international cause or on behalf of a foreign government" (Gurr 1989b). Many scholars use the term *international terrorism* instead of transnational terrorism. Whatever term it goes by, such terrorism captures headlines many times a year and imperils people worldwide (Hoffman 1998).

Several acts of transnational terrorism in the recent past have hit U.S. targets, both human and property. Two were cited at the outset of this chapter: the 1993 World Trade Center bombing and the 1988 Pan Am bombing over Scotland. In the World Trade Center bombing, a truck bomb exploded in the building's underground garage and killed 6 people and injured more than 1,000 (Dwyer 1994). Four Middle Eastern defendants were convicted in federal court in March 1994 of the bombing, and each was sentenced to 240 years in prison without parole. After a nine-month trial, a federal jury in October 1995 later convicted ten other defendants implicated in the bombing with plotting to commit several terrorist acts to avenge U.S. policy in the Middle East. Another defendant had pleaded guilty before the trial. The acts that the group allegedly plotted included assassinating political leaders and bombing other sites in New York City, such as the United Nations headquarters, the George Washington Bridge, and the Lincoln and Holland tunnels under the Hudson River. Two defendants received life terms in prison, while the others received sentences of up to 57 years.

In the 1988 Pan Am bombing, the 747 airplane, flying to New York, exploded in mid-air over Lockerbie, Scotland, killing all 259 people on board, including 189 Americans and 11 people on the ground. The bomb had been hidden in a radio cassette player inside a suitcase. The United States and Great Britain later accused two Libyan intelligence agents with the crime. When Libya refused to turn over the two men, the United Nations imposed sanctions on that nation in April 1992. The United States charged that Libya had ordered the Pan Am bombing to avenge U.S. bombing raids on the nation in 1986. Those raids had been in response to Libya's suspected involvement in a bombing in a Berlin club earlier in the year that killed two U.S. soldiers. Libyan agents had earlier been suspected of a 1989 bombing of a French plane over Niger that killed 171 people.

A decade earlier, Omega 7, an anti-Castro organization composed of Cuban Americans, was "one of the most active international terrorist groups on American soil in the late 1970s and early 1980s" (Smith 1994:134). The group is thought to have committed more than fifty bombings and assassination attempts in the United States against Cuban diplomats and businesses involved with Cuba. The founder of the group claimed that the CIA had trained him in the use of explosives and other terrorist tactics. Their bombing targets included the Venezuelan Consulate in New York City in 1975; the Cuban delegation to the United Nations in 1976; a Soviet ship docked at the New Jersey coast, also in 1976; several travel agencies in New Jersey in 1977 and 1978; New York City's Lincoln Center in 1978; and both the Cuban Mission to the United

Nations and a Soviet airlines ticket office in New York in 1979. Omega 7 members also assassinated a Cuban official at the United Nations in 1980. The Omega 7 founder was later arrested, convicted, and sentenced to life in prison, while other Omega 7 members were given ten-year terms.

Despite Americans' fears over transnational terrorism occurring in the United States, this form of terrorism is much more common outside of the United States. The prime example is Middle Eastern terrorism, which has spread into Western Europe as "the battle over the Palestinian question and other Middle Eastern issues has moved beyond the Middle East" (White 1991:193). Most of the terrorist acts have been directed against other Middle Eastern groups and individuals, but others have been aimed at European and U.S. targets. From 1980 to 1985, for example, an estimated 233 Middle Eastern terrorist acts occurred in Western Europe. Of these, more than 60 percent of the targets were Arab or Palestinian, 17 percent were Israeli, 16 percent were European, and 5 percent were American (White 1991). One of the most active transnational terrorist groups has been Abu Nidal, which was founded in the early 1970s and which has targeted moderate Arabs as well as Israelis. It has assassinated or tried to kill officials from Egypt, Jordan, Kuwait, and Syria, and in 1985 hijacked an Egyptian plane and killed 59 people on board. Later that year, it shot airport passengers in Rome and Vienna and the next year killed 21 people when it bombed a synagogue in Turkey (Melman 1986; Wege 1993).

Two other Middle Eastern groups that have engaged in transnational terrorism are the Hizbollah and Islamic Jihad. Hizbollah is centered in Iran and Lebanon and controls Islamic Jihad, which is based in Lebanon. Both groups have engaged in suicide bombings, while Islamic Jihad has also bombed cars and ambushed and kidnapped many people, including more than 20 from Western Europe and the United States (Brooks 1993; Rapoport 1988; Taylor and Ryan 1988).

State Terrorism

As noted earlier in the chapter, when we hear the term *terrorists,* we typically think of individuals acting on their own behalf. But governments can also be terrorists. In state terrorism, a government uses random violence to terrorize its own citizens. The purpose here is to stifle dissent. State terrorism takes the form of mass murder, individual assassinations, execution without due process, and beatings and torture. In this century, far more people have been killed and injured by state terrorism than by all other types of terrorism combined (Bushnell 1991; Claridge 1998; Glover 1991). Despite this toll, most terrorism experts have focused on the types of terrorism already discussed, leaving state terrorism understudied.

The most extreme type of state terrorism is **genocide,** the systematic extermination of a whole people because of their race, religion, ethnicity, or national origin (Chalk and Jonassohn 1993). Undoubtedly the most heinous example of genocide in modern times is the Holocaust during World War II, which resulted in the deaths of about 6 million Jews and 6 million other people, including gypsies and homosexuals (Gilbert 1987). In 1915, Turkey committed genocide against 1 million Armenians by forcing them into the desert, where they died from thirst, starvation, or other reasons (Nazian 1990). In the late 1970s, the Cambodian government slaughtered hundreds of thousands of Cambodians in an effort to solidify its rule (Martin 1994). In 1994, Rwandan governmental troops slaughtered up to 1 million Tutsis, a major ethnic group in that African nation (Lynch 1995).

Although almost all genocide has been committed by authoritarian regimes, some critics say the United States has also committed it. They have in mind at least two examples. The first concerns U.S. troop involvement in the slaughter of Native Americans in the 1800s. As noted earlier in the chapter, settlers and troops killed tens of thousands of Native Americans; some critics liken government involvement in this mass killing to genocide (Brown 1971). The other example concerns the U.S. war against Vietnam in the 1960s and 1970s. The war claimed almost 2 million Vietnamese lives, including many civilians; critics then and now charge that the United States committed genocide against the Vietnamese (DeBenedetti and Chatfield 1990). The continuing controversy over the nature of U.S. killings of Native Americans and Vietnamese, and in particular over whether they constituted genocide, demonstrates the emotions that both episodes still excite.

Most state terrorism doesn't go as far as genocide, but it still involves much death, injury, misery, and fear. Perhaps the most discussed example of state terrorism in this century occurred under Joseph Stalin in the Soviet Union in the 1930s and 1940s. To protect his power, Stalin ordered the execution of thousands of rival Communist Party leaders and other citizens (Conquest 1990; Parrish 1996). Much more recently, Chinese troops gunned down several thousand unarmed protesters at Tiananmen Square in Beijing in June 1989. Several hundred died while others were arrested and imprisoned and a few were executed (Black 1993).

This Stalinist and Chinese state terror occurred in Communist countries, but right-wing regimes have also engaged in considerable state terrorism. Much of this has occurred in Latin America, where most acts, as noted previously, have been committed *by* the government, not *against* the government. Right-wing regimes there have been all too willing to have police and secret death squads terrorize the citizenry. In the last few decades, tens of thousands have been kidnapped, tortured, murdered, and otherwise terrorized, with some of the worst abuses occurring in Argentina, Guatemala, and Colombia. U.S. involvement in these abuses has long been documented, as the United States has helped install Latin American dictators, trained their military police in terrorist tactics, and otherwise supported their authoritarian rule (Blum 1995; Brysk 1994; Chomsky 1985; Giraldo 1996; Goti 1996; Perera 1993).

The United States has also used state terror against its own citizens. Recall the U.S. troop massacres of Native Americans a century ago. Genocide or not, these massacres still fit the definition of state terror. The labor movement discussed previously also saw its share of official violence. During an 1897 coal-mining strike in Pennsylvania, for example, deputies shot into a group of peaceful miners, killing 18 and wounding 40; many of the victims were shot in the back (Taft and Ross 1990). Another official massacre occurred in Ludlow, Colorado, in 1914, when Colorado Fuel and Iron Company guards and National Guard troops machine-gunned mining families as they fled from a tent city that the guards and troops had set afire. Nineteen miners and their families, including 13 children, lay dead when the smoke cleared (McGovern and Guttridge 1972).

In two more recent examples of state terror, local police and state troops murdered or beat hundreds of civil rights activists in the South during the early-to-mid 1960s. In one of the most notorious incidents, Birmingham, Alabama, police clubbed unresisting demonstrators, sprayed them with fire hoses, and attacked them with police dogs (McAdam and Moore 1989). A few years later, the Panthers were also targeted by police with lethal violence (Churchill and Wall 1990). In one of the worst incidents, Chicago police raided the Chicago residence of Panther leader Fred Hampton in December 1969 and shot him in his bed. Another Panther leader also died in the raid. Later evidence suggested that neither Hampton nor Clark had fired a bullet, and critics charged they'd been murdered in cold blood.

State terrorism raises some fascinating if troubling questions for the social sciences (Slann 1993; Stohl and Lopez 1984). Although we usually think of terrorism as illegal behavior, it is committed by the very state that makes the laws; hence, it is "legal" in the technical sense of the word. In Western political theory, the state is created by citizens to establish and maintain social stability and otherwise improve their lives. To have a state terrorize its own citizens is thus a fundamental contradiction of what states should ideally be all about. Seen in this light, state terrorism challenges our common notions of what "terrorism" is and underscores terrorism's political objectives no matter who engages in it.

Despite its frequency and importance, state terrorism has received much less attention from social scientists than other types of terrorism. As one scholar put it, "One searches in vain through the thousands of articles and books written by political scientists, political sociologists, economists, and anthropologists for references to the awful and bloody deeds of governments and for explanations of how and why these deeds are done" (McCamant 1984:11). Although this lament was written more than 15 years ago, it remains largely true today, as most scholarly treatments and popular discussions of terrorism neglect the state variety in favor of the other types discussed here. Ironically, state terrorism sometimes motivates insurgent and multinational terrorists to respond in kind (Slann 1993). Additional understanding of state terrorism would thus enhance understanding of the other types that receive far more attention.

Explaining Terrorism

If terrorism is difficult to define, it's perhaps even more difficult to explain. The different types of terrorism discussed here differ widely from each other despite some overall similarities; thus, it's difficult to come up with a comprehensive explanation that applies to all terrorism (Laqueur 1987). However, certain explanations seem to make more sense than others. Because state terrorism remains understudied, most explanations focus on insurgent, transnational, and sometimes vigilante terrorism. Accordingly, most of the next discussion concerns terrorism by individuals rather than terrorism by government, although the context for state terrorism also is discussed.

Earlier chapters noted that we can try to explain either why individuals commit collective violence or why collective violence occurs. These two levels of analysis are related, of course, but they yield very different sorts of explanations that, together, provide a more comprehensive explanation of collective violence than either level of analysis can by itself. The same is true for terrorism, as we must ask both why individuals commit it *and* why it occurs, regardless of who's involved. Both levels of explanation are necessary for the most complete understanding of terrorism. Although some individuals might be more predisposed than others to terrorism, they would still be less likely to engage in it if certain historical and political conditions precipitating terrorism did not exist. At the same time, although these conditions might make terrorism more likely, the fact remains that only a few individuals engage in terrorism even under these conditions.

For better or worse, in many ways it is easier to explain why terrorism occurs than why individuals become involved in it. As you might guess, it's difficult to study individual terrorists. Social scientists who wish to study terrorists must first be able to find them to ask them questions. Not surprisingly, terrorists don't like to be found, and, in any event, they aren't as likely as the other people that social scientists study to be willing to sit down and fill out a questionnaire or submit to intensive interviews. We might be able to learn in other ways about their upbringing and other aspects of their background, but that's no substitute for more tried-and-true methods of social research. With this caveat in mind, let's review some of the leading explanations for terrorism.

Psychological and Social-Psychological Views

As with other explanations of collective violence, a basic distinction in terrorism explanations lies between psychological views and structural or sociopolitical approaches (Crenshaw 1992; Ross [Jeffrey] 1998b; Sederberg

1998). Influenced by media coverage, most Americans probably favor a psychological approach instead of a structural one. In a psychological perspective, individuals commit terrorism because they have psychological states or problems that predispose them to do so (Reich 1990; Schmid and Jongman 1988) (recall Chapter 2). Within this psychological framework, different explanations emphasize different psychological processes. Because terrorism, however defined, involves wanton violence, some formulations stress that an individual who is drawn to terrorism must suffer from psychological abnormalities that lead to a sadistic and/or paranoid personality—in short, a "terrorist personality"—that in turn compels the person to commit such violence (Fromm 1973; Storr 1991). As one writer summarizes this view, "From this perspective, certain people will be driven by their inner demons to engage in terrorism" (Sederberg 1998:24). Terrorism is thus thought to be a symptom of a psychopathological mind.

There are at least three problems with this psychopathological viewpoint. First, and probably most important, the available evidence indicates that most terrorists do *not* suffer from psychopathology and do not have terrorist personalities. While some individual terrorists may indeed be mentally unstable in the ways specified here, just as some nonterrorists may be mentally unstable, most are as psychologically "normal" as the average person (Sederberg 1989). As one writer puts it, "Most terrorists are no more or less fanatical than the young men who charged into Union cannonfire at Gettysburg or those who parachuted behind German lines into France. They are no more or less cruel and coldblooded than the Resistance fighters who executed Nazi officials and collaborators in Europe, or the American GI's ordered to 'pacify' Vietnamese villages" (Rubenstein 1987:5).

As this comment suggests, people are quite capable of committing extreme violence without being psychologically disturbed. This was true of the Nazi doctors who performed some of the most hideous experiments imaginable (Lifton 1986), and it is certainly true of the individuals who commit the many types of terrorism discussed in this chapter. If we are willing to assume (as many of us would be), that the dictators and their henchmen who order and carry out state terrorism do so in a rational, cold, and calculated way, however bloodthirsty, why should we believe anything less of other kinds of terrorists?

The second problem with the psychopathological viewpoint can be summarized more easily. Even if it were true that terrorists tend to suffer from psychopathological personalities that compel them to terrorism, that does not explain why their personalities do not compel them to other forms of destructive behavior, for example, common violence. A psychopathological viewpoint can at most explain why someone turns to violence, but it cannot readily explain why they turn to *terrorist* violence.

The third problem with this viewpoint is a bit more abstract. A psychopathological perspective takes attention away from the historical, political, and other structural conditions that underlie terrorism and suggests that terrorism is an abnormal rather than a normal, if usually undesirable and often abhorrent, reaction to these conditions. As Peter C. Sederberg (1998:25) puts it, "While psychopathology may offer some intriguing insights, it tends to discount the significance of the social and political environment. Indeed, under certain conditions, such as those of the [Nazi] death camps, terrorist acts may become the norm, and the deviant personality may be the one who resists committing acts of terrorism."

Another psychological approach to terrorism connects psychological states to structural conditions and thus could be considered a social-psychological approach (Benesh 1998; Sederberg 1998). In this approach, terrorism is best considered one of the many possible reactions to discontent. Without discontent, no one would be unhappy, and no terrorism—or for that matter, other forms of social protest—would occur. The question then is what social and political conditions and processes lead to discontent. As discussed in Chapter 2, scholars trying to answer this question focus on such concepts as alienation, relative deprivation, and rising expectations. Although most such investigations focus on various types of collective and political violence and not just on terrorism, they have obvious implications for terrorism. Yet, as shown in Chapter 2, the importance of the social-psychological processes for collective violence and other protest remains disputed. If it is not clear how well they explain collective action in general, then it is, unfortunately, also not clear how well they explain terrorism.

One problem is that these social-psychological states "cannot explain by themselves why people choose to respond with acts of severe coercion" (Sederberg 1998:25). Many other types of responses are certainly possible. Thus some scholars emphasize that terrorism is unlikely to occur unless individuals adopt ideologies that justify the use of extreme violence to achieve political goals. For such adoption to occur, these ideologies must be transmitted through friendship networks and other means (Rapoport 1988; Wilkinson 1986). Such ideologies can also explain how and why state terrorism happens. For example, the Nazi terror depended on the transmission and adoption of a "bioideology" that branded Jews as subhuman (Gilbert 1987; Lifton 1986). A similar set of ideologies may also underlie vigilante terrorism. Thus in the South, a "racist ideology" that dehumanized blacks by portraying them as sinister threats to white society was a necessary condition for the several thousand lynchings that occurred after the Civil War and during the first three decades of this century (Beck and Tolnay 1995; Myers, 1995).

Structural Views

Scholars who take a *structural* approach to terrorism and other collective violence see these behaviors as *rational* responses to structural (i.e., economic, political, and social) conditions. According to this view, collective violence and other forms of protest are simply "politics by other means" (Gamson 1990) that are invoked when the affected group perceives threats to its economic, political, and social well-being. Thus much insurgent and transnational terrorism is a response to what the individuals involved view as governmental oppression. Just as the American colonists revolted against England because of "a long train of abuses and usurpations" (as the Declaration of Independence so eloquently puts it), so do groups as different as the IRA, PLO, and others commit terrorism because they see a similar situation in their own homelands. Whether their terrorism is justified or not, often objective evidence exists to support their charges of oppression and inequality.

In such a political framework, state terrorism can likewise be seen as a response to dissent that threatens the "well-being" of those in power. Vigilante terrorism can be viewed in a similar manner as an effort to preserve the status quo, and thus the well-being of those committing such terrorism, by striking out at disadvantaged groups that pose a threat to established interests. For vigilante terrorism that targets racial minorities, this conception is consistent with theories of racial prejudice that connect white prejudice and punitive treatment of racial minorities to the threat that such minorities pose to whites' economic and political well-being (Blalock 1967; Bonacich 1972).

The Southern lynchings are best understood in this context. They increased when the economy worsened—when the price of cotton was falling and when inflation was rising—and decreased when the economy improved. They also happened more often in Southern counties with higher proportions of blacks than in those with lower proportions, as long as blacks did not outnumber whites. In counties in which blacks were a majority, lynchings were less common (Beck and Tolnay 1995; Corzine, Creech, and Corzine 1988; Tolnay and Beck 1995).

For lynchings and other racial violence, the interracial competition described here combines with the racist ideology discussed previously to form two of the four necessary conditions for racial violence to occur (Beck and Tolnay 1995). The other two are state permissiveness and some threshold event. By "state permissiveness" is meant the willingness of state officials to look the other way when racial violence is committed or even to encourage its use. When such state permissiveness exists, racial violence is more common. A "threshold event" is a real or imagined event that "provides the immediate justification for violent action directed toward the target group" (Beck and Tolnay 1995:123). For lynchings, such threshold events typically included rumors that blacks had committed rape or other offenses against whites.

The emphasis here on state permissiveness complements other work from a political opportunity perspective, outlined in Chapter 2, that sees collective action more likely when a regime has weakened social control or is otherwise vulnerable to protest (McAdam, McCarthy, and Zald 1988). In such regimes, nonstate terrorism should be more likely. Such states can be either democratic or authoritarian; the key factor is whether the political system is stable or unstable and even volatile.

Media Coverage of Terrorism

One possible facilitator of terrorism not yet mentioned is news media coverage. In most nations in which state terrorism exists, the government largely or even totally controls the media and thus can count on the media either not to report state terrorism or to report it in a way that suggests that the terrorism's victims got what they deserved. Nonstate terrorists don't control the media, but insurgent and transnational terrorists typically count on media coverage to help spread the fear and intimidation that are so often their primary goals. The more the media cover terrorism, the more the public becomes afraid of terrorism and the more pressure the government then feels to alter its policies. Thus the media can play an unwitting role not only in facilitating terrorism, but also in helping it to succeed (Schmid and Graaf 1982; Weimann and Winn 1994). This is especially true in democratic regimes, where the media are free to report terrorism and, because of terrorism's sensationalism, are apt to report it heavily (Hoffman 1998). Thus the news media "provide 'the oxygen of publicity' on which terrorism thrives" (Kidder 1998:149). Recognizing this, some terrorist groups have become virtual public relations experts as they send out press releases, hold news conferences, and provide videotapes of hostages and various terrorist acts.

What Would You Do?

Suppose that you are the news director for one of the major TV networks. You get a report that terrorists have taken two dozen people hostage in a U.S. embassy in a nation with whom the United States has had hostile relations. The terrorists demand that the U.S. government end its military aid to their government in return for the release of the hostages. The United States, reiterating its policy of never negotiating with terrorists, refuses. A standoff begins. Naturally, you send your lead news anchor and several reporters to cover the situation, as do all of your competitors.

Two days later, your anchor says that she was approached by a spokesperson for the terrorist group. The spokesperson offered to give the anchor an exclusive, one-hour interview with the head of the group, who is inside the embassy. You will be allowed to ask how the hostages are doing and to briefly interview some of them, but most of your interview would have to be devoted to asking the terrorist leader about the reasons for why his group is holding the embassy workers hostage.

> You realize that if you consent to the interview, your network will be giv-
> ing the terrorists an international forum for their views and that to a large
> extent your coverage will be orchestrated by the terrorists to yield the most
> favorable impression possible about them. But you also realize that the inter-
> view will lead to unprecedented high ratings for your network and that if you
> decline to do the interview, one of your competitors will likely end up with this
> dubious honor.
> What would you do?

Media leaders, public officials, and scholars continue to debate the
extent to which the media should cover terrorism, especially in the television
age when broadcasts of terrorist actions can be sent around the world in seconds (Livingston 1994; Nacos 1994). Defenders of media coverage feel that
it enhances public understanding of terrorism and reinforces public hostility
toward terrorists. If the media in a democratic society are truly free, they say,
they must be allowed to cover terrorism without restriction. Critics of media
coverage feel that it gives "terrorists a megaphone through which to spread
their message of fear to their ultimate target," the public; that it increases terrorism via a "contagion" effect as new terrorists come along to engage in
"copycat" acts; and that it may even make some terrorists into folk heroes
akin to Robin Hood (Kidder 1998:149).

Not surprisingly, the issue of media coverage often raises serious dilemmas for the media, as they must decide how much coverage is appropriate
(Zulaika 1996). As one example, when a TWA plane was hijacked in Beirut,
Lebanon, in 1985, the terrorists involved offered television networks the
chance to interview the hostages for $12,500 or to tour the plane for $1,000.
The U.S. and British governments called on the media to limit their coverage. Despite that urging, U.S. television networks covered the hijacking
almost nonstop. After the incident ended, the London *Times* charged that
"the behavior of the American television crews was a disgrace" (Finn
1998:154; Kidder 1998).

Unfortunately, systematic studies of the actual impact of media coverage
are relatively scant. Some evidence suggests that it does increase public fear
and concern about terrorism, and limited evidence suggests that a contagion
effect does exist, as media coverage of terrorism sometimes seems to inspire
other terrorist acts (Mazur 1982; Schmid and Graaf 1982). However, there is
little evidence that media coverage increases public support for terrorist goals;
more likely, it decreases such support (Martin 1985; Weimann and Winn
1994). One reason for this latter effect is that the media generally ignore the
reasons for terrorist violence and depict it negatively, while positively portraying governmental efforts to thwart such violence (White 1991).

Women and Terrorism

Efforts to explain terrorism are beginning to focus on the role that gender plays (Neuburger, Valentini, and Campling 1996; Schmemann 1998; Vetter and Perlstein 1991). Although women have over the years played important roles in revolutionary and terrorist movements, terrorism generally has been much more a male activity than a female one. This gender difference raises two related questions: Why are men so much more involved in terrorism, and why are women so much less involved? Most explanations of collective violence ignore gender, so we turn to the criminology literature for some possible answers to these questions. If we can understand why gender differences exist in conventional crime, including common violence, then perhaps we can understand why gender differences in terrorism exist.

Early explanations of gender differences in crime focused on the supposed biological nature of the two sexes (Klein 1973). Males were "naturally" assertive and even aggressive, and females were "naturally" nonassertive, with some scholars tracing these differences to the mobility of sperm and the relative immobility of the egg. Some psychoanalytical thinkers thought that when girls and women did commit crime, they did so either because they were suffering from "penis envy" and wanted to be more like men or because they were frustrated over not having a boyfriend. In 1950, one scholar even argued that women committed more crime than was known about because they were naturally deceitful (because they hide evidence of their menstrual periods and fake orgasms) and thus were adept at hiding evidence of their crimes (Pollak 1950). A more recent biological explanation focuses on testosterone, which men obviously have much more of than women and which is said to increase aggressive behavior (Booth and Osgood 1993).

Today most criminologists reject these biological and psychoanalytical explanations of gender differences in criminality and instead favor more sociological ones (Barkan 1997; Cullen, Golden, and Cullen 1979; Rosenbaum 1987). The key factors here are said to be socialization and opportunity. We raise our boys to be assertive and dominant, both traits that are conducive to criminality, and we raise our girls to be more nurturing and passive. We also give our boys more freedom during adolescence to be outside the home, where they have more opportunity to commit crime, and practice a double standard for girls that confines them to the home. If gender differences in socialization and opportunity underlie gender differences in crime, including violent crime, then they could also account for gender differences in terrorism.

One interesting question is whether women are now more involved in terrorism than they used to be. This question is difficult to answer, because we don't have good historical or contemporary data on the extent of women's involvement (Vetter and Perlstein 1991). Some anecdotal evidence indicates that women are more involved now than before the 1960s, but we do not really know how reliable this evidence is. If women are more involved, it may be due to the changing female socialization patterns in contemporary societies (Neuburger, Valentini, and Campling 1996). But analogous work in criminology suggests caution in making this assumption. During the 1970s, some scholars and many members of the media heralded the "rise of the new female criminal" (Adler 1975; Simon 1975) and traced this rise to changing female socialization patterns prompted by the women's liberation movement. Yet subsequent studies cast serious doubt on whether women's crime rates were rising substantially at all and, even if some rates were rising, whether the women's movement was responsible (Barkan 1997; Steffensmeier 1980). Certainly further research is needed before we can make firm conclusions about whether women have become more involved in terrorism and the reasons for any increase that might have occurred.

Countering Terrorism

The terrorism literature is filled with recommendations and debates concerning the best ways to counter terrorism, and the term *counterterrorism* has made its way into popular usage. Almost all work on counterterrorism addresses only two of the four types of terrorism discussed earlier in this chapter. These two types are insurgent and transnational terrorism. As noted previously, discussions of terrorism typically ignore the vigilante variety and often neglect the state variety, and the counterterrorism literature is no exception. This section sketches the major points of the counterterrorism debate on the first two types and turns later to the latter two.

The question that all counterterrorism discussions try to answer is how can we best deal with the terrorist threat. This question is difficult to answer. As Richard E. Rubenstein (1987:229) observes, "Since serious terrorist movements are locally rooted and politically diverse, there is no unified terrorist threat to discuss, and no possibility of prescribing an all-purpose response. One's reaction to any particular terrorist campaign will depend on the nature of the attacking group, the precise situation presented, and one's own political ideas." Other writers also emphasize that the diversity of terrorism makes it difficult to come up with any all-encompassing solution to it. Thus Sederberg (1989) says that the response to insurgent terrorism must at a minimum consider the goals of the groups committing it and the degree to which those groups enjoy public support.

Most counterterrorism experts have answered this question by advocating a law enforcement or military approach to terrorism (Carr 1998; Turner 1991; Wardlaw 1989). In this approach, the law, legal system, and military are used to try to prevent terrorism and to punish terrorists. Here we can distinguish between offensive and defense strategies (Vetter and Perlstein 1991). Offensive strategies include economic and diplomatic sanctions, military strikes, harsh prison terms, and so on. Defense strategies typically take the form of **target hardening,** which involves efforts to make potential terrorist targets secure and safe. Airport metal detectors are perhaps the most familiar example of target hardening.

How successful are such counterterrorism measures? Although target hardening has helped in many cases, determined terrorists can still succeed. The effectiveness of the offensive strategies is even more debatable (Heymann 1998). Although there is some evidence that police crackdowns have weakened or eliminated some terrorist groups in the United States and Western Europe, other groups, especially in the Middle East, persist despite repeated military strikes and other punitive measures (Hewitt 1984; Sederberg 1989). This fact makes several experts question the value and advisability of such measures, with one saying flatly that "terrorist movements cannot be eliminated by a policy of assassination and disruption" (Rubenstein 1987:231). Moreover, often these harsh measures have the unintended effect of increasing the resolve of terrorists, as well as popular support for their cause, while doing nothing to address the political, social, and economic conditions underlying at least some examples of terrorism (Sederberg 1989; White 1991).

Another problem raised by harsh counterterrorist measures in democratic societies is the threat they pose to civil liberties (Charters 1994; Heymann 1998). In any democratic society, tension always exists between the goals of keeping the society safe (e.g., from crime and terrorism) and keeping the society free. As one writer notes, "Responding to terrorism exposes a conflict between our need for survival, the most urgent objective, and our commitment to democracy, our highest purpose" (Finn 1998:157). A recent example of the civil liberties debate surrounding counterterrorism occurred after the Oklahoma City bombing discussed previously. The public, media, and government at first suspected Middle Eastern terrorists, and Congress soon considered legislation designed to crack down on terrorism. Critics charged that several provisions in the legislation would cut away at civil liberties guaranteed by the Bill of Rights (Rubin 1995).

In a related area, several counterterrorism experts believe the United States and other democracies need to restrict media coverage of terrorism. In response, other observers charge that such restrictions would undermine the freedom of the press guaranteed in the First Amendment (Finn 1998). Britain, which does not have the freedom of the press tradition that the United States enjoys, does restrict media coverage of terrorism, and observers there and elsewhere continue to debate the merits of British law in this regard (Miller 1993).

An alternative to conventional counterterrorism measures stems from the political explanation of terrorism discussed previously and focuses on the social, economic, and political causes of terrorism. If inequality, oppression, and other such ills lie at the heart of much insurgent and transnational terrorism, then efforts to reduce or eliminate these problems should reduce terrorism (Sederberg 1989; Stohl 1988; White 1991). This is especially the case when terrorist groups "have a broad base of support and substantive grievances"

(Sederberg 1989:154). However, such efforts are less likely to succeed when terrorist groups enjoy little public support and have goals unrelated to structural problems in their society.

Perhaps the key question concerning the use of such structural reform to deal with terrorism is whether this approach will placate terrorists and would-be terrorists or instead encourage them to commit even more terrorism. Christopher Hewitt (1984) thinks that both effects could occur. On the one hand, terrorists may regard these efforts as concessions and increase their terrorism because they perceive that their previous actions have succeeded. If so, addressing the underlying causes of terrorism may, ironically, increase it in the short run. On the other hand, addressing the social roots of terrorism may in the long run meet the intended goal of reducing or eliminating terrorist activity.

Rubenstein (1987:235) argues that much insurgent and transnational terrorism today derives from U.S. imperialism: "American diplomats, soldiers, and businesspeople are prime targets for terrorist attack because they are considered representatives of imperialist oppression . . . by a frighteningly broad array of groups subjected to American power." He thus feels that an end to U.S. involvement in other nations would do much to end terrorism.

What about vigilante terrorism and state terrorism? An examination of historical and contemporary vigilante terrorism in the United States shows that much of it takes place when economic conditions are worsening and when public officials indicate through word or deed their approval, or at least a lack of stern disapproval, of such terrorism. To the extent that both factors underlie vigilante terrorism, an improved economy and a practice of zero tolerance for such violence should help reduce, if not eliminate, it (Rubenstein 1987).

State terrorism is a different matter altogether. Because the government itself commits this sort of violence, we cannot count on the government to do anything about it. That is why groups such as Amnesty International continue to publicize the worst examples of governmental violence. The long-term solution to state terrorism is not easy. As Sederberg (1989:155) notes, it probably means that "the character of the regime itself must change." Some terrorist governments might be vulnerable to external pressure, such as economic boycotts, and thus might be induced by such pressure to at least lessen their repressiveness. As an example, the international economic boycott of South Africa, because of its notorious apartheid policy, is often cited as one factor that helped end apartheid in the 1990s (Klotz 1995).

Most often, however, external pressure is not enough to force governments to lessen or end their repression. The international community usually disagrees on using such pressure, and repressive governments typically resist. Even in South Africa, the key factor in ending apartheid was by all accounts the political struggle of the South Africans that apartheid tyrannized (Juckes 1995). For better or worse, the historical record worldwide indicates that often the only way to end state terrorism is for the people subjected to it to revolt against it. Indeed, it's fair to say that most revolutions, violent or nonviolent, in the last few centuries occurred precisely because a populace abhorred state terrorism and other governmental abuses. The fact that revolution might be necessary to end state terrorism underscores how serious and unyielding this form of terrorism is.

Conclusion

Because terrorism so often seems so senseless, it remains difficult for us to comprehend. When innocent victims die or are maimed, what purpose can terrorism serve?

In discussing terrorism, this chapter continued the theme of the preceding ones, that of the essential rationality of collective violence. If riots and revolution are violent acts of primarily rational actors protesting often grievous conditions, then so is terrorism. For better or worse, terrorism has played a central role in the struggle between political regimes and their opponents. The fact that terrorism is such a common tactic in political struggle underscores its essentially political nature. This observation doesn't necessarily make terrorism any more justifiable, but at least it helps put it into an understandable context.

Although this discussion of terrorism echoes the theme of previous chapters, it also departs from them in one very important way. While previous chapters emphasized collective violence committed *against* the state or other established interests, this chapter introduced the idea of collective violence committed *by* the state against its own citizens in the form of state terrorism. This distinction is important for several reasons, not the least of which is that it reminds us that collective violence can work both ways. In the long run, in fact, state terrorism poses a much bigger threat—in the forms of death, injury, fear, and misery—to the global community than does all other terrorism combined. To think that revolution might be the only practical solution to state terrorism is a sobering thought. Certainly the enormity of state terrorism warrants far more attention than it has received so far from the media and from scholars.

6

Cults, Militia, and Hate Groups

Cults, militia, survivalist, and hate groups are not easily explained by the structural perspective emphasized in previous chapters. To many scholars, the motivation for their formation seems more psychological than structural, and the violence that these groups sometimes commit is not easily understood by analyzing existing social conditions. Instead, one must look to the study of group dynamics and social psychology to understand how the need to solve an unsolvable problem or the dislike for a person one hardly knows can become the overarching behavioral motivation in one's life. The aim of this chapter is to explain the origins of these small, intense groups, the reasons for the decisions to join them, and the groups' dynamics and outcomes. As will be shown, all of these groups share certain similarities that help us understand why they exist and why they commit collective violence.

Cults

Most cults aren't violent, but when a cult does turn to violence, it often shocks us, if only because many cults begin with seemingly innocent and even altruistic motives. Let's first look at what cults are and why people join them.

What Is a Cult?

A **cult** is a small, tightly organized group that forms to alleviate some problem for which it thinks society has no set cure or answer. Most cults are usually viewed as a special type of religious organization with a set of beliefs and practices that differ sharply from more conventional religious tenets and behaviors (Collins 1991). As with many more conventional religious groups, cults involve people who are trying to find spiritual meaning in the world. A cult is typically led by a charismatic leader, someone who is thought by cult members to have a special talent or an exceptional character (Galanter 1989; Singer 1995). Sometimes the cult members even think their leader has divine or supernatural powers. Many cults impose strict discipline on their members and are thought to control their behavior and even their thoughts quite severely, although scholars disagree on the extent to which such control exists.

Cults have a very negative image, so some scholars prefer to call them "new religious movements" because of the negative connotation of the term *cult*. This image notwithstanding, cults have played a very important role in the development of religious thought and organization throughout the world. As an example, some Christian sects began as cults 2,000 years ago. As some cults grow larger and acquire more legitimacy, they often turn into sects and, later, into established religions (Finke and Stark 1992).

Charismatic Leadership in Cults

Let's return for a moment to the charismatic leadership that guides many cults. Max Weber, a German sociologist, discussed such leadership extensively in his writings (Weber 1959). He said that the charismatic person, or prophet, exerts authority simply by virtue of his or her special gifts rather than through the process of legitimation bestowed through societal certification such as divinity school. The holders of charisma often demand obedience and a following by virtue of their mission. Their charismatic claim breaks down if their mission is not recognized by those to whom they feel that they have been sent, that is, their followers. It is the duty of their followers to recognize them as their charismatically determined leaders.

Charismatic leadership is a very important element of the social structure of the cult. In fact, the influence of charismatic leaders is so important that many scholars prefer to call cults "charismatic groups" (Galanter 1989). The charismatic leader may symbolize the movement in its entirety or in part. Typically, the leader represents the group's revolt against convention, the cult members' inner struggles in their own lives, or their personal independence and power of resolute action. As a cult evolves, its leader might become ineffectual. If this happens, the cult tends to either disintegrate or, instead, remove its leader and replace him or her with one that more closely reflects the cult's current ideological position.

One of the most valuable assets that charismatic leadership brings to the cult is the ability to focus members' attention so that the group can develop an intense social cohesiveness. The cult is held together via a system of shared beliefs that are usually taught by the leader and reinforced by other high-ranking group members, such as counselors (Galanter 1989). The leader often induces various states of altered consciousness through techniques such as physical and sensory deprivations, hallucinatory drugs, meditation, and time distortion. The state of altered consciousness induced in these ways helps to destabilize old attitudes and to prepare the cult members to accept the group's beliefs. It acts to enlarge the group's cohesiveness, stabilize and even enhance a member's acceptance of group goals, and legitimate the use of violence, if it is needed. It can also serve as a medium to attract members to join the group. For example, the use of hallucinogens such as LSD or rock music have served as recruitment techniques as well as enhancers of group dynamics (Linedecker 1993).

How and Why People Join Cults

A basic question about cults is how and why people join them. *Recruitment* is typically a major function of the group's leader, who often makes both national and international excursions to find new followers. The recruitment technique of the Branch Davidians, a cult that lost many members in a fiery stand with federal agents in Waco, Texas, in 1993, is a good example. David Koresh, the cult's leader, made trips to California, Hawaii, England, Israel, Canada, and Australia to recruit new followers. Special audiences are often targeted during such trips. Again using the Branch Davidians as an example, they recruited mainly from the ranks of Seventh Day Adventists, maintained large mailing lists, and regularly sent out tapes and literature expounding Koresh's teachings (Tabor and Gallagher 1995).

Sometimes members with special qualities prove to be valuable in the cult's recruiting process. For example, two Branch Davidian members with theological training used their special talents in rock music and public speaking to draw people into the group. One of them was Marc Breault, whom Koresh recruited in California in early 1986. Breault played the keyboard in Koresh's band and became his right-hand man. He later recruited a friend and University of Hawaii religion professor, Steve Schneider, into the cult. Schneider was an effective speaker and once recruited 20 people when he traveled to England in 1988 (Tabor and Gallagher 1995).

While Branch Davidian members were recruited largely from one religious group, the Seventh Day Adventists, other cults draw a diverse following of recruits who join for many different reasons. Galanter (1989) found that members reported four different routes of induction into the Unification Church (Moonies) cult: (1) as a result of *subterfuge* on the part of church members; (2) after experiencing their own protracted searches as *seekers* of an acceptable creed; (3) because of an attraction to the group, which offered the opportunity to *identify* with an admired figure or ideal; and (4) because the group *compelled* them to accept church dogma, which they initially had opposed (Galanter 1989:134–140).

To expand on the use of subterfuge, cult recruitment sometimes operates as an inverse pyramid scheme whereby members are gradually brought into the group through a series of invitations to participate in workshops and study sessions that increasingly involve the participants in the cult's belief system. Beginning with general topics such as helping the world's poor, the sessions become increasingly focused on the group's divine mission and its ideals of universal brotherhood. Groups often encourage the best recruits to become instructors or workshop leaders in order to bring them over the final threshold and into the group.

Other recruits, or *converts* as they are often called, have experienced long careers as seekers of spiritual quests as they search for a way to resolve their inner conflicts about life's meaning (Galanter 1989:53). Some authors such as Galanter (1989) and Collins (1991) feel that people growing up in countercultures such as the hippie subculture of the 1960s were in essence seeking a guiding philosophy and were easily drawn into various cults and sects: "Yet, for many seekers, the specifics of ideology in the sects they joined were apparently less relevant in their particular choice than coincidences surrounding their initial encounters with the group. That is, if the time, people, and place were right, any movement might have caught their attention" (Galanter 1989:53).

Much of the literature on cult membership has concentrated on how the conversion process works rather than the reason why a particular person chooses to join a cult or which characteristics predispose one to cult membership. For example, Lofland (1966) suggested that prospective members are indoctrinated via promotion vehicles and strategies that actively encourage their entry into the group. He says conversion is a seven-step selection process that focuses on specific candidates with the following traits: (1) are suffering with acute "tension," (2) are easily distracted by alternative solutions to their problems, (3) have a history of religious seekership, (4) are at a critical turning point in life, (5) are willing to develop cult-affective bonds, (6) are willing to disassociate "extra" cult bonds, and finally (7) enter total conversion through intensive interaction with cult members (pp. 31–57).

Once they join, cult members typically develop intense feelings of commitment to their new group and friendships within the group. This pattern is no different from that in other small, intense groups such as communes. Kanter (1972) emphasizes the development of commitment to such groups. In these groups, processes such as sacrifice, surrender to a larger reality, reeducation, a sense of the eternal, testimonials by group members, self-investment, mortification, and renunciation play an important role in the development of membership commitment.

Interaction with other cult members, typically involving casual contact, or "hooking," also plays an essential role (Collins 1991). In this step, the invitee arrives at a designated location to find that each person has been assigned "buddies," who gather information on the invitees to reveal what each individual is seeking so that these qualities can be used to hook the person into the group. Next, the cult members attempt to "surround" the invitee, filling all waking moments with systematic indoctrination into the cult. Members also display "excessive affection" toward the invitee in the effort to win that person into the group and to intensify the person's commitment (Collins 1991). As this discussion suggests, recruitment into cults is in large part due to the efforts of cult members to add to the cult's membership (Snow, Zurcher, and Ekland-Olson 1980).

So far, the focus has been on the *how* of joining cults. Now let's look at the *why*. To answer this question, a few studies have attempted to identify specific characteristics of people who join cults. For example, Melton (1982) claimed that the Eastern, or occult, religious groups that were popular during the 1970s attracted primarily single young adults (aged 18–25) with middle or upper socioeconomic (SES) backgrounds. Universities were popular recruiting grounds for members from mainly Protestant and Jewish backgrounds. Pattick's (1997) research on women attracted to the New Age mysticism found that many well-educated young women with the potential for successful careers and happy home lives chose to pursue spiritual quests in the new religious movements (NRMS) of the seventies and eighties. She concluded that the NRMs met the women's spiritual needs and values of safety, self-esteem, and empowerment, as well as the need for an environmental awareness within spirituality. In his review of cult research, Collins (1991) concluded that people who are more likely to join cults are looking for a sense of community; access to special, or divine, power; a desire for dependence; and a sense of unspoiled purity and simplicity in their lives. Thus, many of the studies of cults find that their members have apparently led normal, stable lives before joining their cult and join in order to find spiritual guidance and fulfillment.

Other studies suggest that cult members have experienced personal crises or difficulties in their lives before joining their cults. Downton's (1976) study of the Divine Light Mission group found that half of his sample had experienced family difficulties, such as divorce, while Galanter's (1989) study on the Moonies revealed that 86 percent of all members reported uncontrollable substance abuse problems before joining the cult. Findings such as these support the popular view that people who join cults are apt to be experiencing personal problems or crises that they think the cult will help resolve (Lofland 1966).

This view was reinforced after the Heaven's Gate cult gained notoriety a few years ago (see later in the chapter), and various reports chronicled the personal backgrounds of its members. Some had been with the group from its beginning in 1975, whereas others had only recently joined, in the 1990s. Most were highly educated, holding such jobs as computer trainers and consultants, masseur, car salesperson, local TV personality, medical assistant, ex-paratrooper, artist, musician, and paralegal. Many of the members were reported to be shy or loners with private lives, and many were attracted to the cult when they were going through difficult periods in their lives, such as experiencing the loss or death of a loved one, job insecurity, or a shattered marriage. A few of the members joined in conjunction with a loved one such as a spouse. The description of one of the most recent members, Alphonzo Foster, 44, a bus driver, seems to typify the complex backgrounds of the cult's members:

> On the surface he was full of promise. Intelligent and handsome, he devoured books on philosophy and spirituality. But, says James Hannon, who roomed with Alphonzo Foster in Minneapolis in the '70s, he didn't do so well on the practical details of his life. A free spirit who was rarely able to hold a job, Foster sank into a deep depression after his mother died in 1980. Hannon wasn't surprised when Foster joined Heaven's Gate in 1994 after talking on the phone with [the Heaven's Gate leader] for 20 minutes. He didn't like much about life in this dimension, says Hannon. He wanted to go beyond. (*People Weekly*, 1997:43)

Two other popular views of cults are that their members suffer from mental illness or are often brainwashed into joining their cult. However, Eileen Barker (1984) found in her study of the Moonies that people who joined the cult exhibited no more symptoms of mental illness than did people who didn't join the Moonies. She also found no evidence that recruits to the Moonies had been in any way "brainwashed" into joining. Her findings suggest that popular beliefs in mental illness and brainwashing as reasons for cult joining could be myths that reflect the generally negative image of cults in modern society.

In sum, the research on the characteristics of cult members produces an ambiguous picture. Although many members have had personal problems and join cults to help them deal with those problems, many also have led fairly stable, normal lives. Although some come from economically poor backgrounds, many come from much wealthier backgrounds. Overall, people join cults for the same reason that other people join more established religions: They seek spiritual meaning in their lives, and they seek the fellowship of like-minded people. Even if some people joining cults have had personal difficulties in their lives, people in established religions have experienced similar problems. Given the many similarities between cult members and church members, research on cults does not yet help us understand adequately the reasons that people join cults instead of established religions.

Little has been said so far about the structural roots of cults. That's because little research tries to uncover their structural origins. However, some scholars do think that cults proliferate in periods of rapid social change and transition (Lofland 1966). Brandt (1994), for example, argues that cults appear when value systems fail to adequately transmit norms from one generation to the next. He predicts that *intentional communities* (another term for cults) will become more attractive in the future due to social and economic problems. He sees cults as a type of emergency response mechanism in social systems that are in need of repair.

Cults and Violence

The violence that some cults commit contributes to their negative image. A few examples of such violence should indicate why so many people fear cults. In 1987, the *Aum Shrinrikyo* ("Supreme Truth") movement was founded in Japan to "obtain self enlightenment through Tibetan Buddhism with a touch of Hinduism" (Strasser and Post 1995:41). Eight years later, thousands of innocent subway riders became acquainted with members of this cult when in March 1995 they released bombs of deadly Sarin nerve gas in several Tokyo subway lines, killing 10 and injuring more than 5,000. The cult's leader, Shoko Asahara, who used the title Venerated Master, had encouraged the cult to stockpile chemicals needed to make Sarin and its antidotes for use against some future enemy. Conflict between the cult and Japanese authorities prompted the group to brace for a confrontation. After the police raided its Osaka headquarters, the cult's leaders warned its members that "there would be more death coming" and that their only options were to "be a slave or die" (Strasser and Post 1995:40).

The Branch Davidian cult captured headlines in 1993 in Waco, Texas, when its armed compound was attacked by federal agents. A fire broke out and killed 80 members of the cult, including 19 children. Debate continues over the origins of the fire. Some believe that the federal agents started it, while others believe that it was ordered by Koresh, who reportedly opposed surrender to the government (McCarry 1999; Tabor and Gallagher 1995). Although it's unclear whether the Waco deaths resulted from mass suicide, other cults have definitely directed violence toward their own members.

Perhaps the most notorious act of mass suicide by a cult involved Jim Jones and his People's Temple of the Disciples of Christ, which he formed in the early 1950s. Jones's congregation became known for good work regarding homeless and other needy people. During the 1960s, Jones became obsessed with apocalyptic ideas, declaring that nuclear war would break out. He moved his church to one of the U.S. "safe" locations, Uhriah, California, and continued to encourage his followers to engage in heavy community involvement. Church membership continued to grow and outreach expanded into Africa. By the mid-1970s, the People's Temple had become politically active and Jones became more and more obsessed with the encroaching evils of racism and holocaust to the point that he began recommending mass suicide as the only path to salvation (Galanter 1989).

In the late 1970s, criticism by journalists and cult defectors prompted Jones to move his group to Guyana. A member of the House of Representatives, Leo Ryan, and a NBC News crew obtained Jones's permission to visit the cult. Once there, however, they were attacked and killed by cult members, who feared the demise of the People's Temple. Jones saw his leadership role as ended and ordered a mass suicide. Recording his ultimate power trip for posterity, Jones taped himself during the collective death ritual. He said, "We win when we go down" (Stoen 1997). After taking poison, 914 people died. There was also evidence that some of the cult members murdered other members during the suicide ritual before killing themselves.

What Would You Do?

A few years ago, the Heaven's Gate cult also captured national attention. Assume that you are a parent who has a 19-year-old in this cult. You go to a cult expert who tells you the following story about the group.

The leader of the group, Marshall Herff Applewhite, formed it approximately 25 years earlier with the help of a former nurse, Bonnie Nettles, whom he might have met in the course of his medical treatment for a nervous breakdown (Hoffman and Burke 1997). They became known to the group as Do and Ti. Called formerly the Human Individual Metamorphosis (HIM) and, later, Total Overcomers Anonymous, the Heaven's Gate cult did a bit of metamorphosizing of its own by beginning as an offshoot of the UFO cult movement of the 1970s and then incorporating New Age mysticism, science fiction paranoia, purification through self-denial (including castration), and biblical apocalypticism. It also used sophisticated computer technology and the Internet to spread the message of the group, recruit new members, and finance its activities (Miller 1997).

The charismatic duo of Applewhite and Nettles lived out their own nightmarish fantasies that evolved through Nettles's obsession with astrology and science fiction and Applewhite's humiliation and self-hatred from being discharged from several academic positions because of his blatant homosexual affairs with students (Hoffman and Burke 1997; Thomas 1997). The cult went underground for more than a decade (due to a windfall inheritance from one of the members and the loss of many participants due to several failed predictions of a spaceship rendezvous), resurfacing in the 1990s to proclaim itself as a UFO group with a "final order." During the cult's period of hiding, Nettles had died of liver cancer and the cults' apocalyptic tone had increased and deepened. The group changed its name to Heaven's Gate and delved deeply into technology, using elaborately designed World Wide Web pages to spread their message about such topics as "the public's last chance to advance beyond human" and a computer programming company named Higher Source to produce greater wealth for itself than it had ever imagined. A client of the firm, Nick Matazorkis, summed up the group's efforts: "[I]ts workers were weird . . . dressing identically and calling themselves monks. But their work was superb" (Hoffman and Burke 1997:183).

But the charismatic Do was not happy. He had a castration operation that went badly, was rumored to be in poor health, and believed that he was dying. He said repeatedly that "He felt imprisoned in his body" (Miller 1997:42). The discovery of the Hale-Bopp comet was like a wish come true for the unhappy leader. He seized on the fact that a rare comet would visit Earth, calling it a heavenly signal for a mass suicide.

Having now heard about the Heaven's Gate group, what would you do? Would you make every effort to get your 19-year-old child out of the group, or would you decide that your son or daughter was now too old for you to try to take such action? What would you do?

Postscript: In March 1997, 39 members of the Heaven's Gate cult killed themselves in their posh California rental home. Do ordered the group to "exit their earthly containers" and, with much anticipation and preparation, 21 women and 17 men complied with his order and killed themselves.

Cult Beliefs and Cult Violence

Although these examples aren't typical of most cults, many cults do often put themselves in roles that very likely will lead to conflict with governmental authorities. The literature on cult violence attributes the violence to three related processes, all of them involving cult beliefs and ideologies (Wright 1995). First, cults adopt violent strategies due to the tension between their apocalyptic beliefs and the external political order. Second, the group dynamics of the cult involve powerful motivations such as fear and anger to maintain the social distance between it and the real world. This can easily lead to internal violence. Third, violence can become an integral part of the cult experience if the leadership attempts to take over the minds and bodies of cult members and use them to perpetuate its pursuit of power and wealth.

One type of cult, known as *millennial* or *doomsday,* seems to be particularly prone to violent ends (Lofland 1979; Miller 1985). These cults either begin, or later adopt, a goal to deal with the belief that Armageddon, a world war, or some other cataclysmic event will occur and only cult members will go on to heaven, paradise, or a similar place as they die defending against the encroaching evil forces. Goals related to violence, even only defensive ones, inspire the development of elaborate ideologies to justify the violence (Singer 1995). These ideologies in turn ensure that any attempt to impose law and order on the group will legitimate the leadership's claim that the cataclysmic event has occurred. Thus, a self-fulfilling prophecy is set in motion, and the cult members end up labeling governmental authorities as evil enemies. It's a short step from that to engaging in violence in an effort to maintain the cult members' special status as the "chosen" ones.

Many cults also prepare for a "Day of Reckoning," on which powerful forces will be overthrown by the faithful cult members (Robbins and Anthony 1995). Governmental forces are easily categorized as the enemy, since they are usually the ones responsible for keeping the group in line. Past persecution of religious groups by governmental agents adds to their reputation as evil doers, so cults are likely to consider any governmental interference as a warning signal that persecution is about to occur.

Although much research on cult violence emphasizes the importance of cult beliefs for such violence, some scholars say that the presence of a charismatic leader is a more important factor in determining a cult's potential for violence than are the beliefs that cult members hold (Robbins and Anthony 1995). They argue that if the leader advocates violence, some cult members will heed such calls, but others might try to leave the cult. If they do leave, a violence-prone groupthink is even more likely to dominate the cult. Norris Johnson (1980) describes a similar process in his study of riots as a "risky" or group-induced shift to the extreme. If a riot appears about to begin, people who would likely counsel restraint leave the scene out of fear that violence might occur, thereby increasing the likelihood that the remaining people will decide to use violence.

It's also true that this process can work in reverse in cults. If a cult leader is more violent than most of the cult's members and can't convince them to believe otherwise, the leader might leave the cult, along with its violence-prone members. If this happens, the remaining cult is more uniformly opposed to violence than it was previously.

If it's true, then, that charismatic leadership is the glue that welds the group into a cult, it's also possible that charismatic leaders of cults can induce members into being violent. Determining the relative importance of cult beliefs versus cult leadership on a cult's potential for violence (or lack of it) remains an important issue for future research.

The History of Cults in the United States

Singer (1995) states that at least 11 types of cults have existed in the United States and can be grouped into the categories listed in Table 6.1. In the 1990s, examples of these types were found in U.S. society and throughout the world

TABLE 6.1   *Types of Cults in the United States, 1600–1995*

Religious	*Mystical*	*Pseudo-Social Scientific*
Neo-Christian	Spiritualist	Racial
Hindu/Eastern	Zen/Sino-Japanese	Psychological
Satanic/Occult	Philosophical-Mystical	Political
		Self-Help
		Flying Saucer/UFO

Sources: Galanter 1990; Singer 1995

as well. Other scholars use different classifications of cults. For example, Barrett (1996) distinguishes five types: Christian, Eastern, Esoteric, Neopagan, and Personal Development. Whatever classification scheme is used, no one is really sure how many cults exist in the United States. Scholarly estimates range from a low of 500 to 600 to a high of 3,000 to 5,000, and the number of people estimated to be involved in cults over the last two decades ranges from about 200,000 to 20 million (Hicks 1991; Singer 1995).

Cults have a long, rich history in the United States, as they do elsewhere in the world. Reports about the existence of cults have circulated since the days of the Greek city-states and the Roman Empire. In the United States, cults have existed since colonial times, when they were imported by the immigrants who crossed the seas. Some groups began as cults and then grew and mainstreamed. One example was the Society of Friends (Quakers), which came to what is now Pennsylvania early in the colonial period to establish a holy community based on Quaker beliefs of pacifism, simplicity, and especially the view that there is "that of God" inside every person. The Society of Friends, founded in England by George Fox, was persecuted in both England and Massachusetts Bay for their religious beliefs (Auerbach 1983).

Although the Quakers practiced nonviolence in all aspects of their lives and certainly were not a violent cult, other colonial cults were more violent. All of us have heard of the Salem witch trials, which took place when Satan and his followers were reported to be in business in Salem, Massachusetts, in 1692. There, a Barbados slave, Tituba, reportedly recruited village girls for Satan and his followers who resided in the community. More than twenty people eventually were executed on charges of witchcraft (Zellner 1995). The Salem witch trials opposed magic as a source of authority. However, they showed how arbitrary the labeling of extralegal control could be, since an outbreak of similar behavior in Boston at the same time was called a "religious awakening" rather than the work of an evil cult of Satanists (Auerbach 1983). More than three hundred years later, Satanic cults continue to exist worldwide. We discuss them further later.

From 1820 through 1860, a period known as the Second Great Awakening in cult history, numerous religious cults existed. Singer (1995) points out that people in many walks of life became involved in the revivalist movement. Some of the cults that began during this time later grew into sects such as the Millerites and the Seventh-Day Adventists, while others such as the Oneida Community evolved into unique enterprises (Kephart and Zellner 1995). Others moved west with the California gold rush.

In the 1960s, the formation of a sizable counterculture provided a fertile recruitment ground for cults such as the Hare Krishnas and the Moonies. Many Eastern-style cults emerged and were followed by awareness cults and neo-Christian cults. The Divine Light Mission is an example of the latter. Formed to bring greater spiritual awareness to its members, it claimed that people could know God directly and quickly "since as the source of all things

God is really primordial energy—the Divine Light" (Collins 1991:19). The leader of the group, Guru Maharaj Ji, aged 13, did not wish to form a new religion; rather he wanted to make the members of any religion more perfect believers in their God. His cult movement grew quickly, with some estimates putting its U.S. membership as high as 50,000 people, but it broke down when its most devoted followers became disillusioned with their leader. As Maharaj Ji matured, he adopted the ways of American teens and finally was deposed by his mother when he married his Caucasian secretary. By breaking his own rule of celibacy, Maharaj Ji lost more than 50 percent of his most devoted followers (Collins 1991).

Since the 1960s, new religious movements have proliferated, many combining elements of psychology, mysticism, and occultism (Singer 1995). Computer technology and UFOs have also been combined with cataclysmic beliefs. The growth of cults has led to an anticult movement that has, for better or worse, increased the chances of cult violence.

The Anticult Movement

The antiwar, drug subculture of the 1960s led to the defection of many middle-class hippies to cults and other nontraditional religious groups, as well as to self-help groups that formed in that time period. A countermovement among parents and relatives of the new cult members developed almost immediately to combat the influence of these groups on their children. Some deprogrammers forcibly abducted members of cults and other nontraditional groups, locked them up in motel rooms, and assaulted their beliefs until they gave up their religious faith (Lewis 1996).

The anticult movement (ACM) began in earnest during the late 1970s when several grassroots organizations formed a coalition and then a national confederation. The ACM came down hard on cult groups, claiming that they were profit-making organizations that manipulated and programmed members to the extent that they could not function on their own (Shupe and Bromley 1980). Religious scholars and the nontraditional religious groups countered with charges that deprogrammers were little more than vigilantes who attempted to manipulate the cult's media image for their own personal gain (Lewis 1995; Shupe and Bromley 1980). Cult watchdog groups also formed during the late seventies. One, originally termed the Citizens Freedom Foundation and then the Cult Awareness Network (CAN), developed a symbiotic relationship with the deprogrammers by acting as a referral service for people seeking work as a deprogrammer. Kickbacks from such recommendations have been alleged (Lewis 1995). CAN grew throughout the years, despite the slightly tarnished image that it developed, by using techniques similar to those used by the cults themselves. It claimed more than eighteen hundred deprogrammings in 1992 (Brandt 1994).

Just as the suicide poisoning of hundreds of people at Jonestown, Guyana refueled the ACM when it was declining in popularity at the end of the 1970s, the confrontation in Waco, Texas, between the Branch Davidian cult and federal agents refocused public attention on cults and deprogramming in the 1990s. During the last decade, cults and the ACM have fought many legal battles, and cults have won some significant legal victories. For example, CAN was driven out of business by law suits filed against them by the Scientologists (Hofman and Burke 1997).

At the same time, the struggle between cults and their opponents heightened the chances for violence. One reason for this, say some scholars, is that the ACM has painted an unjustifiably negative picture of cults and violated American standards of religious freedom: "Cultbusters send confusing messages about the dimensions of the cult problem, the power of the cult leader, and the nature of the audience for cults. . . . The anticult activists' claim to support the fundamental values of American democratic society is undermined by their willingness to suppress the exercise of religious freedom" (Tabor and Gallagher 1995:187). Even if anticult activists have returned some individuals to their families, these scholars say, they still have failed to define cult behavior in such a way as to differentiate it from other group behavior.

Satanic Cults in the United States

One type of cult that Americans seem especially to fear is the satanic cult. Although satanic cults have existed for more than two hundred years, their leaders have remained silent and their ideology and procedures have been cloaked in secrecy. In the last few decades, the rise in tele-evangelism and religious fundamentalism has fueled increased concern about Satan and satanic cults (Zellner 1985). At the same time, some journalists, con artists, and thrill-seeking rock stars such as the band, Black Sabbath, have played on people's fear of the devil. Luckily, most reports attributing baby breeding, snuff films, and human sacrifice to satanic cults are erroneous (Hicks 1991; Zellner 1995). People do join satanic cults and commit ugly acts in the name of Satan, but such acts are relatively uncommon.

There are two main organized streams: the Church of Satan, founded in 1966 by Anton LaVey, and the Temple of Set, founded by Michael Aquino and Lilith Sinclair (Hicks 1991). The estimated membership of both groups combined is two to three thousand, with the Church of Satan being about twice as large as the Temple of Set (Hicks 1991; Zellner 1995). Novices in the Church of Satan are attracted to the cult with promises of instruction in magic and the black arts. They also are encouraged to speak of their evil thoughts and deeds and are then praised by cult members for doing so (Hicks 1991).

Self-professed witches, pagans, and Wiccans are also included in the satanic category even though their group associations and lifestyles can differ radically from that of the satanists (Melton 1982). Witches organize in covens, which meet in the home of the leader on the new and full moons (*esbats*), while neopagans form groves, nests, and circles. Ritual magicians form lodges and temples. Modern magic is a mixture of many different activities and ideas, such as paganism, astrology, alternative therapies, Kabbalism, mysticism, and rites from a variety of cultures such as Celtic, Greek, and early Egyptian. There is some disagreement in the literature as to whether Wiccans are actually witches but, regardless, technically Wiccans are people who adhere to the Wiccan Redes, a pagan credo or philosophy. Witches may or may not adhere to all parts of the Principles of Wiccan Belief, even though it was adopted in 1974 by the Council of American Witches (Hicks 1991).

Because reports of animal mutilations, ritual murders, and teenage dabblers in sorcery have appeared throughout the United States, a contingent of law enforcement personnel, dubbed "cult cops" by Hicks (1991), has begun to offer costly in-service seminars that cover investigative techniques, portfolios of satanalia, and lurid tales of occult rituals and animal sacrifices. Cult survivors are often presented at the seminars as proof that such practices occur. For example, Lauren Stratford, author of *Satan's Underground,* has appeared at many seminars. However, cult survivor stories are often filled with many inconsistencies and unprovable assertions (Hicks 1991).

Another problem found in research and literature on satanic cult violence is that of guilt by association. For example, a mystical, pagan cult known as The Druidry is often suspected of evil doings by the authorities or local religious communities. While Neopaganism is usually associated with evil and destruction, many groups form who have little violent potential. The Druids are an excellent example of guilt by association with satanism. Although they are chiefly based in the United Kingdom, Orders of Druids are based also in the United States and throughout the rest of the world. Their ritual robes resemble those of witchcraft and their focus is on symbolism and magic, but Druids worship knowledge, nature, and renewal. Present-day Druid groups are based on ancient Druidism, which existed thousands of years ago, but are part of the Neopagan strand of cults that began in the late 1960s and expanded during the 1990s. Most of the Druid Orders are based on a love of nature, such as the mighty oak tree, and the land. Their goal is to unite their natural earthly selves with their spiritual selves as they work to protect the environment (Kendrick 1994).

Another problem is overreaction when dealing with satanism. For example, in 1985, a Bakersfield, California, jury sentenced a young woman who worked in a fast-food restaurant to 405 years in prison for molesting children. Some children in the community claimed that she was a member of a satanic cult that killed and mutilated babies (Hicks 1991). Despite a flawed investigation, the young woman and several others were given the longest sentences in California legal history.

Militia and Survivalist Groups

Survivalist groups are a popular contemporary alteration of the traditional cult structure. In general, they are formed to join together "superior" people who would survive an apocalypse brought on by modern problems of overpopulation, nuclear holocaust, drug use, and so on. The belief that separates survivalists from traditional apocalyptic cults is that they expect to *witness and survive* the collapse of modern civilization, rather than be rewarded with a special place of honor in the hereafter. The term *survivalist*, coined by author Kurt Saxon during the 1960s, denotes a person able to protect him- or herself from attackers (Zellner 1995). Saxon claims that the term is politically neutral and reflects a lack of ties to any organized group. The emphasis, according to Saxon, is on teaching intelligent people how to survive the collapse of modern civilization (Zellner 1995:54). Groups that strongly espouse survivalist beliefs would be less likely to commit suicide than more traditional cults. However, people who espouse these beliefs are likely to have expertise in sophisticated weaponry, so they might be prone to use it when highly provoked.

Militias may be formed by survivalists with either religious or political orientations and sometimes resemble terrorist organizations as much as cults. This is because they exhibit characteristics of both. They are like cults when they wish to retreat from mainstream society and like terrorists when they wish to deliver political messages that are aimed at overthrowing established governments, at either the national or local level. Militia groups with a religious orientation more closely resemble cults, since they form to solve extremely intractable problems, typically focus inward, and more frequently use violence internally rather than externally. Militias who form for religious purposes envision a transformation or the return of the savior on a day of judgment. At this point, such groups believe that the faithful, in this case, the group members, will be rewarded and the unfaithful punished. Such groups are closely allied with violent apocalyptic Christian cults, such as the Branch Davidian cult.

Another strand of the militia movement is populated with former hate group members, such as the skinheads (see later in the chapter), who are anti-Semitic and racist. In addition, some paramilitary groups who espouse survivalist goals have similarities in their belief systems to traditional hate groups. These include The Order and Christian Identity, as well as neo-Nazis such as the Aryan Nations.

Other militia are mainly paramilitary in nature. Wayne LaPierre, an official of the National Rifle Association, says that the network of armed militia that has formed throughout the United States is the ultimate deterrent to crime (LaPierre 1995). For LaPierre, a thoroughly armed people is relatively crime free. Militia groups concentrate on informing the public about armaments and run training exercises and camps that focus on weapons training. They believe that the federal agents who are charged with enforcing federal gun control laws persecute and entrap citizens who have done nothing wrong and would never contemplate doing anything wrong.

Personified by the Bureau of Alcohol, Tobacco, and Firearms (BATF), the U.S. government is portrayed by these militia as composed of mildly inept to outright traitorous people who plan to sell out their country to a new world order (Dees 1996). Most militia groups fit ideologically with the countermovement against gun control. *Newsweek* reported in 1995 that Internet traffic shows that the paramilitary right is fundamentally estranged from the national dialogue and in a world in which conspiracy theories thrive among a "bunch of dumb white guys who like to fantasize about guns and guerrilla war" (*Newsweek* 1995:39). However, the majority of militias confine themselves to running paramilitary exercises rather than move to cult or terrorist status. While smaller militias are found throughout the country, some have developed large state networks. The Militia of Montana, the Michigan Militia, the Viper Militia, and the West Virginia Mountaineer Militia are among the largest groups, several of whom have run into problems with the FBI and the U.S. Department of Justice for conspiracy and weapons charges.

Hate Groups

In addition to cults, survivalists, and militia, hate groups are another example of small, intense groups that sometimes resort to violence to achieve their goals by committing what Chapter 5 referred to as *vigilante terrorism*. Hate groups are born when a group of people join together to oppose and even destroy another group because they believe that the group is responsible for some negative change in their environment. This change could be economic, political, or social, but in general, the hated group is assumed to be in a "do or die" position vis-à-vis the hated group. In hate groups, like-minded people come together to promote their ideology and legitimate their right to move from thought to action, action that is sometimes violent. The basis for a violent attack could be any physical or cultural characteristic which, in the minds of the hate group members, separates the victims from them in a negative way (Jenness and Broad 1997; Levin and McDevitt 1993). It's difficult to know whether most hate crime is committed either by organized hate groups whose members are dedicated to such goals as achieving racial purity or under ordinary circumstances by otherwise unremarkable types of people, with brutal attacks taking place spontaneously without the help of others.

What exactly is *hate crime*? Hamm (1994) feels that hate crime is best understood by looking at the various dimensions of the acts. He finds no consensus in the literature and so settles on hate crime as being illegal acts perpetuated because of what a victim represents (Hamm 1994). Hate crime might evolve from individual resentment, thrill seeking, frustration (for example, from economic competition; see later in the chapter), substance abuse, or a mission to rid the world of the members of a "despised" group (Jenness and Broad 1997; Levin and McDevitt 1993). Staub (1989) believes that a continuum of destruction exists whereby hate groups involve their members in a progression that could lead to heinous actions: "Small, seemingly insignificant acts can involve a person with a destructive system." These initial behaviors, aimed at encouraging an individual to participate in the group, can result in psychological changes that make more serious acts possible.

Why Hate Groups Develop

Perhaps the dominant explanation of hate group violence based on race or ethnicity is the ethnic competition model (see Chapter 2). This model states that ethnic conflict occurs as part of the social modernization process when jobs, housing, and other valued resources become scarce. If the society is composed of multiple cultural entities, the competition between them becomes so intense that conflict, including violent conflict, occurs (Olzak 1992). Belanger and Pinard (1991) have reformulated this model through a critical historical review and survey research on interethnic competition between the French and English Canadians in Quebec, Canada. They conclude that the competition holds only under very limited circumstances, which include the presence of discriminatory acts, the failure to punish such acts, and the perception that the group is *relatively deprived* in comparison to its competitors (see Chapter 2).

Hate groups have at least some, if not all, members who experience relative deprivation vis-à-vis the despised group. The members feel that the despised ones have deprived them of a job, governmental benefits, or other substantial rewards, or even something so small as tax dollars. As they learn to hate, members of hate groups become oversensitized to danger from a particular group. They thus may commit violence if they feel that their physical survival and/or an intolerable reduction in their quality of life is likely to happen, even if the hated group is not directly connected with the threatening events (Perry and Pugh 1978).

The Social Structure of Hate Groups

Hate groups at times in their life cycles might resemble gangs and at other times paramilitary organizations or terrorist groups. Their social structures are usually flexible, transitional, and often decentralized, as in the "leaderless cells" or concentric circles model (see later in the section). Their volatile structures and these methods of leadership, in addition to their violent goals, help make them a dangerous group for agents of social control to handle. Often hate groups form on a hierarchical, paramilitary model only to find that it is self-defeating for their purposes. An example of this situation is the Provisional Wing of the Irish Republican Army (PIRA). PIRA was "initially organized on quasi-military lines with battalions and a well-defined hierarchy of officers and volunteers in each country or town area" (Boyle and Hadden 1994:76). Its members eventually realized, however, that this structure made it too easy for the British and other security forces to find out the names of the leadership through the use of informers. They decided to revamp their organization, replacing it with a cellular structure according to which the number of members in each action unit was small and false names for their immediate superiors were used so that they could not be revealed by a member captured during a mission. These low-level leaders reported to a high-security command, thereby making it more difficult for the authorities to identify leaders and to identify members in charge of supplying weapons and other important items (Boyle and Hadden 1994).

Today, a few U.S. hate groups and militia have adapted the PIRA model to create a *leaderless resistance*. They recruit new members by publishing books and pamphlets, but their other activities are done secretly. Their membership is limited to five or six members per unit, each of which has relative autonomy in deciding what type of resistance efforts that they will mount (Kaplan 1997). During the 1990s, the leaderless resistance model began to emphasize that the cells should encourage their rank and file to emulate the lone-wolf assassin, the solitary berserker, and the fictional heroes of the Phineas Priesthood, who were underground revolutionaries, men with no ties to society, family, or friends and who had the grim purpose of avenging their dying race (Kaplan 1997). Although Kaplan (1997) points out that few men fit this description, Timothy McVey and Terry Nichols, the accused Oklahoma City bombers, bear a chilling and eerie resemblance to it.

A Historical Perspective on Hate Groups

The hatred of people because of their race, ethnicity, and other characteristics is nothing new. Persecution based on such hatred has existed since ancient times when, for example, the Romans fed Christians to the lions. It perhaps reached its darkest hour during the Holocaust of the last century at the hands of the Nazis. Contemporary ethnic conflict likewise derives from ethnic hatred. For example, the violent conflict in the former nation of Yugoslavia between the Serbs, the Bosnian Muslims, and Croats dates back to the Ottoman (Turkish-Muslim) and the Austro-Hungarian Empires in the seventeenth century (Bjornson and Jonassohn 1994). Ethnic conflict comes and goes, but often old animosities and disputes are reborn as a result of current collective fears and uncertainties.

One bit of irony concerning hate groups involves their names. Unlike cult groups, which give themselves unusual religious names such as Heaven's Gate, the Branch Davidians, and Church of Satan, hate groups often have innocent-sounding names that belie their radical ideology of hatred. An example is the contemporary Citizen's Law Enforcement and Research Committee (also known as Posse Comitatus). Another example is the Church of Jesus Christ Christian, which, despite its neutral name, believes that the Jew is the adversary of the white race and God and is a cancer or a satanic disease invading the Aryan race to destroy its culture and purity (Sargent 1995). From a longer historical viewpoint, other hate groups have had names that included such terms as brotherhood, klan, and Christian.

As noted in Chapter 5, hate violence has been common in U.S. history. Brown (1989) argues that the American Revolution served as a model for later violence by Americans in behalf of any cause considered to be upright, proper, or honorable. This model helped ensure, he says, that violence would have a permanent role in American life.

Perhaps the most notorious hate group in American history is the Ku Klux Klan, discussed in Chapter 5. To the casual onlooker, the Klan might seem more like a joke than a hate group. Its members wear ghost-like costumes, use a jargon that emphasizes the letter "k," and consider themselves part of what they call an Invisible Empire. But the Klan, which was conceived by six Confederate veterans as a lark, quickly metamorphosized into a hate group during the Reconstruction Era, when it served as a vehicle to terrify and torture former slaves. Masquerading as a protector of traditional American values, it renewed its terroristic activity after World War I and then again during the Civil Rights movement of the 1950s and 1960s (Toy 1989; Zellner 1995).

The Klan has suffered serious legal setbacks in the last two decades that have weakened its resources and influence. One of these was in 1981, when a jury deadlocked over the guilt of a black man in the murder of a white police officer. The jury's failure to convict the defendant provoked Klansman in Mobile, Alabama, to take the law into their own hands. One Mobile Klan leader reportedly said to his followers, "Get this down: If a black man can kill a white man, a white man should be able to get away with killing a black man" (Zellner 1996:29). Two days later, two members of the Klan allegedly kidnapped nineteen-year-old Michael Donald, an African American, at gunpoint. After beating and torturing him, one of the two allegedly cut Donald's throat three times. He was then hanged from a tree in the front yard of the home of one of his assailants. Despite this evidence, no one from the Klan was prosecuted for the murder.

Because of this legal inaction, the victim's mother sued the Klan and won a huge sum of money in court that seriously weakened the Klan. This legal and financial defeat led the Klan to refocus its attention on promoting institution discrimination through political means such as attacks on affirmative action and immigration laws.

Other hate groups were also active during the twentieth century, with several, like the Klan, still existing today. During the 1920s, the enduring myth of an international Jewish conspiracy was joined to strong anti-immigrant feeling (nativism) in the United States. A politician, Gerald L. K. Smith, attracted a following when he combined this philosophy with a

British quasi-theological theory that became known as Christian Identity, which still exists (Ridgeway 1990). Christian Identity believers hold that European whites were the Lost Tribe of Israel, which dwelt with inferior people. These inferiors were people of color and relatives of Satan who had been sent to Earth as a scourge on God. Christian Identity advocates believe that apocalypse is inevitable and that in this final battle, Earth will be rid of these inferior beings and reserved for the only true Israelite people, White Aryans, whose sign of racial purity is their ability to blush, or to have "blood in the face" (Ridgeway 1990:17).

After a stint as a minister, Smith took to politics and organized for the late Senator Huey Long of Louisiana. After Long was assassinated, Smith began a crusade that attracted many people who would emerge as leaders of the far right in the United States: Wesley Swift of the Christian Identity Church; Richard Butler, leader of Aryan Nations; William Gale, a founding father of the Posse Comitatus; Bob Miles of the New Klan; and Robert Matthews, leader of The Order, a splinter group of Aryan Nations. All of these were graduates of Smith's brand of racist radicalism (Ridgeway 1990; Stock 1997).

The cross-pollination of far-right leaders contributed to the political and social milieu of the 1990s. Robert Miles went on to be Grand Dragon of the Michigan Ku Klux Klan, a spokesman for the Dualist religion, an advisor to more than 15 different churches, and an ambassador of Aryan Nations. He joined with Louis Beam to edit a newsletter that outlined the ideology and goals of the Aryan Nations and other white supremacist groups of the 1980s. One editorial claimed:

> We do not advocate . . . segregation, . . . that was a temporary political measure and that time is past . . . [rather] the Greater White Racialist Movement intends to establish for our White Aryan Race what every other Race on Earth has, a racial homeland . . . Our Order intends to take part in the Physical and Spiritual Racial Purification of All those countries which have traditionally been considered White Lands in Modern Times. . . . We intend to purge this land-area of every Non-white person, idea and influence. . . . In Summary: This continent will be white or it will not be at all. (Ridgeway 1990:88)

As the Christian Identity flourished, many right-wing extremists began to believe that conventional agrarian ways of life and politics are doomed because Zionists already control the federal government and "are actively preparing to enslave all white Christian Americans" (Stock 1997:143). Most members espousing this philosophy also adopt survivalism and think that rural mountain tops are their most likely place for survival. Boundary Country, Idaho, home to many radical groups such as Aryan Nations, is one such area. It provided the backdrop for the Aryan Nations World Congress in the summer of 1986, a meeting that brought many radical right groups to Idaho. Later, Aryan Nations and the New Klan, led by Louis Beam, met at Estes Park, Colorado, where they announced plans to establish "leaderless resistance" to the U.S. government through militia cells that would teach Americans how to prepare for the Zionist Occupational Government (ZOG) assault (Stock 1997).

Founded by Richard Butler in 1979, the Aryan Nations headquarters is in Hayden Lake, Idaho, a guarded compound surrounded by a socially conservative population. The Aryan Nations has spawned several deadly offspring, such as The Order and the Silent Brotherhood. The group's belief system includes portraying homosexuality, pop culture, and immigration as part of a larger ZOG plot to destroy and dilute America's white gene pool. The Holocaust is also thought to be a myth perpetuated by Jewish bankers and intellectuals to justify the killing of millions of white Christians (Stock 1997). Such behavior legitimates a coming race war.

Today, there are signs of "diffusion" among hate groups across national boundaries. As Ridgeway (1990:145) notes:

> By the late 1980s the far right in the United States had begun to forge ties with similar groups abroad. The progress toward an international movement was achieved at first by skinheads, who also struck up an alliance in the United States with the Ku Klux Klan. In addition to the birth of this street-fighting youth movement, the far right began . . . to move successfully into electoral politics. (Ridgeway 1990:145)

In 1989, the Dragon of the Invisible Empire, an offshoot of the Louisiana Klan, initiated an extensive recruitment plan in Western Europe that coincided with the international renaissance of the far right. As the Berlin Wall fell and the Eastern European Communist Union crumbled, anti-Semitism made a reappearance fed by the currents of nationalistic and religious conflict. Skinheads were reported in East Germany in 1988, and their numbers grew rapidly (Ridgeway 1990). They originally emerged from the British mod youth culture movement that began when English teenagers started to define themselves first in terms of their music, such as acid rock and reggae, and later according to their political orientation (Aronowitz 1994). As the movement seemed likely to be co-opted by the larger culture by becoming trendy, those young men with ties to the National Front broke off from the main movement and redefined their goals, emphasizing downward mobility, rejection of consumerism, and expressions of skinhead disaffection (Ridgeway 1990).

Transplanted to the United States via the invitation from the Klan, the more extreme skinhead practices such as slam-dancing and Paki-bashing merged with American tendencies toward violence, racial segregation, and rural bullying. Near the end of the 1980s, Tom Metzger, leader of the 2,000-member White Aryan Resistance (WAR), saw the skinheads as the way to revitalize the White Supremacist Movement with younger members. He helped his son, John, to build the Aryan Youth Movement, the WAR affiliate youth group. Many AYM members were skinheads who quickly allied themselves with other skinhead groups throughout the United States and Western

Europe (Ridgeway 1990). It didn't take long for the older racists to motivate their younger counterparts to violence. Hamm (1994) reports that U.S. skin-head groups were responsible for a sudden increase in right-wing terrorism. They were implicated in a majority of violent assaults against gays and les-bians, a 41 percent rise in anti-Semitic attacks throughout the country, including arson incidents, bombings, and cemetery desecrations, as well as one-half of the violent racial assaults, of which at least a dozen were murders.

Episodes of racial violence continued in the 1990s as the FBI arrested two Aryan Nations members who were plotting to bomb Seattle's largest gay nightclub, as skinhead attacks on Asians became common, and as the Klan began to abandon their robes in favor of camouflage and militarism. The farm crisis in America attracted many rural people to the radical right, which counseled farmers to fight back against bank and governmental foreclosures. Tax evasion also came to the forefront with hard economic times, with the far right continuing to argue its unconstitutionality (Stock 1997).

One of the newest and most popular hate groups is the World Church of the Creator (WCC), which captured national headlines in 1999 when one of its members, Benjamin Nathaniel Smith, went on a shooting rampage over the Fourth of July weekend in Illinois and Indiana. Before killing him-self while being chased by the police, Smith shot and wounded 12 people and killed 2 others. All of his victims were Asian Americans, African Americans, or Jews.

After Smith's shootings, national attention focused on the WCC, which was called "perhaps the fastest-growing and one of the largest hate groups in the country" (Belluck 1999:A1). At the time of the shootings, the WCC was estimated to have 41 chapters in 17 states and a national membership rang-ing from the hundreds to several thousand. Besides Smith, other WCC mem-bers have engaged in hate crime. One was convicted of killing an African American sailor who had just come back from serving in the Persian Gulf War in 1991. Two other members pleaded guilty to beating a black man in Miami, and four others pleaded guilty to beating a video store owner whom they thought was Jewish.

Despite the violence, the WCC does its best to look respectable. As of 1999, it maintained a popular Internet site, which featured among other things a coloring book for children that included white supremacist messages and a crossword puzzle with racist clues. It was also active on college campuses, where it tried to recruit students with leaflets and talk of religious redemption. Several WCC members want to become lawyers so that they can try to use the legal system to advance the cause of white supremacy. In general, WCC lead-ers are young, educated, and articulate and—quite in contrast to groups such as the skinheads—try to present their white supremacist views in a calm, rea-sonable way that's intended to mask their underlying message of hate.

The head of the WCC, Matthew F. Hale, fits this image. A graduate of law school who passed the Illinois bar exam, he was denied a license to practice law because of his racist views and activities. Hale said he didn't approve of Smith's shootings but nonetheless thought Smith was "a martyr for free speech for white people." He noted that his group advocates legal change but does not rule out violence: "Our position is similar to that of Thomas Jefferson. If our Constitution is destroyed, if our right to free speech is denied, then we have the right to use whatever means necessary to survive and to advance our position. If you're cornered in an alley you have the right to defend yourself" (Belluck 1999:A16).

Ethnic Conflict

When the hatred underlying hate crime gets played out on a much larger scale, ethnic conflict develops. Sometimes war between two governments exacerbates ethnic stereotypes and animosities. For example, Moore and Pachon (1985) credit the Mexican-American War of 1846 with instilling hatred of Mexicans into the American Psyche. Americans began to call the Mexicans "yellow-bellied greasers" and to develop the notion that Mexicans were cowards with no moral scruples or sense of fair play. The ensuing myth of racial inferiority conveniently justified the low status of Mexicans in the developing southwestern and far western parts of the United States that continues even today.

Natural disasters and other major problems, such as outbreaks of disease, have caused groups to be stereotyped and persecuted if they are blamed for the problems. For example, in Europe during the Middle Ages (mid-fourteenth century), the appearance of the Black Plague in a village or area could cause an entire ethnic group to be tortured and executed. The plague developed among the corpses of earthquake and flood victims in China and moved into Europe via rats living on the caravan trails; however, infected Russian Tartars blamed Christian merchants of Caffa, Italy, for spreading the disease (Gotteried 1983). The Tartars thus attacked Caffa and later transferred the plague to townspeople by catapulting corpses at them over the town's walls. In Germany, Jews and lepers were blamed for the plague. This led to tortured confessions from and executions of Jews all over Germany. Lepers, who, despite being tolerantly regarded before that period, were then stoned to death or refused entry into the walled cities.

One of the strangest scapegoating situations that occurred during the Black Plague concerned a religious group known as the Flagellants. This group was founded by Italians who became convinced that God was sending plagues and famines to Italy because of their behavior. Thinking that they had to show God their repentance, they began public displays in which half-naked people whipped and tortured themselves. The movement became very popular throughout Western Europe as the Black Plague took hold, but the Flagellants carried the plague from city to city as they proselytized. Public opinion quickly turned against them, thereby causing them to be ostracized and stoned to death (Chalk and Jonassohn 1993).

Ethnic conflict also arises when two or more cultures that have been living side by side in the same society disagree over power distributions and the priority of one system over the other. The problem is that it is extremely difficult, if not impossible, to reach equality in either a bicultural or multi-cultural state. Kitano (1991) says that it has generally been the lot of groups with less power to adapt to changing social realities such as a new economic, employment, or political environment. When ethnic groups decide to promote competing claims rather than to compromise, conflict occurs.

Conclusion

This chapter discussed violence by cults, militia, survivalist, and hate groups. These groups differ in many ways, but they also share several similarities. They are small, intense groups that inspire deep commitment from their members, they are often led by charismatic leaders, and they sometimes commit violence to defend the existing order or to change it.

Social scientists have been able to study cults much more often than militia, survivalist, or hate groups, which are much less receptive to being studied than their cult counterparts. As a result, we know more about cult recruitment and dynamics than we do about the same processes in these other groups. The continuing controversy that all of these groups arouse ensures that they will continue to capture headlines around the nation and the world and that social scientists will continue to try to study them. Such attention is essential to understanding why they exist, why people join them, and what, if anything, can and should be done about them and the violence that they sometimes commit.

7

Conclusion: The Nature and Future of Collective Violence

Now that you've reached the end of this book, what have you learned? At the outset, several themes and issues were introduced in the study of collective violence and addressed further in later chapters. Let's return to these topics to summarize the major strands of knowledge in the study of collective violence. We combine materials in earlier chapters into a coherent whole that provides a good sociological perspective on collective violence.

The Structural Roots of Collective Violence

Chapter 1 distinguished macro roots of collective violence from micro ones. As shown again and again in the book, the macro, or structural, roots of collective violence lie in problems in the social, political, and economic systems and, depending on the type of collective violence, in the opportunities afforded for collective action by weaknesses in state regimes and other state structures.

Even in the presence of these problems and weaknesses, most people don't protest. Thus a social-psychological understanding of collective action is necessary to explain why some people do protest and others do not (Klandermans 1997). Some of this understanding was developed in previous chapters. But the fact remains that most people would have neither the need nor the inclination to protest if structural problems and weaknesses did not exist in the first place. The study of these problems and weaknesses thus remains key to understanding the origins of collective violence and other forms of collective action.

The overview of riots in Chapter 3 offered evidence of these structural roots in studies of why some U.S. cities had riots in the 1960s and others did not. Recall that these studies yielded two conflicting answers to this question. One set of studies found that cities that experienced riots were not worse off economically or in other ways than cities that did not and concluded that conditions of blacks were so negative *everywhere* that a riot ideology had developed throughout the United States (Spilerman 1970; Spilerman 1971; Spilerman 1976; Tomlinson 1968). If the cities with worse conditions were not more riot-prone than cities with better conditions, this line of research concluded, then structural conditions did not explain riot variation in U.S. cities in the 1960s.

Our assessment of this line of research concluded that its rejection of structural conditions was based on very narrow grounds. Even if a riot ideology led to riots in various cities despite structural differences among them, this ideology and the frustration underlying it resulted from the poor conditions in which blacks in all of these cities lived. Structural problems facing blacks thus help explain why they rioted at all, even if they don't explain why some cities experienced riots and others did not.

Underscoring the importance of structural factors, other studies on the 1960s riots found that cities with worse conditions were indeed more likely to experience riots (Downes 1968; Morgan and Clark 1973). Although these studies were criticized on methodological grounds (Spilerman 1976), more recent research using more complete data and more advanced statistical techniques found that cities with greater unemployment and a few other problems were more likely to experience riots (Myers 1997; Olzak and Shanahan 1996; Olzak, Shanahan, and McEneaney 1996).

The best conclusion, then, from research on the 1960s riots is that structural conditions did matter. The same conclusion arises from studies of prison riots. Although prisons are usually terrible places in which to live, most inmates don't riot and most prisons experience riots only rarely, if at all. But when prison riots do occur, they ultimately are reactions to the negative (structural) conditions in which inmates typically live. Often they are, moreover, responses to a worsening of these conditions or a weakening of the social control mechanisms that inmates ordinarily face. To the extent that this is true, structural factors help explain prison riots just as they explain urban riots.

In revolutions, too, structural conditions are significant. Many authoritarian and other regimes exist in which people live in misery and even fear for their lives. While it remains true that most of the time they don't revolt, the revolts that do occur are ultimately reactions to the negative conditions in which their participants live. Another way of saying this is that negative structural conditions are a necessary if not sufficient cause of revolution, just as they are a necessary but not sufficient cause of riots. For revolutions, these structural conditions include not just misery, lack of freedom, and other similar sources of discontent, but also an economic or other crisis in the state that weakens the state's control and makes it vulnerable to revolt (DeFronzo 1996).

Structural factors also help explain at least some types and examples of terrorism. Because insurgent and transnational terrorism is committed, by definition, against governmental targets, hostility to structural conditions and governmental policies thought to promote these conditions often underlies both types of terrorism. Vigilante terrorism is often fueled by ethnic and racial hatred and is more apt to occur in times of economic distress, as minority groups and the other targets of vigilante terrorism become scapegoats for the economic problems of their attackers (Tolnay and Beck 1995). While it's fashionable to depict terrorists as sadistic and senseless madmen, underlying structural conditions and problems often help to explain their terrorist acts as well.

The literature on cults, militia, survivalist, and hate groups is more ambiguous on this score. Studies that examine why these groups exist and why people join them emphasize psychological explanations focusing on personality problems, negative family experiences, and related factors. Yet to the extent that hate groups engage in vigilante terrorism, at least some of their hatred might be fueled by economic problems and competition over jobs and other scarce economic resources (Olzak 1992).

If structural conditions and problems do matter for collective violence, then the question remains *why* they matter. Some scholars feel that economic and other structural problems lead to feelings of deprivation and other types of frustration and that these reactions in turn lead to protest (Gurr 1970). Others feel that structural problems such as unemployment reflect and also reinforce a breakdown in, and thus a weakening of, normal mechanisms of social control, thereby opening the door to norm violation of many types, including collective action (Useem 1998). Assessment of the exact reasons for why structural problems lead to collective violence and other protest remains one of the most important tasks in the study of social movements and will doubtless be guided by a social-psychological understanding of movements and their members (Klandermans 1997; Snow and Oliver 1995).

The Rationality of Collective Violence

This book has emphasized the rationality of collective violence. By this was meant two things. First, collective violence is generally goal-directed. Whatever we think of collective violence, its participants intend their violence to achieve one or more goals having to do with social, political, and/or economic change. In this sense, collective violence is typically as goal-directed, or rational, as is conventional political activity such as voting and running for office. While collective violence doesn't always achieve the ends that it seeks, neither do voting and other conventional political activities.

Second, collective violence actors are rational. They're not psychologically unsound—or at least no more unsound than members of the general population. Some people, of course, commit collective violence because they do have psychological problems or because, perhaps without realizing it, they will have some psychological need met by the violence that they commit. But that is true of people in all walks of life. It might be difficult to think that acts of terrorism and other collective violence can be committed by people who are "in their right minds." As pointed out in previous chapters, however, people can and do commit great acts of violence without necessarily being psychologically unsound. The soldiers who fight in wars and the generals and political officials who give them orders have been responsible for millions of deaths over the years, but we don't ordinarily attribute these deaths to psychologically unsound actors. If that's the case, then we should be open to the possibility that people committing collective violence are at least as psychologically sound as these other actors who also kill and maim.

Emphasizing the rationality of collective violence and the people engaging in it is not meant to imply that collective violence isn't emotional and that the people engaging in it don't act for emotional reasons. People can be both rational and emotional, as readers who have engaged in sports will easily attest. Out on the playing fields, athletes are certainly emotional, but they are also quite rational. Their emotions are often a key to their success, but sometimes a key as well to their failure. On the playing fields, emotion and reason certainly can and do coexist.

Collective violence and other forms of collective action are no different, but the field of collective behavior has been slow to recognize this. As Chapter 2 noted, early collective behavior approaches tended to depict collective action as emotional and irrational. In developing a new paradigm for collective action that sought to counter this view of irrationality, proponents of the resource mobilization theory in the 1970s painted the opposite view, one that involved a mechanical, overly rational picture of the individuals engaged in collective action. These actors were depicted as coldly and carefully calculating the risks and rewards of such engagement. In the world of the resource mobilization theory, the actors' emotions didn't matter and their acts had no emotional components.

That was in the 1970s. Beginning in the 1980s, as was also explored in Chapter 2, collective action scholars using a social constructionist approach rediscovered the social-psychological dimensions of collective action (Ferree and Miller 1985; Gamson 1992; Klandermans 1984; Snow and Oliver 1995). One dimension that they emphasized was emotion. They argued that emotion could be brought back into the study of collective action while avoiding the extreme irrationalism of some of the early collective behavior approaches (Jasper 1998; Snow and Oliver 1995; Taylor 1995). This was necessary, they said, because collective action is, after all, emotional, as are many other kinds of actions. As one sociologist put it, "Emotions pervade all social life, social movements included. . . . Not only are emotions part of our responses to events, but they also . . . shape the goals of our actions. There are positive emotions and negative ones, admirable and despicable ones, public and hidden ones. Without them, there might be no social action at all" (Jasper 1998:398). Two other sociologists similarly observed that "most people participate in crowd behavior and social movement activities because of problems or dilemmas they care about, and these events are often characterized by displays of emotion. . . . Indeed, one is hard-pressed to think of instances of collective behavior gatherings that do not evoke strong sentiments. . . ." (Snow and Oliver 1995:589).

Today, most collective action scholars accept the idea that the behavior they study is both rational and emotional. This observation applies no less to collective violence than to any other forms of collective action. If anything, collective violence is accompanied by more emotion—anger, fear, joy, and so on—than are the other forms. Seeing this emotion displayed leads much of the public to regard both the collective violence itself and the people involved in it as irrational. But the social constructionist perspective suggests that this conclusion is mistaken.

The Consequences of Collective Violence

This book has emphasized that collective violence is goal-directed, or rational. That raises a logical question: How successful is collective violence? Earlier chapters addressed this question, the relevant research is summarized here. Note that most of this research concerns the impact of riots and other types of collective violence that stop far short of revolution. By definition, revolution succeeds in toppling a regime. To this extent, revolution "succeeds" regardless of whether the new regime lives up to the vision that the revolutionaries had for it. But most studies of the impact of collective violence focus on Western democracies, where collective violence is typically more limited in extent and scope, if indeed it occurs at all.

Before the relevant research is reviewed, it should be noted that the field of social movements includes surprisingly few studies of the success of protest, including collective violence, and of the conditions under which protest succeeds (Andrews 1997; Burstein, Einwohner, and Hollander 1995; Giugni 1998). As several authors have noted (e.g., McAdam, McCarthy, and Zald 1988), the field has spent much more time trying to understand the emergence of social movements than what happens after they emerge. This neglect of movements after their emergence means that we know far less than we should about their outcomes and the reasons for their outcomes. This lack of understanding applies no less to collective violence than to other types of protest.

Reflecting this scholarly neglect, a study from 1975 is still, more than 25 years later, "perhaps the most systematic attempt to inquire into the impact and effectiveness of social movements," as a recent review noted (Giugni 1998:375). This study, by William Gamson (1975), investigated the success and failure of several dozen "challenging groups" in U.S. history. As noted in Chapter 1, Gamson found that groups that used disruptive tactics, both violent and nonviolent, were generally more successful than those that did not use such tactics. Although his conclusions were later challenged on methodological and other grounds, his study remains a standard against which to compare other research findings (Burstein, Einwohner, and Hollander 1995; Giugni 1998).

The studies that are available, including Gamson's, support one general but very cautious conclusion. As a recent review put it, "Overall, the use by social movements of disruptive tactics and violence seems to increase their potential for change" (Giugni 1998:376). This is especially true during times of state crises and other weaknesses in state institutions (see later in the chapter). In addition to Gamson's research, other studies, many of them on the 1960s urban riots in the United States, support this overall conclusion (Button 1989; Isaac and Kelly 1981; Mueller 1978). It's also true that the evidence supporting this conclusion is far from unanimous (Burstein, Einwohner, and Hollander 1995). As noted in the Chapter 3 discussion of these studies, they generally found that the riots led to only limited gains for blacks in urban America, or no gains at all, and several studies found that their main effect was to increase police resources to enable a more punitive response to rioting. A study of protest in three Asian countries—Malaysia, the Philippines, and Thailand—in the 1960s and 1970s supports this last conclusion (O'Keefe and Shumaker 1983). Generally, the use of violence by dissident groups in these nations proved counterproductive because it led mainly to violent oppression by police and the military.

Because of these mixed results, it seems fair to say that collective violence is double-edged for dissenters. Although collective violence can achieve some of its goals, it runs the great risk of alienating other dissenters, members of the general public, and important allies and elites in the larger economic and political systems, as well as justifying a repressive response by the state (Tarrow 1998). That risk was an important reason for the conscious effort of the Southern Civil Rights movement to remain nonviolent in the face of vicious violence at the hands of Southern police and citizens. The movement knew that it risked losing legitimacy and support and would suffer additional injuries and deaths if it turned to violence. It also even hoped that the police would overreact with violence that would be so extreme that it would win public support throughout the nation and force the federal government to make concessions (Barkan 1984; Garrow 1986; McAdam 1983). That, of course, is precisely what happened.

The mixed results on the impact of collective violence underscore the need for more research on its effectiveness. Several works indicate that its effectiveness depends on several factors, including the sympathies of third parties, the amount of state resources available to meet the demands of those engaging in collective violence, the scope of the goals of dissident groups, and the relative strength of the state and the nature of its response (see later in the chapter) (Burstein, Einwohner, and Hollander 1995; Button 1978; McAdam, McCarthy, and Zald 1996). Still, more research is needed to assess the conditions under which collective violence succeeds or fails.

Research also needs to address the relative impact of collective violence versus collective nonviolence. As noted in Chapter 4 on revolution, nonviolent revolutions toppled several Communist regimes beginning in 1989, and nonviolent protest has been a common and sometimes successful tactic elsewhere. In general, nonviolent direct action avoids some of the risks of collective violence, in particular the risk of alienating third parties and prompting a violent response from the state. For these reasons, nonviolence might be more effective than collective violence in Western democracies. Despite the rich history of nonviolence directed at social change (Sharp 1973; Tarrow 1998), its impact remains a "black box" in the study of social movements and collective action. Although nonviolence can and does work, the results of the relatively few studies of its effectiveness are at least as mixed as those concerning the impact of collective violence (Burstein, Einwohner, and Hollander 1995). Certainly much more research is needed to understand the impact of nonviolent protest on public policy and other areas and the conditions under which nonviolence succeeds or fails. Until we know more about the impact of both collective violence and collective nonviolence, we cannot know which strategy, if any, is more effective in achieving the social change goals of dissident groups.

Interplay with State Authorities

The preceding discussion touched on the role that the state plays in whether collective violence and other protest succeeds or fails. Previous chapters, and especially Chapter 4 on revolution, included discussions of the role that the state and state authorities play in the origins, dynamics, and outcomes of collective violence. As noted previously, until recently relatively few studies existed of the outcomes of collective violence and of the role that the state's reaction plays in these outcomes. New research has begun to fill in this gap, with special attention being paid to the political opportunity structure, or aspects of the political environment that affect people's expectations for success or failure if they protest (Eisinger 1973; Kriesi 1995; McAdam, McCarthy, and Zald 1996; Tarrow 1998). For example, weak states or national, political, and economic crises could lead people to feel that state officials will have to give in to demands if confronted with sustained protest. Conversely, state repression might signal that protest will meet with quick and even lethal force and other methods of social control and thus may prompt people not to protest.

The political opportunity structure therefore affects both the origins and outcomes of collective action. It affects whether people decide to protest in the first place, and it affects what happens when they do protest. Although research on political opportunity structures has arguably focused more on the origins of collective action than on its outcomes (Giugni 1998), scholars have begun to explore the importance of the state's response for collective action. More specifically, they've begun to examine how and why the state's response affects the outcomes of protest (Barkan 1984; Della Porta 1996; Lichbach 1987; Marx 1979; McAdam 1983; Rasler 1996; Tilly 1978).

This book has shown that revolutions are more likely when certain political opportunities prevail, especially political crises that undermine the power of the state and render it vulnerable to insurgent challenges (Goldstone 1986; Skocpol 1979). In addition, prison riots are sometimes apt to occur when the control of prison authorities weakens because of, among other things, changes in the resources and mechanisms of social control in the prison.

Less time has been spent addressing another key question: To what extent does the response of state officials affect the outcomes of collective violence? Let's now address this question more fully. Research on this issue focuses on the effects of the state's response on the continuation of collective action. Before reviewing this research, let's first look at the ways in which states respond to collective violence and other protest.

Studies typically divide the state's response into two types: *violent control* and *legal control.* **Violent control,** often termed *violent repression,* involves the use of the police, the military, and other armed agents to quell dissent. These agents may threaten protesters with the use of violent force or may actually use it. Violent repression was discussed in Chapter 5, where it was termed *state terrorism.* One example of state terrorism mentioned there occurred in Beijing, China, in 1989 at Tiananmen Square. A democracy movement had challenged China's political officials to effect democratic reforms. When several thousand unarmed demonstrators, many of them students, gathered in Tiananmen Square on June 4, the military opened fire and slaughtered several hundred demonstrators. Others were arrested, imprisoned, and even executed. The violent repression effectively ended the democracy movement (Black 1993; Cherrington 1991). Another example of violent expression nine years earlier had the opposite effect. In the late 1970s, peasants in El Salvador began demanding that the government institute economic reforms to help the poor. In response, government troops assassinated one of the peasants' most vocal supporters, Archbishop Oscar Arnulfo Romero, in March 1980. His death sparked riots throughout the country and remained a rallying cry for dissident forces for several years (Brockman 1982; Goldston 1990).

Legal control of protest involves the use of the legal system—the police, courts, and prisons—to quell dissent (Balbus 1977; Barkan and Cohn 1994; Della Porta and Reiter 1998). Sometimes, legislation is passed that helps thwart dissident goals (Andrews 1997). In more dramatic events, protesters are arrested without undue police violence, tried in fair, or sham, proceedings in the courts, and imprisoned after what is usually a certain conviction. Such legal control, sometimes termed *legal repression* (Balbus 1977), has several aims in democratic and authoritarian regimes alike (Balbus 1977; Barkan 1985; Marx 1979). One aim is to tie up the time and money of the dissenters who are arrested and of the larger movement to which they belong. A second aim is to frighten would-be protesters and to deter them from engaging in dissent, lest they be arrested and prosecuted themselves. A third aim is to use what is often called the "majesty of the law" to legitimate the state's effort to quell dissent and to paint protesters as little better than common criminals who threaten law and order.

These aims were achieved by city officials in the Southern Civil Rights movement. When police used violence against nonviolent Civil Rights protesters, their violence was aired by TV stations across the nation and won many supporters to the Civil Rights cause (McAdam 1983). But when cities merely arrested and prosecuted protesters, their legal response looked much more legitimate in comparison, and they were able to defeat local protest movements or at least tie up their time and money and sap their morale (Barkan 1984).

This brief look at the types of state control of dissent suggests its possible effects on collective violence and other protest. Most research on these effects concerns the impact of violent repression of dissent. What does this research say? Perhaps the safest, if ambivalent, conclusion is that "repression has both positive and negative effects on government opposition" (Rasler 1996:133). As this statement suggests, repression could have two very different effects. First, it might scare people and deter them from new acts of protest. Conversely, it might escalate protest by angering dissidents and inspiring them to commit more protest; it might also win public sympathy for the movement to which the protesters belong and for the cause they represent (Lichbach 1987). As noted with the Tiananmen Square and El Salvador examples, repression can work, but it can also strengthen a movement. Repression can also encourage extremism by dissident groups and spur them into committing violence in return (Koopmans 1993; Tarrow 1998). The effects of repression can also depend on the timing of these effects. Repression might incite new acts in the short run but deter them in the long run or deter them in the short run and ignite them in the long run (Rasler 1996).

The research on repression has explored these many possibilities and, despite mixed results, has yielded at least three conclusions on which there is some consensus (Andrews 1997; Rasler 1996). First, extreme repression tends to stop a movement in its tracks, but moderate repression tends to lead to more protest by strengthening the solidarity of dissident groups and winning them external support (Klandermans 1997). A key variable here is the type of dissent that is being repressed. Violent repression of violent dissent might succeed in its goals, since the public and other parties are apt to agree that violent dissent needs to be repressed. Conversely, violent repression of nonviolent dissent could backfire, as external parties may feel that the state went too far. As noted previously, this dynamic was seen again and again in the Southern Civil Rights movement, as violent responses by white police against nonviolent demonstrators won support for the Civil Rights cause throughout the United States (McAdam 1983).

Second, violent repression tends to discourage peaceful protest, while at the same time igniting violent protest (Tarrow 1998). Donatella Della Porta

(1996) uncovered this effect in a study of protest and policing in Germany and Italy since World War II. When Italian police killed demonstrators who were marching peacefully, protest groups in Italy became more violent. Conversely, the more peaceful protests in Germany during this period reflected a generally tolerant, soft style of protest policing in that country.

Third, whether repression works depends on the timing of repression and its effects. Several studies support this conclusion. In a study of the Iranian revolution, Karen Rasler (1996) found that repression in Iran deterred protest in the short run but escalated it in the long run, as it led to many more contacts among dissidents and thus greater mobilization. In a second study, of peasant rebellion in Central America, Charles Brockett (1993) found that the effects of repression depended on when it occurred in the *protest cycle* of peasant dissent. Repression was effective before a series of protests began and again when they were about to end. But in the middle of a protest cycle, repression escalated protest. In a third study, Kenneth Andrews (1997) examined the impact of violent attacks by whites on the number of black candidates running for and being elected to office in Mississippi in the late 1960s. Whereas white violence earlier in the decade in Mississippi and elsewhere in the South helped mobilize the Civil Rights movement during its heyday, the violence in Mississippi in the latter part of the decade, after the movement had waned, reduced the number of black candidates who ran and were elected.

In sum, violent repression is double-edged for the state, just as the use of collective violence is for dissident groups. Certainly authoritarian governments feel freer than democratic ones to use violent repression, and, if their repression is severe enough, it can be effective, as illustrated by the events in Tiananmen Square. Yet other authoritarian governments, such as those in Iran (see Chapter 4) and El Salvador, have not been able to repress movements through violent means and, instead, their efforts ultimately have inspired more protest and resulted in sympathy for dissenters against their regimes. Ironically, violent repression can beget violent dissent.

More research is needed to determine when repression of collective violence and other protest succeeds in its attempt to quell dissent and when it fails to do so. As Andrews (1997:801–802) notes, "The key issue is sorting out the conditions under which repression diminishes protest and when repression 'backfires,' generating higher levels of mobilization."

The Future of Collective Violence

As we enter our first years of a new century and new millennium, there is both hope and fear. The hope is that the new era will bring with it new discoveries, new ways of addressing the social problems of the past, and new understanding of the disparate needs of the many peoples on Earth. The fear is that none of these things will happen and that the problems of the past will continue and even worsen. There is uncertainty any time a new venture begins, and our new century is no exception.

One thing is certain: If history is any guide to the future, collective violence will continue to mark the political landscape. Riots, rebellion and revolution, terrorism, and violence by cults and other groups have been around for centuries and give no signs of stopping their activities. Indeed, as the 1990s drew to a close, they continued to grab headlines everywhere. On any one day, newspaper readers could find examples of collective violence across the world (Tarrow 1998).

These examples represented the culmination of a wave of worldwide protest, both violent and nonviolent, that began in the 1960s and never really abated. This trend prompted some scholars to argue that protest has become a recurring feature of modern life. We now have, they said, a "movement society" in which protest is as much a part of the political process as are voting, campaigning, and other conventional political activities (Meyer and Tarrow 1998; Tarrow 1998). This expansion of protest stems from several factors, including increasing education and the rapid diffusion of protest ideologies and tactics via electronic communication and mass media coverage. Through the media and the Internet, collective violence and other protest that occur in one country quickly become known in many others. Protest in one country thus can quickly inspire protest in others, and activists around the world can learn from each other's successes and failures. The globalization of the world community that seems to be a hallmark of modern times thus includes a globalization of collective violence and other forms of protest.

As we move into the new century, the structural and cultural problems that lead to collective violence—poverty, exploitation, and hatred, to name a few—have not diminished. Thus, we'd be foolish to expect collective violence to go away. We'd also be wise to understand its roots, dynamics, and consequences as much as possible. The purpose of this book has been to help you reach this understanding.

Is collective violence just? This is a question this book has ignored, for it is a question that social scientists cannot answer. Pacifists feel that collective violence inevitably undermines the very ends that it is pursuing and makes its practitioners no better than the official agents of state violence. As we consider how best to seek social change, they urge that we become, in Albert Camus's (1986 [1947]) famous words, "neither victims nor executioners." Proponents of collective violence disagree. They say that such violence is sometimes a just and necessary act to address perceived injustices and grievances and is more effective than its nonviolent alternative.

Recall what was noted at the outset of this book: Collective violence can have both good and bad outcomes. It has enabled people worldwide to free themselves of the misery and oppression that characterizes most authoritarian regimes. It has also subjected other people to injury and death based on their race, ethnicity, religion, and other characteristics. It has alerted societies to perceived grievances and injustice, but it has also reminded us of the hatred that continues to guide too much of social life. Terrorism continues to frighten, maim, and kill many innocent victims, and violence by cults, militia, and hate groups continues to threaten the civil order and public safety.

As the problems of the last century carry over into the new one, people and states around the world must decide how they will meet the issues that still confront us. For better or worse, collective violence will be a common response. How will the world community deal with such violence? The answer to this question is critical in the years ahead.

References

Abrahamian, Ervand. 1986. "Structural Causes of the Iranian Revolution." Pp. 119–127 in *Revolutions: Theoretical, Comparative, and Historical Studies*, edited by J. A. Goldstone. San Diego: Harcourt Brace Jovanovich.

Abrahams, Naomi. 1992. "Towards Reconceptualizing Political Action." *Sociological Inquiry* 62:327–347.

Adler, Freda. 1975. *Sisters in Crime: The Rise of the New Female Criminal*. New York: McGraw-Hill.

Alter, Jonathan. 1995. "Jumping to Conclusions." *Newsweek* May 1:55.

Anbinder, Tyler Gregory. 1992. *Nativism and Slavery: The Northern Know-Nothings and the Politics of the 1850s*. New York: Oxford University Press.

Andrews, Kenneth D. 1997. "The Impacts of Social Movements on the Political Process: The Civil Rights Movement and Black Electoral Politics in Mississippi." *American Sociological Review* 62:800–819.

Aronowitz, Alexis. 1994. "Germany's Xenophobic Violence: Criminal Justice and Social Responses." Pp. 37–70 in *Hate Crime: International Perspectives on Causes and Control*, edited by M. Hamm. Cincinnati: Anderson Publishing Co.

Auerbach, Jerold S. 1983. *Justice Without Law*. Oxford: Oxford University Press.

Bachman, Ronet, and Linda E. Saltzman. 1995. *Violence Against Women: Estimates from the Redesigned Survey*. Washington, D.C.: Bureau of Justice Statistics, U.S. Department of Justice.

Balbus, Isaac. 1977. *The Dialectics of Legal Repression*. New York: Transaction Books.

Ball-Rokeach, Sandra J. 1972. "The Legitimation of Violence." In *Collective Violence*, edited by James F. Short and Marvin E. Wolfgang. Chicago: Aldine.

Barkan, Steven E. 1984. "Legal Control of the Southern Civil Rights Movement." *American Sociological Review* 49:552–565.

Barkan, Steven E. 1985. *Protesters on Trial: Criminal Prosecutions in the Southern Civil Rights and Vietnam Antiwar Movements*. New Brunswick, NJ: Rutgers University Press.

Barkan, Steven E. 1997. *Criminology: A Sociological Understanding*. Upper Saddle River, NJ: Prentice Hall.

Barkan, Steven E., and Steven F. Cohn. 1994. "Racial Prejudice and Support for the Death Penalty by Whites." *Journal of Research in Crime and Delinquency* 31:202–209.

Barker, Eileen. 1984. *The Making of a Moonie: Choice or Brainwashing*. New York: Oxford University Press.

Barrett, David V. 1996. *Sects, "Cults," and Alternative Religions*. London: Blandford Press.

Bart, Pauline B., and Eileen Geil Moran (eds.). 1993. *Violence Against Women: The Bloody Footprints*. Thousand Oaks, CA: Sage Publications, Inc.

Beck, E. M., and Stewart E. Tolnay. 1995. "Violence Toward African Americans in the Era of the White Lynch Mob." Pp. 121–144 in *Ethnicity, Race, and Crime: Perspectives Across Time and Place*, edited by D. F. Hawkins. Albany, NY: State University of New York Press.

Belanger, Sarah, and Maurice Pinard. 1991. "Ethnic Movements and the Competition Model: Some Missing Links." *American Sociological Review* 56:446–457.

Belluck, Pam. 1999. "A White Supremacist Group Seeks a New Kind of Recruit." *The New York Times* July 7:A1.

Benesh, Peter. 1998. "Many Terrorists Are Seduced by Thoughts of Becoming a Martyr." Pp. 29–31 in *Violence and Terrorism 98/99*, edited by B. Schechterman and M. Slann. Guilford, CT: Dushkin Publishing Group.

Benford, Robert D. 1997. "An Insider's Critique of the Social Movement Framing Perspective." *Sociological Inquiry* 67:409–430.

Bennett, David Harry. 1988. *The Party of Fear: From Nativist Movements to the New Right in American History*. Chapel Hill: University of North Carolina Press.

Berk, Richard A. 1972. "The Controversy Surrounding Analyses of Collective Violence: Some Methodological Notes." Pp. 112–118 in *Collective Violence*, edited by James F. Short and Marvin E. Wolfgang. Chicago: Aldine-Atherton.

Berk, Richard A. 1974. "A Gaming Approach to Crowd Behavior." *American Sociological Review* 39:355–373.

Bernstein, Iver. 1990. *The New York City Draft Riots: Their Significance for American Society and Politics in the Age of the Civil War*. New York: Oxford University Press.

Bianco, Lucien. 1971. *Origins of the Chinese Revolution, 1915–1949*. Stanford: Stanford University Press.

Bjornson, Karin, and Kurt Jonassohn. 1994. "The Former Yugoslavia: Some Historical Roots of Present Conflicts." Montreal: Concordia University.

Black, George. 1993. *Black Hands of Beijing: Lives of Deviance in China's Democracy Movement*. New York: John Wiley.

Blalock, Hubert. 1967. *Toward a Theory of Minority-Group Relations*. New York: John Wiley.

Bloombaum, Milton. 1968. "The Conditions Underlying Race Riots as Portrayed by Multidimensional Analysis: A Re-analysis of Lieberson and Silverman's Data." *American Sociological Review* 33:76–91.

Blum, William. 1995. *Killing Hope: U.S. Military and CIA Interventions Since World War II*. Monroe, ME: Common Courage Press.

Blumer, Herbert. 1939. "Collective Behavior." Pp. 221–279 in *Outline of the Principles of Sociology*, edited by R. E. Park. New York: Barnes & Noble.

Boin, R. Argen, and Menno J. Van Duin. 1995. "Prison Riots as Organizational Failures: A Managerial Perspective." *Prison Journal* 75:357–389.

Bonacich, Edna. 1972. "A Theory of Ethnic Antagonism: The Split-Labor Market." *American Sociological Review* 37:547–559.

Booth, Alan, and D. Wayne Osgood. 1993. "The Influence of Testosterone on Deviance in Adulthood: Assessing and Explaining the Relationship." *Criminology* 31:93–117.

Boyle, Kevin, and Tom Hadden. 1994. *Northern Ireland: The Choice*. London: Penguin Books.

Bragg, Rick. 1998. "Abortion Clinic Hit by 2 Bombs; Six are Injured." Pp. 136–137 in *Violence and Terrorism 98/99*, edited by B. Schechterman and M. Slann. Guilford, CT: Dushkin Publishing Group.

Bramson, Leon, and George W. Goethals. 1968. *War: Studies from Psychology, Sociology, Anthropology*. New York: Basic Books.

Brandt, Daniel. 1994. "Cults, Anti-Cultists, and the Cult of Intelligence." *NameBase Newsline (Internet)*, April–June.

Braswell, M., S. Dillingham, and R. Montgomery, Jr. (eds.). 1985. *Prison Violence in America*. Cincinnati: Anderson Publishing Co.

Brinton, Crane. 1938. *The Anatomy of Revolution*. New York: Vintage Books.

Brockett, Charles. 1993. "A Protest Cycle Resolution of the Repression/Popular-Protest Paradox." *Social Science History* 17:457–484.

Brockman, James R. 1982. *The Word Remains: A Life of Oscar Romero.* Maryknoll, NY: Orbis Books.

Broehl, Wayne G., Jr. 1964. *The Molly Maguires.* Cambridge: Harvard University Press.

Brooks, David. 1993. "Israel's Deadly Game of Hide-and-Seek." Pp. 47–49 in *Violence and Terrorism,* edited by B. Schechterman and M. Slann. Guilford, CT: Dushkin Publishing Group.

Brown, Dee Alexander. 1971. *Bury My Heart at Wounded Knee: An Indian History of the American West.* New York: Holt, Rinehart, and Winston.

Brown, Richard Maxwell. 1975. *Strain of Violence: Historical Studies of American Violence and Vigilantism.* New York: Oxford University Press.

Brown, Richard Maxwell. 1989. "Historical Patterns of Violence." Pp. 23–61 in *Violence in America: Protest, Rebellion, Reform,* vol. 2, edited by T. R. Gurr. Newbury Park, CA: Sage Publications.

Brown, Richard Maxwell. 1990. "Historical Patterns of American Violence." Pp. 4–15 in *Violence: Patterns, Causes, Public Policy,* edited by Neil A. Weiner, Margaret A. Zahn, and Rita J. Sagi. San Diego: Harcourt Brace Jovanovich.

Brownmiller, Susan. 1975. *Against Our Will: Men, Women, and Rape.* New York: Simon and Schuster.

Bruce, Robert V. 1959. *1877: Year of Violence.* Indianapolis: Bobbs-Merrill.

Brysk, Alison. 1994. *The Politics of Human Rights in Argentina: Protest, Change, and Democratization.* Stanford: Stanford University Press.

Burstein, Paul, Rachel L. Einwohner, and Jocelyn A. Hollander. 1995. "The Success of Political Movements: A Bargaining Perspective." Pp. 275–295 in *The Politics of Social Protest: Comparative Perspectives on States and Social Movements,* edited by J. C. Jenkins and B. Klandermans. Minneapolis: University of Minnesota Press.

Bushnell, Timothy. 1991. *State Organized Terror: The Case of Violent Internal Repression.* Boulder, CO: Westview Press.

Button, James. 1989. "The Outcomes of Contemporary Black Protest and Violence." Pp. 286–306 in *Violence in America: Protest, Rebellion, Reform,* vol. 2, edited by Ted R. Gurr. Newbury Park, CA: Sage Publications.

Button, James W. 1978. *Black Violence.* Princeton: Princeton University Press.

Camus, Albert. 1986 (1947). *Neither Victims nor Executioners.* Philadelphia: New Society Publishers.

Cannon, Lou. 1998. *Official Negligence: How Rodney King and the Riots Changed Los Angeles and the LAPD.* New York: Times Books.

Capeci, Dominic J., Jr. 1977. *The Harlem Riot of 1943.* Philadelphia: Temple University Press.

Caplan, Nathan, and J. M. Paige. 1968. "A Study of Ghetto Rioters." *Scientific American* 219:15–21.

Caputi, Jane, and Diana E. H. Russell. 1992. "Femicide: Sexist Terrorism against Women." Pp. 13–21 in *Femicide: The Politics of Woman Killing,* edited by J. Radford and D. E. H. Russell. New York: Twayne Publishers.

Card, Claudia. 1991. "Rape as a Terrorist Institution." Pp. 296–319 in *Violence, Terrorism, and Justice,* edited by R. G. Frey and C. W. Morris. Cambridge: Cambridge University Press.

Carr, Caleb. 1998. "Terrorism as Warfare: The Lessons of Military History." Pp. 196–206 in *Violence and Terrorism 98/99,* edited by B. Schechterman and M. Slann. Guilford, CT: Dushkin Publishing Group.

Chalk, Frank, and Kurt Jonassohn. 1993. "Genocide: An Historical Overview." Pp. 72–76 in *Violence and Terrorism,* edited by B. Schechterman and M. Slann. Guilford, CT: Dushkin Publishing Group.

Chalmers, David M. 1965. *Hooded Americanism: The First Century of the Ku Klux Klan, 1865–1965.* Garden City, NY: Doubleday.

Champion, Dean J. (ed.) 1997. *The Roxbury Dictionary of Criminal Justice*. Los Angeles: Roxbury Publishing Company.

Charters, David (ed.). 1994. *The Deadly Sin of Terrorism: Its Effect on Democracy and Civil Liberty in Six Countries*. Westport, CT: Greenwood Press.

Chavarria, Ricardo E. 1986. "The Revolutionary Insurrection." Pp. 152–159 in *Revolutions: Theoretical, Comparative, and Historical Studies*, edited by J. A. Goldstone. San Diego: Harcourt Brace Jovanovich.

Cherrington, Ruth. 1991. *China's Students: The Struggle for Democracy*. London: Routledge.

Chomsky, Noam. 1985. *Turning the Tide: U.S. Intervention in Central America and the Struggle for Peace*. Boston: South End Press.

Churchill, Ward, and Jim Vander Wall. 1990. *Agents of Repression: The FBI's Secret Wars Against the American Indian Movement and the Black Panther Party*. Boston: South End Press.

Claridge, David. 1998. "State Terrorism? Adopting a Definitional Model." Pp. 64–72 in *Violence and Terrorism 98/99*, edited by B. Schechterman and M. Slann. Guilford, CT: Dushkin Publishing Group.

Clarity, James F. 1992. "For All Its Bombs, the I.R.A. Is No Closer to Goals." *The New York Times* December 13:3.

Clarke, James W. 1982. *American Assassins: The Darker Side of Politics*. Princeton: Princeton University Press.

Clemetson, Lynnette, and T. Trent Gegax. 1998. "The Abortion Wars Come Home." *Newsweek* November 9:34.

Cobban, Helena. 1985. *The Palestinian Liberation Organization: People, Power, and Politics*. Cambridge: Cambridge University Press.

Collins, John J. 1991. *The Cult Experience: An Overview of Cults, Their Traditions, and Why People Join Them*. Springfield, IL: Charles C. Thomas.

Collins, Randall. 1994. *Four Sociological Traditions*. New York: Oxford University Press.

Colvin, Mark. 1982. "The 1980 New Mexico Riot." *Social Problems* 29:449–463.

Colvin, Mark. 1992. *The Penitentiary in Crisis: From Accommodation to Riot in New Mexico*. Albany: State University of New York Press.

Conquest, Robert. 1990. *The Great Terror: A Reassessment*. New York: Oxford University Press.

Corzine, Jay, James Creech, and Lin Corzine. 1988. "The Tenant Labor Market and Lynching in the South: A Test of Split Labor Market Theory." *Sociological Inquiry* 58:261–278.

Coser, Lewis. 1977. *Masters of Sociological Thought*. New York: Harcourt, Brace, Jovanovich.

Crenshaw, Martha. 1992. "Current Research on Terrorism: The Academic Perspective." *Studies in Conflict and Terrorism* 15:1–11.

Cullen, Francis T., Kathryn M. Golden, and John B. Cullen. 1979. "Sex and Delinquency: A Partial Test of the Masculinity Hypothesis." *Criminology* 17: 301–310.

Cullen, Kevin. 1996. "Sides Push to Restore Irish Truce: No Accord on How to Proceed." *The Boston Globe* February 12:1.

Cullen, Kevin, and Brian McGrory. 1994. "Abortion Violence Hits Home: Gunman Opens Fire in Brookline Clinics, Kills 2 and Wounds 5." *The Boston Globe* December 31:1.

Currie, Elliott, and Jerome H. Skolnick. 1970. "A Critical Note on Conceptions of Collective Behavior." *Annals of the American Academy of Political and Social Science* 391:34–45.

Curtius, Mary. 1994. "Report Blasts Global Abuse of Women's Rights." *The Boston Globe* March 8:2.

Darnovsky, Marcy, Barbara Epstein, and Richard Flacks (eds.). 1995. *Cultural Politics and Social Movements*. Philadelphia: Temple University Press.

Davies, James Chowning. 1962. "Toward a Theory of Revolution." *American Sociological Review* 27:5–19.

DeBenedetti, Charles, and Charles Chatfield. 1990. *An American Ordeal: The Antiwar Movement of the Vietnam Era*. Syracuse: Syracuse University Press.

Dees, Morris. 1996. *Gathering Storm: America's Militia Threat*. New York: HarperCollins.

DeFronzo, James. 1996. *Revolutions and Revolutionary Movements*. Boulder, CO: Westview Press.

Della Porta, Donatella. 1996. "Social Movements and the State: Thoughts on the Policing of Protest." Pp. 62–92 in *Comparative Perspectives on Social Movements: Political Opportunities, Mobilizing Structures, and Cultural Framings*, edited by D. McAdam, J. D. McCarthy, and M. N. Zald. Cambridge: Cambridge University Press.

Della Porta, Donatella, and Herbert Reiter. 1998. "Policing Protest: The Control of Mass Demonstrations in Western Democracies." Minneapolis: University of Minnesota Press.

DiIulio, John, Jr. 1987. *Governing Prisons: A Comparative Study of Correctional Management*. New York: Free Press.

Dollard, John, Leonard W. Doob, Neal E. Miller, O. H. Mowrer, and Robert R. Sears. 1939. *Frustration and Aggression*. New Haven: Yale University Press.

Downes, Bryan T. 1968. "The Social Characteristics of Riot Cities: A Comparative Study." *Social Science Quarterly* 49:504–520.

Downes, Bryan T. 1970. "A Critical Reexamination of the Social and Political Characteristics of Riot Cities." *Social Science Quarterly* 51:349–360.

Downton, James V. 1976. *Sacred Journeys: The Conversion of Young Americans to the Divine Light Mission*. New York: Columbia University Press.

Drake, Richard. 1995. *The Aldo Muro Murder Case*. Cambridge: Harvard University Press.

Duff, Ernest, and John McCamant. 1976. *Violence and Repression in Latin America*. New York: Free Press.

Dwyer, Jim. 1994. *Two Seconds Under the World: Terror Comes to America: The Conspiracy Behind the World Trade Center Bombing*. New York: Crown Publishers.

Edwards, Lyford P. 1927. *The Natural History of Revolution*. Chicago: University of Chicago Press.

Eisinger, Peter K. 1973. "The Conditions of Protest Behavior in American Cities." *American Political Science Review* 67:11–28.

Evans, Will. 1998. "Wash Your Hands." *The Humanist* 58:31–33.

Feagin, Joe R., and Harlan Hahn. 1973. *Ghetto Revolts: The Politics of Violence in American Cities*. New York: Macmillan.

Feldberg, Michael. 1980. *The Turbulent Era: Riot and Disorder in Jacksonina America*. New York: Oxford University Press.

Ferree, Myra Marx, and Frederick D. Miller. 1985. "Mobilization and Meaning: Toward an Integration of Social Psychological and Resource Perspectives on Social Movements." *Sociological Inquiry* 55:38–61.

Feuer, Lewis S. 1969. *The Conflict of Generations*. New York: Basic Books.

Finke, Roger, and Rodney Stark. 1992. *The Churching of America*. New Brunswick, NJ: Rutgers University Press.

Finn, John E. 1998. "Media Coverage of Political Terrorism and the First Amendment: Reconciling the Public's Right to Know with Public Order." Pp. 153–157 in *Violence and Terrorism*, edited by B. Schechterman and M. Slann. Guildford, CT: Dushkin Publishing Group.

Fitzpatrick, Sheila. 1994. *The Russian Revolution*. New York: Oxford University Press.

Flacks, Richard. 1970–1971. "Review Article: Feuer's Conflict of Generations." *Journal of Social History* 4:141–153.

Fogelson, Robert M. 1971. *Violence as Protest: A Study of Riots and Ghettos*. Garden City, NY: Anchor Books.

Foster, John. 1974. *Class Struggle and the Industrial Revolution: Early industrial Capitalism in Three English Towns*. London: Weidenfeld and Nicholson.

Freud, Sigmund. 1967 (1921). *Group Psychology and the Analysis of the Ego*. New York: Liverwright Publishing.

Frey, R. Scott, Thomas Dietz, and Linda Kalof. 1992. "Characteristics of Successful American Protest Groups: Another Look at Gamson's Strategy of Social Protest." *American Journal of Sociology* 98:368–387.

Fried, Joseph P. 1998. "Sheik and 9 Followers Guilty of Conspiracy of Terrorism." Pp. 130–133 in *Violence and Terrorism 98/99*, edited by B. Schechterman and M. Slann. Guildford, CT: Dushkin Publishing Group.

Fromm, Erich. 1973. *The Anatomy of Human Destructiveness.* New York: Holt, Rinehart, and Winston.

Galanter, Marc. 1989. *Cults, Faith Healing, and Coercion.* New York: Oxford University Press.

Gamson, Joshua. 1996. "The Organizational Shaping of Collective Identity: The Case of Lesbian and Gay Film Festivals in New York." *Sociological Forum* 11:231–261.

Gamson, William A. 1975. *The Strategy of Social Protest.* Homewood, IL: Dorsey Press.

Gamson, William A. 1990. *The Strategy of Social Protest.* Belmont, CA: Wadsworth Publishing Company.

Gamson, William A. 1992. "The Social Psychology of Collective Action." Pp. 53–76 in *Frontiers in Social Movement Theory,* edited by A. D. Morris and C. M. Mueller. New Haven: Yale University Press.

Garrow, David J. 1986. *Bearing the Cross: Martin Luther King, Jr., and the Southern Christian Leadership Conference.* New York: Vintage Books.

Geschwender, James A., and Benjamin D. Singer. 1971. "The Detroit Insurrection: Grievance and Facilitating Conditions." Pp. 353–360 in *The Black Revolt: The Civil Rights Movement, Ghetto Uprisings, and Separatism,* edited by J. A. Geschwender. Englewood Cliffs, NJ: Prentice Hall.

Gibbs, Jack P. 1989. "Conceptualization of Terrorism." *American Sociological Review* 54:329–340.

Gilbert, Martin. 1987. *The Holocaust: A History of the Jews of Europe during the Second World War.* New York: Henry Holt and Company.

Gilligan, James. 1997. *Violence.* New York: Vintage Books.

Giraldo, Javier. 1996. *Colombia: The Genocidal Democracy.* Monroe, ME: Common Courage Press.

Giugni, Marco G. 1998. "Was It Worth the Effort? The Outcomes and Consequences of Social Movements." *Annual Review of Sociology* 24:371–393.

Glover, Jonathan. 1991. "State Terrorism." Pp. 256–275 in *Violence, Terrorism, and Justice,* edited by R. G. Frey and C. W. Morris. Cambridge: Cambridge University Press.

Goldston, James. 1990. *A Year of Reckoning: El Salvador a Decade after the Assassination of Archbishop Romero.* New York: Americas Watch Committee.

Goldstone, Jack A. 1980. "The Weakness of Organization: A New Look at Gamson's The Strategy of Social Protest." *American Journal of Sociology* 85:1017–1042.

Goldstone, Jack A. 1986. "Introduction: The Comparative and Historical Study of Revolutions." Pp. 1–17 in *Revolutions: Theoretical, Comparative, and Historical Studies,* edited by J. A. Goldstone. San Diego: Harcourt Brace Jovanovich.

Goldstone, Jack A. 1991a. *Revolution and Rebellion in the Early Modern World.* Berkeley: University of California Press.

Goldstone, Jack A. 1991b. "An Analytic Framework." Pp. 37–51 in *Revolutions of the Late Twentieth Century,* edited by J. A. Goldstone, T. R. Gurr, and F. Moshiri. Boulder, CO: Westview Press.

Goode, Erich. 1992. *Collective Behavior.* Fort Worth: Harcourt Brace Jovanovich.

Goodwin, Jeff. 1996. "How to Become a Dominant American Social Scientist: The Case of Theda Skocpol." *Contemporary Sociology* 25:293–295.

Goti, Jamie E. Malamud. 1996. *Game Without End: State Terror and the Politics of Justice.* Norman, OK: University of Oklahoma Press.

Gottfried, Robert S. 1983. *The Black Death: Natural and Human Disaster in Medieval Europe.* New York: Free Press.

Gould, Roger V. 1991. "Multiple Networks and Mobilization in the Paris Commune, 1871." *American Sociological Review* 56:716–729.

Green, Jerrold D. 1986. "Countermobilization in the Iranian Revolution." Pp. 127–138 in *Revolutions: Theoretical, Comparative, and Historical Studies,* edited by J. A. Goldstone. San Diego: Harcourt Brace Jovanovich.

Greene, Thomas H. 1990. *Comparative Revolutionary Movements.* Englewood Cliffs, NJ: Prentice Hall.

Griffin, Susan. 1971. "Rape: The All-American Crime." *Ramparts.* September. Pp. 26–35.

Grimshaw, Allen D. 1972. "Interpreting Collective Violence: An Argument for the Importance of Social Structure." Pp. 35–46 in *Collective Violence*, edited by James F. Short and Marvin E. Wolfgang. Chicago: Aldine-Atherton.

Groebel, Jo, and Robert A. Hinde. 1989. *Aggression and War: Their Biological and Social Bases*. Cambridge: Cambridge University Press.

Grynspan, Devora. 1991. "Nicaragua: A New Model for Popular Revolution in Latin America." Pp. 88–115 in *Revolutions of the Late Twentieth Century*, edited by J. A. Goldstone, T. R. Gurr, and F. Moshiri. Boulder, CO: Westview Press.

Guillemin, Jeanne. 1989. "American Indian Resistance and Protest." Pp. 153–172 in *Violence in America: Protest, Rebellion, Reform*, vol. 2 edited by Ted Robert Gurr. Newbury Park, CA: Sage Publications.

Gurney, Joan Neff, and Kathleen J. Tierney. 1982. "Relative Deprivation and Social Movements: A Critical Look at Twenty Years of Theory and Research." *Sociological Quarterly* 23:33–47.

Gurr, Ted Robert. 1970. *Why Men Rebel*. Princeton: Princeton University Press.

Gurr, Ted Robert. 1989a. "Historical Trends in Violent Crime: Europe and the United States." Pp. 21–54 in *Violence in America: The History of Crime*, vol. 1, edited by T. R. Gurr. Newbury Park, CA: Sage Publications.

Gurr, Ted Robert. 1989b. "Political Terrorism: Historical Antecedents and Contemporary Trends." Pp. 201–230 in *Violence in America: Protest, Rebellion, Reform*, vol. 2, edited by T. R. Gurr. Newbury Park, CA: Sage Publications.

Gurr, Ted Robert. 1989c. "Protest and Rebellion in the 1960s: The United States in World Perspective." Pp. 101–130 in *Violence in America. Volume 2: Protest, Rebellion, Reform*, edited by T. R. Gurr. Newbury Park, CA: Sage Publications.

Hacker, Andrew. 1992. *Two Nations: Black and White, Separate, Hostile, Unequal*. New York: Scribner's.

Halperin, Ernst. 1976. *Terrorism in Latin America*. Newbury Park, CA: Sage Publications.

Hamm, Mark S. 1993. *American Skinheads: The Criminology and Control of Hate Crime*. Westport, CT: Praeger Publishers.

Hamm, Mark S. 1994 (ed.). *Hate Crime: International Perspectives on Causes and Control*. Cincinnati: Anderson Publishing Company.

Heise, Lori. 1994. "The Global War Against Women." Pp. 151–153 in *Annual Editions: Sociology 1994/95*, edited by K. Finsterbusch. Guilford, CT: Dushkin Publishing Group.

Henry, David. 1963. *A History of the Haymarket Affair*. New York: Collier.

Herman, Edward. 1983. *The Real Terror Network*. Boston: South End Press.

Hester, Marianne. 1992. "The Witch-craze in Sixteenth- and Seventeenth-Century England as Social Control of Women." Pp. 27–39 in *Femicide: The Politics of Woman Killing*, edited by J. Radford and D. E. H. Russell. New York: Twayne Publishers.

Hewitt, Christopher. 1984. *The Effectiveness of Anti-Terrorist Policies*. Landham, MD: University of America Press.

Heymann, Philip B. 1998. *Terrorism and America: A Commonsense Strategy for a Democratic Society*. Cambridge: MIT Press.

Hicks, Robert D. 1991. *In Pursuit of Satan: The Police and the Occult*. Buffalo: Prometheus Books.

Hing, Bill Ong. 1993. *Making and Remaking Asia America Through Immigration Policy, 1850–1990*. Stanford: Stanford University Press.

Hobsbawn, Eric. 1962. *The Age of Revolution, 1789–1848*. New York: New American Library.

Hoerder, Dirk. 1977. *Crowd Action in Revolutionary Massachusetts, 1765–1780*. New York: Academic Press.

Hoffman, Bruce. 1993. "Terrorism in the United States: Recent Trends and Future Prospects." Pp. 220–225 in *Violence and Terrorism*, edited by B. Schechterman and M. Slann. Guilford, CT: Dushkin Publishing Group.

Hoffman, Bruce. 1998. *Inside Terrorism*. New York: Columbia University Press.

Hoffman, Bill, and Kathy Burke. 1997. *Heaven's Gate Cult Suicide in San Diego*. New York: Harper Paperbacks.

Hopper, Rex. 1950. "The Revolutionary Process: A Frame of Reference for the Study of Revolutionary Movements." *Social Forces* 28:270–279.

Irwin, John. 1980. *Prisons in Turmoil*. Boston: Little, Brown.

Isaac, Larry, and William R. Kelly. 1981. "Racial Insurgency, the State, and Welfare Expansion: Local and National Evidence from the Postwar United States." *American Journal of Sociology* 86:1348–1386.

Jacobs, Sally. 1999. "On the Front Line: Abortion Provider Soldiers on in a Charged Climate." *The Boston Globe* January 5:A1.

Jasper, James M. 1998. "The Emotions of Protest: Affective and Reactive Emotions In and Around Social Movements." *Sociological Forum* 13:397–424.

Jelavich, Barbara. 1987. *Modern Austria: Empire and Republic, 1815–1986*. Cambridge: Cambridge University Press.

Jenkins, Philip. 1995. "Home-Grown Terror." *American Heritage*, September:38–44.

Jenness, Valerie, and Kendal Broad. 1997. *Hate Crimes: New Social Movements and the Politics of Violence*. Hawthorne, NY: Aldine de Gruyter.

Johnson, Norris. 1980. "Collective Behavior as Group-Induced Shift." Pp. 54–63 in *Collective Behavior: A Source Book*, edited by M. D. Pugh. St. Paul: West Publishing Co.

Johnston, Hank, and Bert Klandermans. 1995a. "The Cultural Analysis of Social Movements." Pp. 3–40 in *Social Movements and Culture*, edited by H. Johnston and B. Klandermans. Minneapolis: University of Minnesota Press.

Johnston, Hank, and Bert Klandermans. 1995b. "Social Movements and Culture." Minneapolis: University of Minnesota Press.

Jordan, Donald A. 1976. *The Northern Expedition*. Honolulu: University Press of Hawaii.

Juckes, Tim J. 1995. *Opposition in South Africa: The Leadership of Z. K. Mathews, Nelson Mandela, and Stephen Biko*. Westport, CT: Praeger Publishers.

Kanter, Rosabeth. 1972. *Commitment and Community: Communes and Utopias in Sociological Perspective*. Cambridge: Harvard University Press.

Kaplan, David E., and Andrew Marshall. 1996. *The Cult at the End of the World: The Terrifying Story of the Aum Doomsday Cult, from the Subways of Tokyo to the Nuclear Arsenals of Russia*. New York: Crown Publishers.

Kaplan, Jeffrey. 1997. *Radical Religion in America*. Syracuse: Syracuse University Press.

Kappeler, Victor E., Mark Blumberg, and Gary W. Potter. 1996. *The Mythology of Crime and Justice*. Prospect Heights, IL: Waveland Press.

Kendrick, T. D. 1994. *The Druids*. London: Senate Editions, LTD.

Kephart, William M., and William W. Zellner. 1995. *Extraordinary Groups*. New York: St. Martin's Press.

Kerner Commission. 1968. *Report of the National Advisory Commission on Civil Disorders*. New York: Bantam Books.

Kidder, Rushworth M. 1998. "Manipulation of the Media." Pp. 148–152 in *Violence and Terrorism*, edited by B. Schechterman and M. Slann. Guilford, CT: Dushkin Publishing Group.

Kim, Hyung-Chan. 1994. *A Legal History of Asian Americans, 1790–1990*. Westport, CT: Greenwood Press.

Kimmel, Michael S. 1990. *Revolution: A Sociological Interpretation*. Philadelphia: Temple University Press.

Kitano, Harry H. L. 1991. *Race Relations*. Englewood Cliffs, NJ: Prentice Hall.

Klandermans, Bert. 1984. "Social Psychological Expansions of Resource Mobilization Theory." *American Sociological Review* 49:583–600.

Klandermans, Bert. 1997. *The Social Psychology of Protest*. Oxford: Blackwell Publishers.

Klandermans, Bert, and Dirk Oegema. 1987. "Potentials, Networks, Motivations, and Barriers: Steps Towards Participation in Social Movements." *American Sociological Review* 52:519–531.

Klein, Dorie. 1973. "The Etiology of Female Crime." *Issues in Criminology* 8:3–30.

Kleist, Trina. 1997. "42 Killed in Mexican Massacre." Associated Press.

Klotz, Audie. 1995. *Norms in International Relations: The Struggle Against Apartheid*. Ithaca: Cornell University Press.

Koopmans, Ruud. 1993. "The Dynamics of Protest Waves: West Germany, 1965 to 1989." *American Sociological Review* 58:637–658.

Kornhauser, William. 1959. *The Politics of Mass Society*. New York: Free Press.

Koss, Mary P., Lisa A. Godoman, Angela Browne, Louise F. Fitzgerald, Gwendolyn Puryear Keita, and Nancy Felipe Russo. 1994. *No Safe Haven: Male Violence Against Women at Home, at Work, and in the Community*. Hyattsville, MD: American Psychological Association.

Kressel, Neil J. 1996. *Mass Hate: The Global Rise of Genocide and Terror*. New York: Plenum.

Kriesi, Hanspeter. 1995. "The Political Opportunity Structure of New Social Movements: Its Impact on Their Mobilization." Pp. 167–198 in *The Politics of Social Protest: Comparative Perspectives on States and Social Movements*, edited by J. C. Jenkins and B. Klandermans. Minneapolis: University of Minnesota Press.

Kurzman, Charles. 1996. "Structural Opportunity and Perceived Opportunity in Social-Movement Theory: The Iranian Revolution of 1979." *American Sociological Review* 61: 153–170.

Lakshmanan, Indira A. R. 1998. "Indonesians Take to Streets Over Economy." *The Boston Globe* February 13:A1.

Lang, Kurt. 1972. *Military Institutions and the Sociology of War: A Review of the Literature with Annotated Bibliography*. Beverly Hills: Sage Publications.

LaPierre, Wayne. 1995. *Guns, Crime, and Freedom*. New York: Harper Perennial.

Laqueur, Walter. 1987. *The Age of Terrorism*. Boston: Little, Brown.

Laqueur, Walter. 1977. *Terrorism*. London: Weidenfeld and Nicolson.

LeBon, Gustave. 1978. "The Mind of the Crowds." Pp. 6–11 in *Collective Behavior and Social Movements*, edited by L. E. Genevie. Itasca, IL: F. E. Peacock.

Lens, Sidney. 1973. *The Labor Wars: From the Molly Maguires to the Sitdowns*. Garden City, NY: Doubleday.

Levin, Jack, and Jack McDevitt. 1993. *Hate Crimes: The Rising Tide of Bigotry and Bloodshed*. New York: Plenum Publishing Corporation.

Lewis, I. M. 1996. *Religion in Context: Cults and Charisma*. New York: Cambridge University Press.

Lichbach, Mark Irving. 1987. "Deterrence or Escalation: The Puzzle of Aggregate Studies of Repression and Dissent." *Journal of Conflict Resolution* 31:266–297.

Lieberson, Stanley, and Arnold K. Silverman. 1965. "The Precipitants and Underlying Conditions of Race Riots." *American Sociological Review* 30:887–898.

Lieske, Joel A. 1978. "The Conditions of Racial Violence in American Cities: A Developmental Synthesis." *American Political Science Review* 72:1324–1340.

Lifton, Robert Jay. 1986. *The Nazi Doctors: Medical Killing and the Psychology of Genocide*. New York: Basic Books.

Linedecker, Clifford. 1993. *Massacre at Waco, Texas*. New York: St. Martin's Press.

Livingston, Steven. 1994. *The Terrorism Spectacle*. Boulder, CO: Westview Press.

Lofland, John. 1966. *Doomsday Cult: A Study of Conversion, Proselytization, and Maintenance of Faith*. New York: Irvington.

Lofland, John. 1979. "White-Hate Mobilization: Strategies of a Millenarian Movement." Pp. 157–166 in *The Dynamics of Social Movements*, edited by M. N. Zald and J. D. McCarthy. Cambridge: E. Winthrop Publishers.

Lofland, John. 1996. *Social Movement Organizations: Guide to Research on Insurgent Realities*. New York: Aldine de Gruyter.

Lomasky, Loren E. 1991. "The Political Significance of Terrorism." Pp. 86–115 in *Violence, Terrorism, and Justice*, edited by R. G. Frey and C. W. Morris. Cambridge: Cambridge University Press.

Lynch, Colum. 1995. "Amnesty International Faults Rwanda War Crimes Tribunal." *The Boston Globe* April 6:14.

MacLean, Nancy. 1994. *Behind the Mask of Chivalry: The Making of the Second Ku Klux Klan.* New York: Oxford University Press.

Mahan, Sue. 1985. "An 'Orgy of Brutality' at Attica and the 'Killing Ground' at Santa Fe." Pp. 73–78 in *Prison Violence in America*, edited by M. Braswell, S. Dillingham, and R. Montgomery. Cincinnati: Anderson Publishing Co.

Mahan, Sue, and Richard Lawrence. 1996. "Media and Mayhem in Corrections: The Role of the Media in Prison Riots." *Prison Journal* 76:420–441.

Malecki, Edward S. 1973. "Theories of Revolution and Industrialized Societies." *Journal of Politics* 35:948–985.

Marin, Peter. 1987. "The Weather Men, Twenty Years On." *Harper's Magazine* December.:26–28.

Martin, L. John. 1985. "The Media's Role in International Terrorism." *Terrorism* 8:44–58.

Martin, Marie Alexandrine. 1994. *Cambodia: A Shattered Society.* Berkeley: University of California Press.

Martin, Randy, and Sherwood Zimmerman. 1990. "A Typology of the Causes of Prison Riots and an Analytical Extension to the 1986 West Virginia Riot." *Justice Quarterly* 7:711–737.

Marx, Gary T. 1972. "Issueless Riots." Pp. 47–59 in *Collective Violence*, edited by James F. Short and Marvin E. Wolfgang. Chicago: Aldine.

Marx, Gary T. 1979. "External Efforts to Damage or Facilitate Social Movements: Some Patterns, Explanations, Outcomes, and Compilations." Pp. 94–125 in *The Dynamics of Social Movements*, edited by M. N. Zald and J. D. McCarthy. Cambridge: Winthrop.

Marx, Gary T., and Douglas McAdam. 1994. *Collective Behavior and Social Movements: Process and Structure.* Englewood Cliffs, NJ: Prentice Hall.

Marx, Gary T., and James L. Wood. 1975. "Strands of Theory and Research in Collective Behavior." *Annual Review of Sociology* 1:363–428.

Marx, Karl. 1906 (1867). *Capital.* New York: Random House.

Marx, Karl, and Friedrich Engels. 1962 (1848). "The Communist Manifesto." Pp. 44 in *Marx and Engels: Selected Works*, vol. 2. Moscow: Foreign Language Publishing House.

Mazur, Allan. 1982. "Bomb Threats and the Mass Media: Evidence for a Theory of Suggestion." *American Sociological Review* 47:407–410.

McAdam, Doug. 1982. *Political Process and the Development of Black Insurgency, 1930–1970.* Chicago: University of Chicago Press.

McAdam, Doug. 1983. "Tactical Innovation and the Pace of Insurgency." *American Sociological Review* 48:735–754.

McAdam, Doug, John D. McCarthy, and Mayer N. Zald. 1988. "Social Movements." Pp. 695–737 in *Handbook of Sociology*, edited by N. J. Smelser. Newbury Park, CA: Sage Publications.

McAdam, Doug, John D. McCarthy, and Mayer N. Zald (eds.). 1996. *Comparative Perspectives on Social Movements.* Cambridge, MA: Cambridge University Press.

McAdam, Doug, and Kelly Moore. 1989. "The Politics of Black Insurgency, 1930–1975." Pp. 255–285 in *Violence in America: Protest, Rebellion, Reform*, vol. 2, edited by Ted Robert Gurr. Newbury Park, CA: Sage Publications.

McAdam, Doug, and David A. Snow (eds.). 1997. *Social Movements: Readings on Their Emergence, Mobilization, and Dynamics.* Los Angeles: Roxbury Publishing Company.

McCamant, John F. 1984. "Governance Without Blood: Social Science's Antiseptic View of Rule; or, The Neglect of Political Repression." Pp. 11–42 in *The State as Terrorist: The Dynamics of Governmental Violence and Repression*, edited by M. Stohl and G. A. Lopez. Westport, CT: Greenwood Press.

McCarry, Charles. 1999. "Waco, Forever Unresolved." *The New York Times* September 5:Wk 11.

McCarthy, John D., and Mayer N. Zald. 1977. "Resource Mobilization and Social Movements: A Partial Theory." *American Journal of Sociology* 82:1212–1241.

McCorkle, Richard C., Terance D. Miethe, and Kriss A. Drass. 1995. "The Roots of Prison Violence: A Test of Deprivation, Management, and 'Not-So-Total' Institution Models." *Crime and Delinquency* 41:317–331.

McGovern, George S., and Leonard F. Guttridge. 1972. *The Great Coalfield War*. Boston: Houghton Mifflin.

McPhail, Clark. 1971. "Civil Disorder Participation: A Critical Examination of Recent Research." *American Sociological Review* 36:1058–1073.

McPhail, Clark. 1994. "The Dark Side of Purpose: Individual and Collective Violence in Riots." *Sociological Quarterly* 35:1–32.

McPhail, Clark, and David L. Miller. 1973. "The Assembling Process: A Theoretical and Empirical Examination." *American Sociological Review* 38:721–735.

Melman, Yossi. 1986. *The Master Terrorist: The True Story of Abu-Nidal*. New York: Adama Books.

Melton, J. Gordon. 1982. *Magic, Witchcraft, and Paganism in America: A Bibliography*. New York: Garland Press.

Melucci, Alberto. 1989. *Nomads of the Present: Social Movements and Individual Needs in Contemporary Society*. Philadelphia: Temple University Press.

Messerschmidt, James W. 1997. *Crime as Structured Action: Gender, Race, Class, and Crime in the Making*. Thousand Oaks, CA: Sage Publications.

Meyer, David S., and Sidney Tarrow (eds.). 1998. *The Social Movement Society: Contentious Politics for a New Century*. Lanham, MD: Rowman & Littlefield.

Miller, Abraham H. 1993. "Terrorism and the Media: Lessons from the British Experience." Pp. 143–147 in *Violence and Terrorism*, edited by B. Schechterman and M. Slann. Guilford, CT: Dushkin Publishing Group.

Miller, David L. 1985. *Introduction to Collective Behavior*. Springfield, IL: Waveland Press.

Miller, Mark. 1997. "Secrets of the Cult." *Newsweek* April 14:28–36.

Mirowsky, John, and Catherine Ross. 1981. "Protest Group Success: The Impact of Group Characteristics, Social Control, and Context." *Sociological Focus* 14:177–192.

Montgomery, Reid H., Jr. 1997. "Bringing the Lessons of Prison Riots into Focus." *Corrections Today* 59:28–32.

Moore, Joan, and Harry Pachon. 1985. *Hispanics in the United States*. Englewood Cliffs, NJ: Prentice Hall.

Morgan, William R., and Terry N. Clark. 1973. "The Causes of Racial Disorders: A Grievance-Level Explanation." *American Sociological Review* 38:611–624.

Morris, Roger. 1983. *The Devil's Butcher Shop: The New Mexico Prison Uprising*. New York: Franklin Watts.

Moshiri, Farrokh. 1991a. "Iran: Islamic Revolution Against Westernization." Pp. 116–135 in *Revolutions of the Late Twentieth Century*, edited by J. A. Goldstone, T. R. Gurr, and F. Moshiri. Boulder, CO: Westview Press.

Moshiri, Farrokh. 1991b. "Revolutionary Conflict Theory in an Evolutionary Perspective." Pp. 4–36 in *Revolutions of the Late Twentieth Century*, edited by J. A. Goldstone, T. R. Gurr, and F. Moshiri. Boulder, CO: Westview Press.

Mueller, Carol McClurg. 1978. "Riot Violence and Protest Outcomes." *Journal of Political and Military Sociology* 6:49–63.

Muller, Edward N. 1979. *Aggressive Political Participation*. Princeton: Princeton University Press.

Mullins, Wayman C. 1993. "Hate Crime and the Far Right: Unconventional Terrorism." Pp. 121–169 in *Political Crime in Contemporary America: A Critical Approach*, edited by K. D. Tunnell. New York: Garland Publishing, Inc.

Murphy, Raymond J., and James M. Watson. 1971. "Level of Aspiration, Discontent, and Support for Violence: A Test of the Expectation Hypothesis." Pp. 360–372 in *The Black Revolt: The Civil Rights Movement, Ghetto Uprisings, and Separatism*, edited by J. A. Geschwender. Englewood Cliffs, NJ: Prentice Hall.

Myers, Daniel J. 1997. "Racial Rioting in the 1960s: An Event History Analysis of Local Conditions." *American Sociological Review* 62:94–112.

Nacos, Brigitte Lesbens. 1994. *Terrorism and the Media: From the Iran Hostage Crisis to the World Trade Center Bombing*. New York: Cambridge University Press.

Nazian, Florence. 1990. *Why Genocide? The Armenian and Jewish Experiences in Perspective.* Ames: Iowa State University Press.

Neuburger, Luisella de Cataldo, Tiziana Valentini, and J. O. Campling. 1996. *Women and Terrorism.* New York: St. Martin's Press.

Neuffer, Elizabeth. 1998. "40,000 Jobless Germans Protest." *The Boston Globe* February 6:A2.

Oberschall, Anthony. 1967. "The Los Angeles Riot of August 1965." *Social Problems* 15:322–341.

Oberschall, Anthony. 1973. *Social Conflict and Social Movements.* Englewood Cliffs, NJ: Prentice Hall.

O'Keefe, M., and Paul D. Shumaker. 1983. "Protest Effectiveness in Southeast Asia." *American Behavioral Scientist* 26:375–394.

Olzak, Susan. 1989. "Labor Unrest, Immigration, and Ethnic Conflict in Urban America, 1880–1914." *American Journal of Sociology* 94:1303–1333.

Olzak, Susan. 1992. *The Dynamics of Ethnic Competition and Conflict.* Stanford: Stanford University Press.

Olzak, Susan, and Suzanne Shanahan. 1996. "Deprivation and Race Riots: An Extension of Spilerman's Analysis." *Social Forces* 74:931–961.

Olzak, Susan, Suzanne Shanahan, and Elizabeth H. McEneaney. 1996. "Poverty, Segregation, and Race Riots: 1960 to 1993." *American Sociological Review* 61:590–613.

Paige, Jeffery. 1975. *Agrarian Revolution.* New York: Free Press.

Paige, Jeffery M. 1971. "Political Orientation and Riot Participation." *American Sociological Review* 36:810–820.

Pareto, Vilk. 1935 (1916). *The Mind and Society.* New York: Harcourt Brace and Company.

Park, Robert E., and Ernest W. Burgess. 1921. *Introduction to the Science of Sociology.* Chicago: University of Chicago Press.

Parrish, Michael. 1996. *The Lesser Terror: Soviet State Security, 1939–1953.* Westport, CT: Praeger.

Pattick, Elizabeth. 1997. *Women in New Religions.* New York: St. Martin's Press.

Perera, Victor. 1993. *Unfinished Conquest: The Guatemalan Tragedy.* Berkeley: University of California Press.

Perry, Joseph B., Jr., and M. D. Pugh. 1978. *Collective Behavior: Response to Social Stress.* St. Paul: West Publishing Co.

Pettee, George S. 1938. *The Process of Revolution.* New York: Harper and Row.

Piven, Frances Fox, and Richard A. Cloward. 1979. *Poor People's Movements: Why They Succeed, How They Fail.* New York: Vintage Books.

Pollak, Otto. 1950. *The Criminality of Women.* Philadelphia: University of Pennsylvania Press.

Polletta, Francesca. 1997. "Culture and Its Discontents: Recent Theorizing on the Cultural Dimensions of Protest." *Sociological Inquiry* 67:431–450.

Rand, Michael. 1998. *Criminal Victimization 1997: Changes 1996–97 with Trends 1993–97.* Washington, DC: Bureau of Justice Statistics, U.S. Department of Justice.

Ransford, H. Edward. 1967. "Isolation, Powerlessness, and Violence: A Study of Attitudes and Participation in the Watts Riot." *American Journal of Sociology* 73:581–591.

Rapoport, David (ed.). 1988. *Inside Terrorist Organizations.* New York: Columbia University Press.

Rasler, Karen. 1996. "Concessions, Repression, and Political Protest in the Iranian Revolution." *American Sociological Review* 61.

Read, Christopher. 1996. *From Tsar to Soviets: The Russian People and Their Revolution, 1917–1921.* New York: Oxford University Press.

Reich, Walter. 1990. *The Origins of Terrorism.* New York: Cambridge University Press.

Ridgeway, James. 1990. *Blood in the Face: The Ku Klux Klan, Aryan Nations, Nazi Skinheads, and the Rise of a New White Culture.* New York: Thunder's Mouth Press.

Ringel, Cheryl. 1997. *Criminal Victimization 1996.* Washington, DC: U.S. Department of Justice.

Robbins, Thomas, and D. Anthony. 1995. "Sects and Violence." Pp. 236–262 in *Armageddon in Waco,* edited by S. Wright. Chicago: University of Chicago Press.

Rogers, Patrick. 1994. "Is Murder 'Justifiable Homicide'?" *Newsweek* August 8:22.

Rosenbaum, Jill Leslie. 1987. "Social Control, Gender, and Delinquency: An Analysis of Drug, Property and Violent Offenders." *Justice Quarterly* 4:117–142.

Rosenfeld, Michael J. 1997. "Celebration, Politics, Selective Looting and Riots: A Micro Level Study of the Bulls Riot of 1992 in Chicago." *Social Problems* 44:483–502.

Ross, Jeffrey Ian. 1998. "A Model of the Psychological Causes of Oppositional Political Terrorism." Pp. 48–53 in *Violence and Terrorism 98/99*, edited by B. Schechterman and M. Slann. Guilford, CT: Dushkin Publishing Group.

Ross, John. 1998. "After Massacre, Wider Trouble Looms in Mexico." *National Catholic Reporter* 34:13.

Rubenstein, Richard E. 1970. *Rebels in Eden: Mass Political Violence in the United States.* Boston: Little, Brown.

Rubenstein, Richard E. 1987. *Alchemists of Revolution: Terrorism in the Modern World.* New York: Basic Books.

Rubin, Peter. 1995. "Terror Struck: Gutting Habeas Corpus." *The New Republic.* September 4. Pp. 17–19.

Rudwick, Elliott M. 1964. *Race Riot at East St. Louis: July 2, 1917.* Carbondale, IL: Southern University Illinois Press.

Rule, James B. 1988. *Theories of Civil Violence.* Berkeley: University of California Press.

Russakoff, Dale, and Serge F. Kovaleski. 1998. "Two Angry Men." Pp. 109–121 in *Violence and Terrorism 98/99*, edited by B. Schechterman and M. Slann. Guilford, CT: Dushkin Publishing Group.

Salert, Barbara. 1976. *Revolutions and Revolutionaries.* New York: Elsevier.

Salyer, Lucy E. 1995. *Laws Harsh as Tigers: Chinese Immigration and the Shaping of Modern Immigration Law.* Chapel Hill: University of North Carolina Press.

Sargent, Lyman Tower (ed.). 1995. *Extremism in America: A Reader.* New York: New York University Press.

Schmemann, Serge. 1998. "20 Jailed Arab Women Say No to Israeli Offer of Freedom." Pp. 141–142 in *Violence and Terrorism 98/99*, edited by B. Schechterman and M. Slann. Guilford, CT: Dushkin Publishing Group.

Schmid, Alex P., and Janny de Graaf. 1982. *Violence as Communication: Insurgent Terrorism and the Western News Media.* Beverly Hills: Sage Publications.

Schmid, Alex P., and Albert J. Jongman. 1988. *Political Terrorism.* Amsterdam: North-Holland Publishing Company.

Schram, Sanford F., and Patrick Turbett. 1983. "Civil Disorder and the Welfare Explosion." *American Sociological Review* 48:408–414.

Scott, James C. 1977. "Peasant Revolution: A Dismal Science." *Comparative Politics* 9:231–248.

Sears, David O., and T. M. Tomlinson. 1971. "Riot Ideology in Los Angeles: A Study of Negro Attitudes." Pp. 375–388 in *The Black Revolt: The Civil Rights Movement, Ghetto Uprisings, and Separatism*, edited by J. A. Geschwender. Englewood Cliffs, NJ: Prentice Hall.

Sederberg, Peter C. 1989. *Terrorist Myths: Illusion, Rhetoric, and Reality.* Englewood Cliffs, NJ: Prentice Hall.

Sederberg, Peter C. 1994. *Fires Within: Political Violence and Revolutionary Change.* New York: HarperCollins.

Sederberg, Peter C. 1998. "Explaining Terrorism." Pp. 24–26 in *Violence and Terrorism*, edited by B. Schechterman and M. Slann. Guilford, CT: Dushkin Publishing Group.

Segaller, Stephen. 1987. *Invisible Armies: Terrorism into the 1990s.* San Diego: Harcourt Brace Jovanovich.

Sharp, Gene. 1973. *The Politics of Nonviolent Action.* Boston: Porter Sargent.

Shaw, Martin (ed.). 1984. *War, State, and Society.* New York: St. Martin's Press.

Shillinger, Kurt. 1998. "Wave of Political Turmoil Sweeps Zimbabwe." *The Boston Globe* February 8:A10.

Short, James F., Jr., and Marvin E. Wolfgang. 1972. "Perspectives on Collective Violence." Pp. 3–32 in *Collective Violence*, edited by James F. Short and Marvin E. Wolfgang. Chicago: Aldine-Atherton.

Shupe, Anson D., and David Bromley. 1980. *The New Vigilantes: Deprogrammers, Anti-Cultists, and the New Religions*. Beverly Hills: Sage Publications.

Simon, Rita James. 1975. *Women and Crime*. Lexington, MA: Lexington Books.

Singer, Benjamin D. 1968. "Mass Media and Communication Processes in the Detroit Riot of 1967." *Public Opinion Quarterly* 34:236–245.

Singer, Margaret. 1995. *The History of Cults in the United States*. New York: Columbia University Press.

Skocpol, Theda. 1979. *States and Social Revolutions: A Comparative Analysis of France, Russia, and China*. New York: Cambridge University Press.

Skocpol, Theda. 1994. *Social Revolutions in the Modern World*. New York: Cambridge University Press.

Skocpol, Theda, and Ellen Ray Trimberger. 1978. "Revolutions and the World- Historical Development of Capitalism." *Berkeley Journal of Sociology* 22:101–113.

Skolnick, Jerome H. 1969. *The Politics of Protest*. New York: Simon and Schuster.

Skorneck, Carolyn. 1992. "683,000 Women Raped in 1990, New Government Study Finds." *The Boston Globe* April 24:1.

Slann, Martin. 1993. "The State as Terrorist." Pp. 68–71 in *Violence and Terrorism*, edited by B. Schechterman and M. Slann. Guilford, CT: Dushkin Publishing Group.

Smelser, Neil J. 1963. *Theory of Collective Behavior*. New York: Free Press.

Smith, Brent L. 1994. *Terrorism in America: Pipe Bombs and Pipe Dreams*. Albany, NY: State University of New York Press.

Snow, David A., and Robert D. Benford. 1992. "Master Frames and Cycles of Protest." Pp. 133–155 in *Frontiers in Social Movement Theory*, edited by A. D. Morris and C. M. Mueller. New Haven: Yale University Press.

Snow, David A., E. Burke Rochford, Jr., Steven K. Worden, and Robert D. Benford. 1986. "Frame Alignment Processes, Micromobilization and Movement Partici-pation." *American Sociological Review* 51:456–481.

Snow, David A., Louis A. Zurcher, Jr., and Sheldon Ekland-Olson. 1980. "Social Networks and Social Movements: A Microstructural Approach to Differential Recruitment." *American Sociological Review* 45:787–801.

Snow, David E., and Pamela E. Oliver. 1995. "Social Movements and Collective Behavior: Social Psychological Dimensions and Considerations." Pp. 571–599 in *Sociological Perspectives on Social Psychology*, edited by K. S. Cook, G. A. Fine, and J. S. House. Boston: Allyn and Bacon.

Snyder, David, and William R. Kelly. 1976. "Industrial Violence in Italy, 1878–1903." *American Journal of Sociology* 82:131–162.

Southern Poverty Law Center. 1994a. "Anti-Immigrant Violence Rages Nationwide: White Supremacists Exploiting Fear of Immigrants." *Intelligence Report* August:1.

Southern Poverty Law Center. 1994b. "The Hidden Victims: Hate Crime Against American Indians Under-Reported." *Intelligence Report* October:1.

Southern Poverty Law Center. 1994c. "Violent Hate Crime Remains at Record Levels Nationwide." *Intelligence Report* March:1.

Spilerman, Seymour. 1970. "The Causes of Racial Disturbances: A Comparison of Alternative Explanations." *American Sociological Review* 35:627–649.

Spilerman, Seymour. 1971. "The Causes of Racial Disturbances: Tests of an Explanation." *American Sociological Review* 36:427–442.

Spilerman, Seymour. 1976. "Structural Characteristics of Cities and the Severity of Racial Disorders." *American Sociological Review* 41:771–793.

Stacey, Judith. 1983. *Patriarchy and Socialist Revolution in China*. Berkeley: University of California Press.

Staub, Ervin. 1989. *The Roots of Evil*. Cambridge: Cambridge University Press.

Steedly, Homer and John Foley. 1979. "The Success of Protest Groups: Multivariate Analyses." *Social Science Research* 8:1–15.

Steffensmeier, Darrell. 1980. "Sex Differences in Patterns of Adult Crime, 1965–77: A Review and Assessment." *Social Forces* 58:1080–1108.

Steffensmeier, Darrell, and Emilie Allan. 1995. "Criminal Behavior: Gender and Age." Pp. 83–113 in *Criminology: A Contemporary Handbook*, edited by J. F. Sheley. Belmont, CA: Wadsworth Publishing Company.

Stock, Catherine McNichol. 1997. *Rural Radicals*. New York: Penguin Books.

Stoen, Tim. 1997. "The Most Horrible Night of My Life." *Newsweek* April 7:44–45.

Stohl, Michael (ed.). 1988. *The Politics of Terrorism*. New York: Dekker.

Stohl, Michael, and George A. Lopez. 1984. "The State as Terrorist: The Dynamics of Government Violence and Repression." Westport, CT: Greenwood Press.

Storr, Anthony. 1991. *Human Destructiveness*. New York: Grove Weidenfeld.

Strasser, Steven, and Tom Post. 1995. "A Cloud of Terror—and Suspicion." *Newsweek* April 3:36.

Straus, Murray A., and Richard J. Gelles. 1986. "Societal Change and Change in Family Violence from 1975 to 1985 as Revealed by Two National Surveys." *Journal of Marriage and the Family* 48:465–479.

Tabor, James D., and Eugene V. Gallagher. 1995. *Why Waco? Cults and the Battle for Religious Freedom in America*. Berkeley: University of California Press.

Taft, Philip, and Philip Ross. 1990. "American Labor Violence: Its Causes, Character, and Outcome." Pp. 174–186 in *Violence: Patterns, Causes, Public Policy*, edited by N. A. Weiner, M. A. Zahn, and R. J. Sagi. San Diego: Harcourt Brace Jovanovich.

Tarrow, Sidney. 1998. *Power in Movement: Social Movements and Contentious Politics*. New York: Cambridge University Press.

Taylor, Maxwell, and Helen Ryan. 1988. "Fanaticism, Political Suicide, and Terrorism." *Terrorism* 11:91–111.

Taylor, Verta. 1995. "Watching for Vibes: Bringing Emotions into the Study of Feminist Organizations." Pp. 223–233 in *Feminist Organizations: Harvest of the New Women's Movement*, edited by M. M. Ferree and P. Y. Martin. Philadelphia: Temple University Press.

Taylor, Verta, and Nancy E. Whittier. 1992. "Collective Identity in Social Movement Communities: Lesbian Feminist Mobilization." Pp. 104–129 in *Frontiers in Social Movement Theory*, edited by A. D. Morris and C. M. Mueller. New Haven: Yale University Press.

Taylor, Verta, and Nancy E. Whittier. 1995. "Analytical Approaches to Social Movement Culture: The Culture of the Women's Movement." Pp. 163–187 in *Social Movements and Culture*, edited by H. Johnston and B. Klandermans. Minneapolis: University of Minnesota Press.

Terry, Dan. 1994. "Anti-war Fugitive Surfaces, His Rage Long Gone." *The New York Times* January 7:A1.

Thaxton, Ralph. 1983. *China Turned Rightside Up*. New Haven: Yale University Press.

Thomas, Evan. 1997. "Web of Death." *Newsweek* April 7:26–37.

Tilly, Charles. 1978. *From Mobilization to Revolution*. Reading, MA: Addison Wesley.

Tilly, Charles. 1986. *The Contentious French: Four Centuries of Popular Struggle*. Cambridge, MA: Harvard University Press.

Tilly, Charles. 1989. "Collective Violence in European Perspective." Pp. 62–100 in *Violence in America: Protest, Rebellion, Reform*, vol. 2, edited by Ted Robert Gurr. Newbury Park, CA: Sage Publications.

Tilly, Charles. 1995. *Popular Contention in Great Britain, 1754–1837*. Cambridge, MA: Harvard University Press.

Tilly, Charles, Louise Tilly, and Richard Tilly. 1975. *The Rebellious Century, 1830–1930*. Cambridge, MA: Harvard University Press.

Tocqueville, Alexis de. 1955 (1856). *The Old Regime and the French Revolution*. Garden City, NY: Doubleday.

Tolnay, Stewart E., and E. M. Beck. 1995. *A Festival of Violence: An Analysis of Southern Lynchings, 1882–1930*. Urbana: University of Illinois Press.

Tomlinson, T. M. 1968. "The Development of a Riot Ideology among Urban Negroes." *American Behavioral Scientist* 11:27–31.

Toy, Eckard V., Jr. 1989. "Right-Wing Extremism from the Ku Klux Klan to the Order, 1915 to 1988." Pp. 131–152 in *Violence in America: Protest, Rebellion, Reform*, vol. 2, edited by Ted Robert Gurr. Newbury Park, CA: Sage Publications.

Trelease, Allen W. 1971. *White Terror: The Ku Klux Klan Conspiracy and Southern Reconstruction*. New York: Harper and Row.

Turner, Ralph. 1969. "The Public Perception of Protest." *American Sociological Review* 34:815–831.

Turner, Ralph H. 1964. "Collective Behavior." Pp. 382–425 in *Handbook of Modern Sociology*, edited by R. E. L. Faris. Chicago: Rand McNally.

Turner, Ralph H., and Lewis M. Killian. 1957. *Collective Behavior*. Englewood Cliffs, NJ: Prentice Hall.

Turner, Ralph H., and Lewis M. Killian. 1972. *Collective Behavior*. Englewood Cliffs, NJ: Prentice Hall.

Turner, Ralph H., and Lewis M. Killian. 1987. *Collective Behavior*. Englewood Cliffs, NJ: Prentice Hall.

Turner, Stansfield. 1991. *Terrorism and Democracy*. New York: Houghton Mifflin.

Useem, Bert. 1980. "Solidarity Model, Breakdown Model, and the Boston Anti-Busing Movement." *American Sociological Review* 45:357–369.

Useem, Bert. 1985. "Disorganization and the New Mexico Prison Riot of 1980." *American Sociological Review* 50:667–688.

Useem, Bert. 1998. "Breakdown Theories of Collective Action." *Annual Review of Sociology* 24:215–238.

Useem, Bert, Camille Camp, and George Camp. 1996. *Resolution of Prison Riots: Strategies and Policies*. New York: Oxford University Press.

Useem, Bert, and Peter Kimball. 1989. *States of Siege: U.S. Prison Riots, 1971–1986*. New York: Oxford University Press.

U.S. News & World Report. 1996. "The FBI vs. the Mountaineer Militia." October 21:22.

Vetter, Harold J., and Gary R. Perlstein. 1991. *Perspectives on Terrorism*. Pacific Grove, CA: Brooks/Cole Publishing Company.

Walker, Thomas W. 1985. *Nicaragua: Land of Sandino*. Boulder, CO: Westview Press.

Walsh, Edward J., and Rex H. Warland. 1983. "Social Movement Involvement in the Wake of a Nuclear Accident: Activists and Free Riders in the TMI Area." *American Sociological Review* 48:764–780.

Walton, John. 1984. *Reluctant Rebels: Comparative Studies of Revolutions and Under-development*. New York: Columbia University Press.

Wanderer, J. J. 1969. "Index of Riot Severity and Some Correlates." *American Journal of Sociology* 74:500–505.

Ward, Colleen A. 1995. *Attitudes Toward Rape: Feminist and Social Perspectives*. Thousand Oaks, CA: Sage Publications.

Wardlaw, Grant. 1989. *Political Terrorism: Theory, Tactics, and Counter-measures*. Cambridge: Cambridge University Press.

Waskow, Arthur I. 1967. *From Race Riot to Sit-In: 1919 and the 1960s*. Garden City, NY: Anchor Books.

Weber, Max. 1959. *The Sociology of Religion*. Boston: Beacon Press.

Weber, Max. 1968(1921). *Economy and Society*. Translated and edited by Guenther Roth and Claus Wittich. Berkeley: University of California Press.

Webster's Ninth New Collegiate Dictionary. 1983. Springfield, MA: G&C Merriam.

Wege, Carol Anthony. 1993. "The Abu Nidal Organization." Pp. 50–54 in *Violence and Terrorism*, edited by B. Schechterman and M. Slann. Guilford, CT: Dushkin Publishing Group.

Wei, William. 1985. *Counterrevolution in China*. Ann Arbor: University of Michigan Press.

Weimann, Gabriel, and Conrad Winn. 1994. *The Theater of Terror: Mass Media and International Terrorism*. New York: Longman.

Weitzer, Ronald. 1995. *Policing Under Fire: Ethnic Conflict and Police-Community Relations in Northern Ireland*. Albany, NY: State University of New York Press.

White, Jonathan R. 1991. *Terrorism: An Introduction*. Pacific Grove, CA: Brooks/Cole Publishing Company.

White, Robert W. 1993. "On Measuring Political Violence: Northern Ireland, 1969–1980." *American Sociological Review* 58:575–585.

Whittier, Nancy. 1995. *Feminist Generations: The Persistence of the Radical Women's Movement*. Philadelphia: Temple University Press.

Wicker, Tom. 1975. *A Time to Die*. New York: Quadrangle Books.

Wilkinson, Paul. 1986. *Terrorism and the Liberal State*. New York: New York University Press.

Wilmington News Journal. 1996. "West Virginia Militia Members Charged in Bomb Plot." October 12:1A.

Wilson, William Julius. 1996. *When Work Disappears: The World of the New Urban Poor*. New York: Alfred A. Knopf.

Wolf, Eric R. 1969. *Peasant Wars of the Twentieth Century*. New York: Harper and Row.

Wood, James L., and Maurice Jackson. 1982. *Social Movements: Development, Participation, and Dynamics*. Belmont, CA: Wadsworth.

Woodward, Ralph Lee, Jr. 1985. *Central America: A Nation Divided*. New York: Oxford University Press.

Wright, Joanne. 1991. *Terrorist Propaganda: The Red Army Faction and the Provisional IRA*. New York: St. Martin's Press.

Wright, Robin. 1986. *Sacred Rage*. New York: Touchstone.

Wright, Stuart A. 1995. *Armageddon in Waco: Critical Perspectives on the Branch Davidian Conflict*. Chicago: University of Chicago Press.

Zellner, William. 1995. *Countercultures: A Sociological Analysis*. New York: St. Martin's Press.

Zimring, Franklin E., and Gordon Hawkins. 1997. *Crime Is Not the Problem: Lethal Violence in America*. New York: Oxford University Press.

Zulaika, Joseba. 1996. *Terror and Taboo: The Follies, Fables, and Faces of Terrorism*. New York: Routledge.

Zurcher, Louis A., and David A. Snow. 1981. "Collective Behavior: Social Movements." Pp. 447–482 in Social Psychology: Sociological Perspectives, edited by M. Rosenberg and R. M. Turner. New York: Basic Books.

Name Index

Abrahamian, Ervand, 61
Abrahams, Naomi, 25
Adler, Freda, 86
Alexander II, Czar of
    Russia, 56
Alger, Horatio, 50
Allan, Emilie, 36
Alter, Jonathan, 63
Anbinder, Tyler Gregory, 32,
    68
Andrews, Kenneth D., 118,
    121, 122, 123
Anthony, D., 98, 99
Applewhite, Marshall Herff,
    97
Aquino, Michael, 102
Arafat, Yasser, 74
Aristotle, 17
Aronowitz, Alexis, 110
Asahara, Shoko, 96
Auerbach, Jerold S., 100

Bachman, Ronet, 69
Balbus, Isaac, 29, 31, 121
Ball-Rokeach, Sandra J., 26
Barkan, Steven E., 9, 10, 26,
    36, 85, 86, 119, 121,
    122
Barker, Eileen, 95
Barrett, David V., 100
Bart, Pauline B., 70
Beam, Louis, 109
Beck, E. M., 22, 67, 81, 82,
    116
Belanger, Sarah, 22, 23, 106
Belluck, Pam, 111, 112
Benesh, Peter, 80
Benford, Robert D., 26
Bennett, David Harry, 68
Berk, Richard A., 11, 12, 17
Bernstein, Iver, 2, 32
Bianco, Lucien, 58
Bjornson, Karin, 107
Black, George, 77, 121
Blalock, Hubert, 82
Bloombaum, Milton, 39
Blum, William, 77
Blumberg, Mark, 45
Blumer, Herbert, 15
Boin, R. Argen, 45

Bonacich, Edna, 22, 82
Booth, Alan, 85
Boyle, Kevin, 107
Bragg, Rick, 69
Bramson, Leon, 3
Brandt, Daniel, 95, 101
Braswell, M., 42
Breault, Marc, 92
Brinton, Crane, 51
Broad, Kendal, 68, 105, 106
Brockett, Charles, 123
Brockman, James R., 121
Broehl, Wayne G., Jr., 71
Bromley, David, 101
Brooks, David, 76
Brown, D. Alexander, 67, 77
Brown, Richard Maxwell,
    32, 34, 70, 71, 108
Browne, Angela, 69
Brownmiller, Susan, 70
Bruce, Robert V., 33
Brysk, Alison, 77
Burgess, Ernest W., 15
Burke, Kathy, 97, 102
Burstein, Paul, 7, 118, 119,
    120
Bushnell, Timothy, 76
Butler, Richard, 109, 110
Button, James W., 7, 34, 41,
    42, 119

Camp, Camille, 45
Camp, George, 45
Campling, J.O., 85, 86
Camus, Albert, 124
Cannon, Lou, 2
Capeci, Dominic J., Jr., 34
Caplan, Nathan S., 35, 37
Capone, Al, 5
Caputi, Jane, 70
Card, Claudia, 70
Carr, Caleb, 86
Carter, Jimmy, 60
Chalk, Frank, 77
Chalmers, David M., 67
Champion, Dean J., 6
Charters, David, 87
Chatfield, Charles, 77
Chavarria, Ricardo E., 59
Cherrington, Ruth, 121

Chiang Kai-shek, 58
Chomsky, Noam, 77
Churchill, Ward, 78
Claridge, David, 76
Clarity, James F., 73
Clark, Terry N., 39, 40, 115
Clarke, James W., 5
Clemetson, Lynnette, 69
Cloward, Richard A., 7
Cobban, Helena, 74
Cohn, Steven F., 121
Collins, John J., 90, 93, 94,
    101
Collins, Randall, 14
Colvin, Mark, 42, 44
Conquest, Robert, 77
Corzine, Jay, 82
Corzine, Lin, 82
Coser, Lewis, 14, 15, 27
Creech, James, 82
Crenshaw, Martha, 79
Cullen, Francis T., 85
Cullen, John B., 85
Cullen, Kevin, 69, 73
Curitus, Mary, 70
Currie, Elliott, 16, 17

Darnovsky, Marcy, 25
Davies, James C., 17, 52, 53
DeBenedetti, Charles, 77
Dees, Morris, 73, 105
DeFronzo, James A., 55, 56,
    57, 58, 61, 115
de Graaf, Janny, 70, 83, 84
Della Porta, Donatella, 10,
    121, 122
Dietz, Thomas, 7
DiIulio, John, Jr., 45
Dillingham, S., 42
Dollard, John, 17
Donald, Michael, 108
Doob, Leonard W., 17
Downes, Bryan T., 34, 39,
    41, 115
Downton, James V., 94
Drake, Richard, 74
Drass, Kriss A., 43
Duff, Ernest, 74
Duin, Menno J. Van, 45
Dwyer, Jim, 75

Edwards, Lyford, 51
Einwohner, Rachel L., 7, 118, 119, 120
Eisinger, Peter K., 39, 120
Ekland-Olson, Sheldon, 20, 94
Engels, Friedrich, 49, 50, 51
Epstein, Barbara, 25
Evans, Will, 2

Feagin, Joe R., 29, 31
Feldberg, Michael, 32
Ferree, Myra Marx, 117
Feuer, Lewis S., 16
Finke, Roger, 90
Finn, John E., 84, 87
Fitzgerald, Louise F., 69
Fitzpatrick, Sheila, 56
Flacks, Richard, 16, 25
Fogelson, Robert M., 31, 33, 34, 35, 39
Foley, John, 7
Foster, Alphonzo, 95
Foster, John, 50
Fox, George, 100
Freud, Sigmund, 14, 15, 28
Frey, R. Scott, 7
Fried, Joseph P., 63
Fromm, Erich, 80

Galanter, Marc, 90, 91, 92, 93, 94
Gale, William, 109
Gallagher, Eugene V., 92, 96, 102
Gamson, William A., 7, 17, 23, 27, 82, 117, 118, 119
Garrow, David J., 26, 119
Gegax, T. Trent, 69
Gelles, Richard A., 69
Geschwender, James A., 37
Gibbs, Jack P., 65
Gilbert, Martin, 77, 81
Gilligan, James, 6
Giraldo, Javier, 77
Giugni, Marco G., 118, 119, 120
Glover, Jonathan, 76
Godoman, Lisa A., 69
Goethals, George W., 3
Golden, Kathryn M., 85
Goldstone, Jack A., 6, 7, 48, 51, 52, 53, 54, 55, 121

Goode, Erich, 16, 19, 20, 21, 22, 30, 35, 36
Goodwin, Jeff, 54
Goti, Jamie E. Malamud, 77
Gotteried, Robert S., 112
Gould, Roger V., 55
Green, Jerrold D., 61
Greene, Thomas H., 49
Griffin, Susan, 70
Grimshaw, Allen D., 4, 10
Groebel, Jo, 3
Grynspan, Devora, 59, 60
Guillemin, Jeanne, 67
Gurney, Joan Neff, 18
Gurr, Ted Robert, 18, 34, 48, 52, 65, 66, 68, 70, 71, 72, 73, 75, 116
Guttridge, Leonard, 78

Hacker, Andrew, 4, 47
Hadden, Tom, 107
Hahn, Harlan, 29, 31
Hale, Matthew F., 111, 112
Halperin, Ernst, 74
Hamm, Mark S., 68, 105, 111
Hampton, Fred, 78
Hannon, James, 95
Hawkins, Gordon, 9
Heise, Lori, 70
Henry, David, 33
Herman, Edward, 74
Hester, Marianne, 70
Hewitt, Christopher, 87, 88
Heymann, Philip B., 87
Hicks, Robert D., 100, 102, 103
Hinde, Robert A., 3
Hing, Bill Ong, 33
Hobsbawn, Eric, 29, 48
Hoerder, Dirk, 70
Hoffman, Bill, 97, 102
Hoffman, Bruce, 64, 73, 75, 83
Hollander, Jocelyn A., 7, 118, 119, 120
Hopper, Rex, 51

Irwin, John, 42, 43
Isaac, Larry, 41, 119

Jackson, Maurice, 22
Jacobs, Sally, 69
Jasper, James M., 17, 24, 117

Jefferson, Thomas, 112
Jelavich, Barbara, 48
Jenkins, Philip, 68
Jenness, Valerie, 68, 105, 106
Johnson, Norris, 99
Johnston, Hank, 25
Jonassohn, Kurt, 77, 107
Jones, Jim, 96
Jongman, Albert J., 64, 80
Jordan, Donald A., 58
Juckes, Tim J., 88

Kalof, Linda, 7
Kanter, Rosabeth, 93
Kaphart, William M., 100
Kaplan, David E., 74
Kaplan, Jeffrey, 107
Kappeler, Victor E., 45
Keita, Gwendolyn Puryear, 69
Kelly, William R., 19, 41, 119
Kerner Commission, 35, 39
Khomeini, Ayatollah Ruhollah, 61
Kidder, Rushworth M., 83, 84
Killian, Lewis M., 6, 16, 28
Kim, Hyung-Chan, 33
Kimball, Peter, 42, 43, 44, 45
Kimmel, Michael S., 49, 50, 51, 52, 53, 54
King, Martin Luther, Jr., 72
King, Rodney, 2, 30, 34
Kitano, Harry H.L., 113
Klandermans, Bert, 10, 23, 24, 25, 114, 116, 117, 121, 122
Klein, Dorie, 85
Kleist, Trina, 2
Klotz, Audie, 88
Koopmans, Ruud, 122
Koresh, David, 92, 96
Kornhauser, William, 20, 35
Koss, Mary P., 69
Kovaleski, Serge F., 63
Kressel, Neil J., 64
Kriesi, Hanspeter, 120
Kurzman, Charles, 61

Lakshmanan, Indira A. R., 24
Lang, Kurt, 3

LaPierre, Wayne, 104
Laqueur, Walter, 64, 79
Lawrence, Richard, 42
LeBon, Gustave, 15, 21, 28, 35
Lens, Sidney, 33, 71
Levin, Jack, 68, 105, 106
Lewis, I.M., 101
Lichbach, Mark Irving, 121, 122
Lieberson, Stanley, 39
Lieske, Joel A., 39
Lifton, Robert Jay, 80, 81
Lincoln, Abraham, 32, 50
Linedecker, Clifford, 92
Livingston, Steven, 84
Lofland, John, 8, 93, 94, 95, 98
Lomasky, Loren E., 65
Long, Huey, 109
Lopez, George A., 78
Louis Philippe, King of France, 48
Lynch, Charles, 71
Lynch, Colum, 77

McAdam, Doug, 6, 8, 10, 17, 20, 21, 23, 26, 38, 41, 48, 78, 82, 118, 119, 120, 121, 122
McCamant, John F., 74, 78
McCarry, Charles, 96
McCarthy, John D., 10, 20, 21, 23, 38, 82, 118, 119, 120
McCorkle, Richard C., 43
McDevitt, Jack, 68, 105, 106
McEneaney, Elizabeth H., 22, 40, 115
McGovern, George S., 78
McGrory, Brian, 69
MacLean, Nancy, 67
McPhail, Clark, 17, 19, 21, 30, 31, 35, 36, 37, 40
McVey, Timothy, 107
Mahan, Sue, 42, 44, 45
Maharaj Ji, 101
Malecki, Edward S., 49
Mao Zedong, 58
Marshall, Andrew, 74
Martin, L. John, 84
Martin, Marie Alexandrine, 77
Martin, Randy, 42, 43, 44

Marx, Gary T., 6, 8, 21, 23, 30, 121
Marx, Karl, 49, 50, 51, 54
Matazorkis, Nick, 97
Matthews, Robert, 109
Mazur, Allan, 84
Melman, Yossi, 76
Melton, J. Gordon, 94, 103
Melucci, Alberto, 25, 27
Messerschmidt, James W., 36
Metzger, John, 110
Metzger, Tom, 110
Meyer, David S., 124
Miethe, Terance, 43
Miles, Robert, 109
Miller, Abraham H., 87
Miller, David L., 17, 35, 98
Miller, Frederick D., 117
Miller, Mark, 97
Miller, Neal E., 17
Mirowsky, John, 7
Montgomery, Reid H., Jr., 42, 45
Moore, Joan, 112
Moore, Kelly, 78
Moran, Eileen Geil, 70
Morgan, J. P., 71
Morgan, William R., 39, 40, 115
Morris, Roger, 44
Moshiri, Farrokh, 49, 61
Mowerer, O. H., 17
Mueller, Carol McClurg, 119
Muller, Edward N., 19
Mullins, Wayman C., 68
Murphy, Raymond J., 35
Myers, Daniel J., 22, 40, 81, 115

Nacos, Brigitte Lesbens, 84
Nazian, Florence, 77
Nettles, Bonnie, 97
Neuburger, Luisella de Cataldo, 85, 86
Neuffer, Elizabeth, 24
Newsweek, 105
Nicholas II, Czar of Russia, 56
Nichols, Terry, 107

Oberschall, Anthony, 10, 17, 23, 35
Oegema, Dirk, 23, 24
O'Keefe, M., 119

Oliver, Pamela E., 10, 17, 19, 24, 25, 27, 116, 117, 118
Olzak, Susan, 22, 40, 106, 115, 116
Osgood, D. Wayne, 85

Pachon, Harry, 112
Paige, Jeffery M., 35, 37, 50, 54
Pareto, Vilfredo, 15
Park, Robert E., 15
Parrish, Michael, 77
Pattick, Elizabeth, 94
People Weekly, 95
Perera, Victor, 77
Perlstein, Gary R., 85, 86
Perry, Joseph B., Jr., 106
Pettee, George S., 51
Pinard, Maurice, 22, 23, 106
Piven, Frances Fox, 7
Pollak, Otto, 85
Polletta, Francesca, 25
Post, Tom, 96
Potter, Gary W., 45
Pugh, M. D., 106

Rand, Michael, 69
Ransford, H. Edward, 37
Rapoport, David, 76, 81
Rasler, Karen, 11, 22, 61, 121, 122, 123
Read, Christopher, 56
Reagan, Ronald, 60
Reich, Walter, 80
Reiter, Herbert, 121
Ridgeway, James, 109, 110, 111
Ringel, Cheryl, 5
Robbins, Thomas, 98, 99
Rochford, E. Burke, Jr., 26
Rogers, Patrick, 69
Romero, Oscar Arnulfo, 121
Rosenbaum, Jill Leslie, 85
Rosenfeld, Michael J., 30, 32
Ross, Catherine, 7
Ross, Jeffrey, 79
Ross, John, 2
Ross, Philip, 33, 71, 78
Rubenstein, Richard E., 4, 31, 34, 80, 86, 87, 88
Rudwick, Elliott M., 33
Rule, James B., 6, 14, 15, 17, 19, 20, 22, 25, 35, 49, 53

Russakoff, Dale, 63
Russell, Diana E. H., 70
Russo, Nancy Felipe, 69
Ryan, Helen, 76
Ryan, Leo, 96

Salert, Barbara, 49, 53
Saltzman, Linda E., 69
Salyer, Lucy E., 33
Santos Zelaya, José, 59
Sargent, Lyman Tower, 108
Saxon, Kurt, 104
Schmemann, Serge, 85
Schmid, Alex P., 64, 70, 80, 83, 84
Schneider, Steve, 92
Schram, Sanford F., 41
Scott, James C., 54
Sears, David O., 36, 37
Sears, Robert R., 17
Sederberg, Peter C., 23, 49, 50, 51, 62, 79–80, 81, 86, 87, 88
Segaller, Stephen, 74
Shah of Iran, 60
Shanahan, Suzanne, 22, 40, 115
Sharp, Gene, 62, 120
Shaw, Martin, 3
Shillinger, Kurt, 24
Short, James F., Jr., 3, 8
Shumaker, Paul D., 119
Shupe, Anson D., 101
Sighele, Scipio, 35
Silverman, Arnold K., 39
Simon, Rita James, 86
Sinclair, Lilith, 102
Singer, Benjamin D., 37, 38
Singer, Margaret, 90, 98, 99, 100, 101
Skocpol, Theda, 54–55, 56, 57, 121
Skolnick, Jerome H., 16, 17, 35
Skorneck, Carolyn, 69
Slann, Martin, 78
Smelser, Neil J., 16, 20–23
Smith, Benjamin Nathaniel, 111, 112
Smith, Brent L., 73, 75
Smith, Gerald L. K., 108–109
Snow, David A., 20, 25, 26, 48, 94
Snow, David E., 10, 17, 19, 24, 25, 27, 116, 117, 118

Snyder, David, 19
Somoza Garcia, Anastasio, 59, 60
Somoza Garcia, Luis, 59
Southern Poverty Law Center, 69
Spilerman, Seymour, 39, 40, 115
Stacey, Judith, 59
Stalin, Joseph, 77
Stark, Rodney, 90
Staub, Ervin, 106
Steedly, Homer, 7
Steffensmeier, Darrell, 36, 86
Stock, Catherine McNichol, 109–110
Stoen, Tim, 96
Stohl, Michael, 78, 87
Storr, Anthony, 80
Strasser, Steven, 96
Stratford, Lauren, 103
Straus, Murray A., 69
Swift, Wesley, 109

Tabor, James D., 92, 96, 102
Taft, Philip, 33, 71, 78
Tarrow, Sidney, 10, 23, 119, 120, 122, 124
Taylor, Maxwell, 76
Taylor, Verta, 17, 25, 27, 117
Thaxton, Ralph, 57
Thomas, Evan, 97
Tierney, Kathleen J., 18
Tilly, Charles, 3, 22, 23, 24, 25, 35, 55, 121
Tocqueville, Alexis de, 17–18, 53
Tolnay, Stewart E., 22, 67, 81, 82, 116
Tomlinson, T.M., 36, 37, 39, 40, 115
Toy, Eckard V., Jr., 67, 68, 108
Trelease, Allen W., 67
Trotsky, Leon, 48
Truman, Harry S., 8
Turbett, Patrick, 41
Turner, Ralph H., 6, 16, 26, 28
Turner, Stansfield, 86

U.S. News & World Report, 2

Useem, Bert, 19, 22, 24, 42, 43, 44, 45, 116

Valentini, Tiziana, 85, 86
Vetter, Harold J., 85, 86

Walker, Thomas W., 59
Wall, Jim Vander, 78
Walsh, Edward J., 24
Walton, John, 54
Wanderer, J. J., 39
Ward, Colleen A., 70
Wardlaw, Grant, 65, 86
Warland, Rex H., 24
Waskow, Arthur I., 33
Watson, James M., 35
Weber, Max, 7, 90
Webster's Ninth New Collegiate Dictionary, 65
Wege, Carol Anthony, 76
Weimann, Gabriel, 83, 84
Weitzer, Ronald, 73
White, Jonathan R., 66, 74, 76, 84, 87
White, Robert W., 73
Whittier, Nancy E., 17, 25, 27
Wicker, Tom, 45
Wilkinson, Paul, 66, 81
Wilmington News Journal, 2
Wilson, William Julius, 47
Winn, Conrad, 83, 84
Wolf, Eric R., 51, 55, 57
Wolfgang, Marvin E., 3, 8
Wood, James L., 21, 22
Woodward, 59
Worden, Steven K., 26
Wright, Joanne, 74
Wright, Robin, 74
Wright, Stuart, 98

Zald, Mayer N., 10, 20, 21, 23, 38, 82, 118, 119, 120
Zellner, William W., 100, 102, 104, 108
Zimmerman, Sherwood, 42, 43, 44
Zimring, Franklin E., 9
Zulaika, Joseba, 84
Zurcher, Louis A., Jr., 20, 25, 94

Subject Index

Abortion violence, 69
Abu Nidal, 76
Acid rock, 110
Activism, 23, 24
African American militants, 71–72
African Americans, 111
  in the cities, 32, 36–37, 39–40, 115
  migration to the North, 67
  political change for, 42–43
  in the South, 68–69, 81, 82
Aggressive behavior, 85
Agrarian societies, 54, 57
Airport metal detectors, 87
Altered states of consciousness, 91–92
American Federation of Labor (AFL), 71
American Party, 68
American Revolution, 2, 62, 70, 108
Amnesty International, 70, 88
Animal sacrifice, 103
Anti-abortion violence, 69
Anti-Catholics, 32
Anticult movement, 101–102
Antidraft riot, 2, 30
Anti-immigration movement, 32, 67, 68, 69, 108, 110
Anti-Semitism, 104, 110
Anti-war movement, 16, 72
Apolitical riots, 16, 30
Armenians, 77
Aryan Nations, 104, 109, 110–111
Aryan Youth Movement (AYM), 110
Asia, 74
Asian Americans, 69, 111
Assassinations, 5, 76, 109, 121
Astrology, 97
Attica, New York, state prison, 45

Attitudes, 23, 36–38
Aum Shrinrikyo (Supreme Truth) movement, 96
Austro-Hungarian Empire, 107
Authoritarian governments, 10, 77

Bakersfield, CA, 103
Beijing, China, 77, 121
Beirut, Lebanon, 84
Beliefs, 36–38
Biblical apocalypticism, 97
Birmingham, AL, 78
Black churches, 68
Black Liberation Army (BLA), 72
Black militants, 71
Black Nationalists, 72
Black Panther Party, 72, 78
Black Plague, 112
Black Power movement, 37, 72
Black pride, 41
Blacks. See African Americans
Black Sabbath, 102
Black September, 74
"Bloody Sunday" massacre, 56
Bolsheviks, 57
Bombings, 1, 2, 63, 69, 72, 73, 74, 75, 76
Bosnian Muslims, 107
Boundary Country, ID, 109
Bourgeoisie, 49
Branch Davidian Cult, 92, 96, 102, 104
Britain, 87
Brown v. Board of Education, 68
Buddhism, 96
Bureau of Alcohol, Tobacco, and Firearms (BATF), 105

Caffa, Italy, 112
Cambodia, 77
Capitalist society, 49, 50–51, 54

Castration, 97
Catholics, 68, 73
Celebration riots, 30
Celibacy, 101
Central America, 59–60, 123
Central Intelligence Agency (CIA), 60, 75
Chiapas, Mexico, 1–2
Chicago Bulls riot, 30
Chicago, IL, 30, 33
China. See People's Republic of China
Chinese Communist Party, 58
Chinese Exclusion Act, 33
Chinese immigrants, 33
Chinese Revolution of 1949, 57–59
Christian Identity, 104, 108
Christianity, 91
Christians, 107
Church of Jesus Christ Christian, 107–108
Church of Satan, 102
Citizens Freedom Foundation, 101
Citizen's Law Enforcement and Research Committee (Posse Comitatus), 107, 109
Civil liberties debate, 87
Civil Rights activists, 68, 71–72, 78
Civil Rights movement, 16, 26, 40, 68, 72, 108, 119, 122, 123
Civil violence, 6
Class consciousness, 50
Collective behavior, 10
  examples of, 6
  genesis and dynamics of, 13, 14
  individual-level explanations of, 13–20
  micro explanations of, 13
  norms of, 16
  recent studies of, 25–27
  social and structural explanations of, 20–25

Collective behavior
    tradition, 15–16
Collective identity, 27
Collective nonviolence, 120
Collective violence
    consequences of, 7,
        118–120
    explaining, 13–28, 79
    future of, 123–125
    history of, 3
    micro and macro
        approaches to, 8–10,
        114–115
    problem of, 1–12
    rationality of, 116–118
    structural roots of,
        114–116
    study of, 3–4, 118–120
    as war, 3
Colonial Period, 31–32,
    70–71, 100
Colorado, 78, 109
Colorado Fuel and Iron
    Company, 78
Communes, 93
Communist countries, 77
Communist Manifesto, The
    (Marx & Engels), 49
Computer technology, 101
Concentric circles model,
    106
Conflict of Generations, The
    (Feuer), 16
Contention, 24
Contra forces, 60
Council of American
    Witches, 103
Countercultures, 93, 100
Counterterrorism, 86–89
Croats, 107
*Crowd, The: A Study of the
    Popular Mind* (LeBon),
    15
Crowd behavior, 17, 117
Cuban Americans, 75–76
Cult Awareness Network
    (CAN), 101
Cult cops, 103
Cults, 90–103
    and authority, 98–99, 103
    beliefs, 98–99
    charismatic leadership in,
        91–92, 99
    classification of, 99–100

conversion process in,
    93–94
defined, 90–91
history of, 99–101
mystical, 99
pseudo-social scientific,
    99
recruitment in, 92–95
religious, 74, 90, 92, 94,
    99, 100
Satanic, 100, 102–103
in the U.S., 99–101
violence and, 6, 90,
    96–98, 99, 100
Cult survivors, 103
Cultural aspects, 25
Czars, 56

Declaration of
    Independence, 2
Democratic governments,
    10
Democratic societies, 21
Department of Justice, U.S.,
    105
Deprivation-frustration-
    aggression theory,
    17–19, 21
Deprogrammers, 101
Detroit, MI, 37, 38
Divine Light Mission, 94,
    100–101
Domestic violence, 69, 70
Doomsday cults, 98
Dowry deaths, 70
Dragon of the Invisible
    Empire, 110
Druids, 103

Eastern-style cults, 96, 99,
    100
East Germany, 110
East St. Louis, IL, 33
Economic boycott, 88
Economic conflict, 50
Economic crises, 53, 55, 57,
    58, 59, 61, 82
Economy, 22, 24
    wartime, 57
Eighteenth century, 31
Eighties, 25
El Salvador, 74, 121, 123
Emergent norm theory, 16
Emotions, 117–118

Ethnic competition model,
    22–23, 40, 106
Ethnic conflict, 107
    hate groups and, 112–113
    history of, 112–113
Ethnic violence, 23, 106
Executions, 77
Expressive violence, 6, 16,
    30

Farm crisis, 111
Far right, 110–111
Federal Bureau of Inves-
    tigation (FBI), 2, 105
Flagellants, 112–113
Food, high cost of, 54, 55
Forceful repression, 41
Framing, 26
France, 2, 14, 17–18
Free speech, right to, 112
French Canadians, 106
French Revolution, 2, 14,
    17–18, 64
Frustration-aggression
    theory, 17–19

Gang violence, 5
Gay rights movement, 27
Gender differences, 36,
    85–86
Generalized beliefs, 21
Genital mutilation, 70
Genocide, 76–77
Georgia Republic Militia, 2
Germany, 18, 24, 56, 57,
    74, 112, 123
Ghetto uprising, 29, 31
Greater White Racialist
    Movement, 109
*Group Psychology and the
    Analysis of the Ego*
    (Freud), 15
Gun control, 105
Gypsies, 77

Hale-Bopp comet, 97
Hallucinogens, 92
Hare Krishnas, 100
Harlem, New York City, 33
Hate crimes, 68–69, 105–106
Hate groups, 105–115
    characteristics of, 104
    development of, 90, 106
    history of, 4, 107–112

international movement
of, 110
leadership in, 106
social structure of,
106–107
violence in, 105, 108
Hayden Lake, ID, 110
Haymarket Riot, 33
Heaven's Gate cult, 94–95,
97–98
Hijacking, Beirut, 84
Hinduism, 96
Hizbollah, 76
Holocaust, 77, 107, 110
Homicides, 9–10, 69
Homosexuals, 68, 77, 97,
110, 111
Hostage situations, 44–45,
61, 74, 84
Human Individual Meta-
morphosis (HIM), 97

Idaho, 109, 110
Ideological differences, 37
Ideologies, 8
Immigrants, 32, 68, 69, 110.
See also Anti-immigration
movement
India, 70
Individual, role of, 23
Individual violence, 2–3,
5–6
Institutional Revolutionary
Party (PRN), 1–2
Instrumental violence, 6,
16, 30
Insurgent terrorism, 66, 70–
74, 86, 87
Intentional communities,
95. See also Cults
International terrorism, 75.
See also Transnational
terrorism
Internet, 105, 111, 124
Interpersonal contacts, 38
Iran, 76
Iranian Revolution of 1979,
60–61, 123
Irish Americans, 32, 71
Irish Catholics, 68
Irish Republican Army
(IRA), 65, 73, 106–107
Irrationality, 8
and involvement, 14–17

versus rationality, 6–8,
116–118
Islamic Jihad, 76

Jews, 68, 108, 111, 112
Jonestown, Guyana, 96–97,
102

Kabbalism, 103
Kenya, 1–12
Know-Nothing Party, 32,
68, 69
Ku Klux Klan (KKK), 66,
67–68, 69, 108, 109,
110, 111

Labor violence, 33, 71, 78
Land reform, 58–59
Latin America, 77
Latinos, 69
Leaderless cells, 106
Leaderless resistance model,
107
Leadership
in cults, 91–92, 99
in hate groups, 106
Lebanon, 76
Legal control, 121
Legal repression, 121
Lepers, 112
Liberation theology
doctrine, 60
Libyan intelligence agents,
75
Lincoln Center, 75
Lockerbie, Scotland, 63, 75
London *Times*, 84
Loner image, 20
Los Angeles, CA, 2, 34, 35,
36–37
Louisiana Klan, 110
Low-income housing, 41
Ludlow, CO, 78
Lynchings, 67, 71, 82

Manchester, England, 73
Marxian theory, 49–51, 53,
54, 58
Massacres, 56, 78
Mass suicide, 96–97, 102
Means of production, 49
Media coverage, effect of,
83–84, 87
Mentally ill, 8

Metal detectors, 87
Mexican-American War of
1846, 112
Mexican rebels, 1–2
Mexicans, 112
Michigan Ku Klux Klan, 109
Michigan Militia, 105
Micro explanations, 13
Middle Ages, 112
Middle Eastern terrorists,
63, 65, 74, 76
Milan, Italy, 74
Military crises, 53
Militia groups, 90, 104–105
and authority, 2, 105
compared to cults, 104
danger of, 4, 73
religious beliefs in, 104
Militia of Montana, 105
Millennial cults, 98
Millerites, 100
Mississippi, 123
Mobile, AL, 108
Mobilization for action,
21–22
Molly Maguires, 71
Montana, 105
Moonies, 92, 94, 95, 100
Moscow, Russia, 57
Munich Olympics, 74
Mysticism, 94, 97, 103

National Guard, 41, 78
National Rifle Association
(NRA), 104
Native Americans, 66–67,
69, 77, 78
Nativist movement, 68, 108
Natural history approach,
51–52
Nazi death camps, 81. See
also Holocaust
Nazi doctors, 80
Neo-Christian cults, 100
Neo-Nazis, 104
Neopagans, 103
New Age mysticism, 94, 97
Newark, NJ, 37
New Klan, 109
New religious movements
(NRMS), 94
News media, 83–84, 87
New World Liberation
Front, 72

New York City, 2, 30, 32, 75
Nian Rebellion, 58
Nicaraguan Revolution of
    1979, 59–60
Nineteenth century, 32–33
Noninstitutional behavior,
    15–16
Nonviolence, 7, 26, 72, 100,
    119, 122
Norm theory, 16
North Atlantic Treaty Orga-
    nization (NATO), 74
Northern Ireland, 1–12, 65,
    73

Objective deprivation, 119
Occult religious groups, 94
Occult rituals, 103
Official IRA, 73
Oil depositories, 60
Oklahoma City Federal
    Building bombing, 63,
    73, 87, 107
Omagh, Northern Ireland,
    1–12
Omega, 7, 75
Oneida Community, 100
Order, The, 104, 109, 110
Ordinary crimes, 5
Organizational contacts, 38
Organizational factors, 55
Organized crime, 5
Ottoman Empire, 107

Pacifists, 123–125
Pagans, 102
Paki-bashing, 110
Pakistan, 70
Palestinian Liberation
    Organization (PLO), 65
Pan American flight 103
    bombing, 63, 75
Paramilitary groups,
    104–105
Paris Commune uprising, 55
Peasant revolts, 54, 55,
    57–58, 123
Peasantry, importance of,
    57, 58, 59
Pennsylvania, 100
People's Republic of China,
    57–59, 77, 121
    protest in, 77, 121, 123

People's Revolutionary
    Army, 74
People's Temple of the Disci-
    ples of Christ, 96–97
Persecution, 107
Petrograd, Russia, 56, 57
Poison-gas attack, Tokyo, 74
Police violence, 72
Political factors, 55
Political opportunity theory,
    23
Political process theory, 23
Political protest, 16–17
Political repression, 61, 122
Political terrorism, 65
Political theory, 23–25
Politics of Mass Society, The
    (Kornhauser), 20
Posse Comitatus, 107, 109
Post–Civil War era, 32–33,
    67
Poverty, 9, 39
Precipitating factors, 21
Prison riots, 30, 42–46
    consequences of, 44–46
    explanation of, 42–44,
        115, 121
    living conditions and, 44,
        45, 46
    rising expectations and,
        43–44
Proletariat, 50
Protest, nonviolent, 7
Protest cycle, 123
Protest groups, 10
Protest riots, 30, 31–34
Provisional Wing of the
    Irish Republican Army
    (PIRA), 73, 106–107
Psychoanalytical viewpoint,
    85
Psychological viewpoint, 80
Psychopathological view-
    point, 80–81
Public policy, changes in, 41
Puerto Rican nationalists,
    71, 72–73

Quakers, 100

Racial bigotry, 67, 81
Racial violence, 33–34, 82,
    110, 111

Radical political change, 70
Railroad strikes, 33
Rape, 69, 70
Rationality
    and involvement, 14–17
    versus irrationality, 6–8,
        81, 116–118
    meaning of, 7
Rebellions, 1–2
Reconstruction, 67, 108
Red Army Faction, 73–74
Red Brigades, 74
Relative deprivation, 17–19,
    37
    defined, 18
    perception of, 18, 106
    rising expectations and,
        17–19, 43–44, 52–53
    theory of, 18–19
Religious bigotry, 67
Religious cults, 74, 90, 92,
    94, 99, 100. *See also*
    Cults
Religious fundamentalism,
    102
Repressive terrorism, 66
Republic of China, 58
Resource mobilization
    theory, 17, 23–25, 55,
    117
Revelous riot, 30
Revivalist movement, 100
Revolution, 48–61
    causes of, 89
    compared to riots, 48
    defined, 5, 48, 118
    economic factors leading
        to, 55
    of 1848 in Europe, 48
    history of, 2, 56–61
    Marx and Engels's theory
        of, 49–51
    natural history approach
        to, 51–52
    relative deprivation and,
        52–53
    structural approach to,
        53–55, 115–116
    theories of, 49–55
    in the twentieth century,
        56
Right-wing death squads,
    74

Right-wing extremists, 109
Right-wing regimes, 77
Right-wing terrorism, 73
Riot Era, 32
Rioters, profile of, 20, 35–38
Riots, 24, 29–46
  apolitical, 30
  categorizing, 30–31
  causes of, 32, 34–41, 115
  compared to revolutions,
    48
  consequences of, 41–42
  defined, 5, 29
  explanations of, 34–41
  history of, 2, 29, 31–34
  spontaneous, 26
  typologies of, 29–31
  underlying conditions for,
    38–41, 99
  in the U.S., 2, 4, 34,
    114–115
  see also Prison riots
Rising expectations, 17–19
  and prison riots, 43–44
  and relative deprivation,
    17–19, 43–44, 52–53
Roman Catholics, 68
Rome, Italy, 74, 76, 107
Rural people, 111
Russian Revolution of 1917,
  2, 51, 53, 56–57
Russian Tartars, 112
Rwanda, 77

Salem witch trials, 100
Sam Melville-Jonathan
  Jackson Unit, 72
Sandinista National
  Liberation Front
  (FSLN), 59–60
Santa Fe, New Mexico, state
  prison, 44
Sarin nerve gas, 96
Satanic cults, 100, 102–103
Satan's Underground
  (Stratford), 103
Savak, 60
Scarce resources, 22, 116
Scientologists, 102
"Scum of the earth"
  perspective, 35
Second Great Awakening,
  100

Sects, 91
Self-denial, 97
Separatist terrorism, 70
Serbs, 107
Seventh Day Adventists, 92,
  100
Seventies, 25, 60, 97, 101–
  102
Sexist terrorism, 70
Sexual assault, 69–70
Shays' Rebellion, 32
Silent Brotherhood, 110
Single-issue terrorism, 70
Sino-Japanese war of 1895,
  58
Sixties, 4, 18–19, 29, 31, 34,
  37, 38–39, 40, 41, 78,
  100, 103, 124
Skinheads, 104, 110–111
Slam-dancing, 110
Social attachments, effect of,
  19–20
Social constructionist
  perspective, 25–27
Social control, 22
Socialism, 51, 56, 58
Social movement behavior,
  17
Social movements, 23, 26,
  118
Social policy changes, 7
Social-psychological
  approach, 79–81, 114
Social revolutionary
  terrorism, 70
Social scientists, 31, 78
Society of Friends
  (Quakers), 100
Socioeconomic conditions,
  38–41
South Africa, 88
South America, 74
Soviet Union, 77
Springfield, MA, 32
State
  interplay of collective
    violence with, 10–11,
    120–123
  in structural view, 54
  vulnerability of, 54, 55
State terrorism, 66, 74,
  76–79, 80, 81, 82, 121
  solution to, 88–89

State terrorism permissive-
  ness, 82
Strikes, 30, 33, 56, 71
Structural conduciveness,
  21
Structural-strain theory,
  20–23, 38–39
Structural view, 114–116
  of revolution, 53–55, 115
  of riots, 115
  of terrorism, 81–83,
    115–116
Students for a Democratic
  Society (SDS), 72
Subjective deprivation, 119
Substance abuse problems,
  94
Suicide, mass, 96–97, 102
Suicide bombings, 76
Survivalists, 90, 104–105,
  109
  defined, 104
  see also Militia groups
Symbionese Liberation
  Army, 72
Symbolic riot, 30

Taiping Rebellion, 58
Taiwan, 58
Tanzania, 1–12
Target hardening, 87
Tarring and feathering, 71
Tax evasion, 111
Television. *See* Media
  coverage
Temple of Set, 102
Terrorism, 29, 63–89
  countering, 86–89
  defined, 5, 64–66
  diversity of, 86
  explaining, 79–89
  historical and contempo-
    rary, 66–79
  insurgent, 66, 70–74, 86,
    87
  irrationality of, 6
  media coverage of,
    83–84, 87
  military approach to,
    86–87
  nonstate, 82–83
  as the norm, 81
  political, 65

Terrorism *(continued)*
  psychological and social-
      psychological views
      of, 79–81
  purpose of, 26
  repressive, 66
  separatist, 70
  single-issue, 70
  social revolutionary, 70
  state, 66, 74, 76–79, 80,
      81, 82, 88, 121
  structural view of, 81–83,
      115–116
  transnational, 66, 74–76,
      82, 86
  vigilante, 66–70, 81, 82,
      88, 105, 116
  women and, 85–86
Terrorist personality, 80
Testosterone, 85
Theory of Collective Behavior
    (Smelser), 16
Tiananmen Square, 77, 121,
    123
Tibetan Buddhism, 96
Tokyo, Japan, 74, 96
Tories, 71
Totalitarian societies, 21
Total Overcomers
    Anonymous, 97
Transnational terrorism, 66,
    74–76, 82, 86
Turbulent Era, 32
Turkey, 76, 77
Tutsis, 77
TWA plane hijacking, 84
Twentieth century, 33–34,
    56–61

UFO cult movement, 97
Uhriah, California, 96–97

Unemployment, 24, 39, 40,
    54, 55
Unification Church cult, 92
United Freedom Front, 72
United Nations, 75
United States, 31–34
  as a capitalist society,
      50–51
  foreign involvement of,
      59–60, 77–78
  imperialism of, 72, 88
  state terrorism in, 78
  types of cults in, 99–101,
      102–103
Urban revolts, 29, 31, 54,
    55
Urban workers' uprisings,
    54
U.S. Army, 41

Vienna, Austria, 76
Vietnam antiwar
    movement, 16, 72
Vietnam War, 77
Vigilante terrorism, 66–70,
    81, 82, 88, 105, 116
  against women, 70
Violent control, 121
Violent repression, 121
Viper Militia, 105

Waco, Texas, 92, 96, 102
War, as collective violence,
    3
Wartime economy, 57
Watts riots, 35, 36–37
Weather Underground, 72
Welfare benefits, 41
Western Europe, 48, 73, 76,
    110
West Germany, 74

West Side Story, 5
West Virginia Mountaineer,
    2, 105, 152
West Virginia State
    Penitentiary (WVSP),
    43, 44
White Aryan Resistance
    (WAR), 108, 110
White backlash, 42
White revolutionaries, 71
White Supremacist
    Movement, 73, 110,
    111
Why Men Rebel (Gurr), 18
Wiccans, 102, 103
Witchcraft, 100, 102, 103
Women
  attracted to cults, 94
  and terrorism, 85–86
  violence against, 69–70
Women's liberation
    movement, 86
Women's rights movement,
    27
Working class, 50
World Church of the
    Creator (WCC), 111
World Trade Center
    bombing, 63, 75
World War II, 56, 58, 60, 77

Yugoslavia, 107

Zapatista National
    Liberation Army
    (EZLN), 1
Zimbabwe, 24
Zionist Occupational
    Government (ZOG),
    110